Holistic Product Development

Holistic Product Development

A Broad Perspective

J. H. Welsch

While it is intended to provide useful and authoritative information on variety of subjects related to the development of new products, this book is sold with the understanding that what works well for one company may not be at all appropriate for another. Therefore, advice rendered herein should be evaluated for suitability before implementation. The author accepts no responsibility for the results of using the methods or suggestions found herein. Furthermore, the author is not qualified to render legal or accounting services. The services of qualified professionals should be sought when such advice is need.

ISBN: ISBN: 978-0-578-46692-7

Dedication and Acknowledgement

This book is dedicated to my late father, Donald E. Welsch, both a loving father and the role model for my life and career. Unable to attend college, he was an apprentice machinist before serving in the infantry in Germany during WWII. Back from the war, he was hired as a machinist at a small manufacturing company that designed and built customized machines. He didn't remain a machinist for long, though; because of his intelligence and dedication, he was soon promoted to foreman. Later, he became chief engineer, vice president and, eventually, president. If his company had believed in patents, he'd have been named as an inventor on many. Spending so many Saturdays at his office inspired me to become an engineer. He financed my education and supported me through every step of my own career. He was encouraging as I began writing this book but, sadly, did not live to see its completion; something I deeply regret.

My eternal gratitude goes to my wife, Linda, who encouraged (and occasionally badgered) me through high school and college, typed every one of my lab reports and term papers, supported both of us during my senior year at Lehigh University, stood by me as a I sacrificed family life for my career and tolerated my countless hours in front of the computer as I wrote this book. (Whew!) Without her love and support, this book, not to mention my career, would not have been possible.

I also wish to thank Linting Xue, Jarmani Dozier and my brother, Tom, for their help with the cover artwork.

CONTENTS

APPENDIX D - INTELLECTUAL PROPERTY 219

APPENDIX E – PRODUCT SAFETY & PRODUCTS LIABILITY 245

Preface

Why, after all these years, have I written my first book? The book has two purposes and each is addressed to a different audience. The first is as a guide for those who are currently participating in some way in the development of new products. Some may want to learn how the process in their organization can be made more effective, some to discover how each part of the organization fits into the picture and some to find ways to improve their own contribution to new product development. The second is as a primary text for students or others who yet have had little or no exposure to product development.

I've spent all but a few years of my long career developing products, first as an engineer doing nuts-and-bolts design, a bit later as a middle manager and eventually as an executive with ultimate responsibility for the process and its results within the company. Over the years, I've worked where there was virtually no formal process at all, where the process was overwhelmingly burdensome and everywhere in between. I implemented a process that was successfully followed and continuously improved for over two decades. Having seen and participated in the excellent, the mediocre and the truly repulsive, I like to think I've learned a thing or two. Consequently, I feel compelled to pass that knowledge along to other practitioners through my modest consulting practice and through this book.

In addition to my "real" job in industry, I served as an adjunct instructor. Over 20 years ago, I was asked to teach a class at my alma mater, Lehigh University. The course description can be summarized as "everything you need to know about the business (as opposed to engineering) aspects of product development." As I was new to teaching, I had no idea how to select the text so I jumped at the department head's offer to choose the text for me. Sadly, I was terribly disappointed in his selection; its author clearly lacked practical experience, and much of what he'd written was in direct conflict to what my own experience had taught me. In subsequent years, I sought my own texts but, finding no single text that addressed the breadth of the material I felt essential, I resorted to relying on two or three for the students' use. Even that was insufficient so I relied on many supplemental texts and my own experiences to get the job done.

Though I have retired from teaching, my second motive for writing this book was to fill the gap.

Just as it is for novices as well as experienced practitioners, the book is for a wide range of disciplines. In many organizations, product development is the responsibility of marketing. In others, responsibility rests with engineering or another technical department. While I wholeheartedly agree that a single **person** must have ultimate responsibility to see that product development is done well, many, and in some cases all, departments have a very real responsibility for its success or failure. That responsibility, furthermore, is not simply "keeping an oar on the water" to see that the department's own interests are served; every department and every person involved in the process must understand the process holistically so that he or she can have the maximum positive impact on the outcome. That is not possible without a knowledge of how it should be done.

To what industries and to what types of products does the book apply? When many people think of product development, they think of high technology. That is most definitely not the case. In its earliest years, the company in which I spent much of my career made nothing more exciting than utensils for commercial kitchens. Yet its founder, Louis Maslow, was awarded no fewer than 47 US patents, the first two of which were for egg whisks[1,2]. It doesn't get more "low tech" than that! The company evolved into one that makes much more interesting products but, for its first several decades, the products were anything but high tech and not one of Maslow's patents had anything to do with what we now call "technology".

Nor is product development applicable only to physical products. Software is a huge business and clearly its products are not physical. Given the rate at which software evolves, however, new products are the very lifeblood of that industry. Taking a broader view, I contend that EVERY organization has one or more "products", though some also carry the label "service". Ponder for a moment the breadth of products (AKA services) offered by banks, insurance companies, credit card companies, universities and consultants. They all have "products" to sell and the good ones, at least, are constantly developing new ones. I've attended product development conferences where executives from such organizations were participants and even presenters.

Neither are products always sold. Though they may not sell them, government and social agencies have their own "products" and, to stay relevant, they must at least occasionally change or supplement their offerings.

Because of the breadth of products considered and the variety of ways that they are engineered and produced, this book almost totally avoids technical topics. The book addresses the non-technical subjects with varying levels of detail but does not attempt to present an exhaustive treatment of any single aspect of product development. Rather, it is intended to offer a basic understanding of the many aspects of the broader subject and, more importantly, how they fit together.

Whether you work in the public or private sector; whether your organization's product is physical or non-physical, this book is for you. It's for you whether you work in finance, operations, marketing, sales, engineering, quality, ... well, you get the idea. If you are an owner or executive, this book is especially for you. And if you are still a student, you cannot now know where your career will lead but, if you want to be on the leading edge of your organization, it's for you as well.

How to use this book

I've written this book to be used in several ways. It can be used as a text for a class aimed at introducing the principles of product development to people destined to any one of many professions. Based on the feedback I've had from my classes at both Lehigh and Wilkes Universities, I think you will find it effective for that application. Likewise, it can be used for independent study or within an organization to introduce those same principles so that all associates involved in the process can gain an appreciation for the whole, exciting process. And lastly, it can be used as a reference manual by experienced practitioners to brush up on new or forgotten topics.

Admittedly, my career in industry has resulted in some of the specifics in this book being directed to physical products; I hope you will forgive me for that. With very little peripheral vision, however, it will be clear that the same principles apply to the entire spectrum of products and services. So, as you read this book, remember to interpret the word "product" to encompass whatever it is you offer to your customers or clients. Likewise, though I will sometimes use the word "company", the word should be interpreted to encompass the broader sense of "organization", whether that be bureau, agency, association, or something else. Most of what is presented here applies to them all.

Let me acknowledge here that, while there are some new tools and techniques here, many of the individual core principles presented here are not. What I believe is unique about this book is its comprehensive treatment of the subject which, again, is aimed at bringing a full appreciation of this broad subject to a broad audience. My intention here, therefore, is to weave together the many disparate principles into the cloth which is new product development.

There are several topics covered in this book that, though an understanding of them is critical, did not fit well into the flow of a discussion of new product development. Therefore, I have included them as appendices. I understand the tendency of many people to skip over or even completely ignore appendices. Unless you already have a firm working knowledge of those topics, though, I strongly suggest that you resist that urge.

Chapter 1 - Innovate or Die!

It is not the strongest or the most intelligent who will survive but those who can best manage change.

— Attributed to Charles Darwin[3]

Innovate or Die! Yes, it's a cliché. Like many clichés, however, it states a fundamental truth. As with living organisms, organizations are either growing or dying; those that fail to evolve are doomed to extinction. For some, it happens slowly, for others with disturbing swiftness. Think of what were once considered "blue chip" companies; those whose stock was a safe bet. Consider names like Bethlehem Steel, Kodak, Polaroid, Blockbuster and Borders. Now think of Google, Apple, Netflix, Keurig and Tesla. The second list is clearly one of innovative companies; those who have a record of developing and introducing innovative new products to stay ahead of or, in the worst case, closely behind, their competitors. Like the dinosaurs, however, those in the first list could not or would not keep up with changing realities.

Clayton Christensen's best-seller, "The Innovator's Dilemma"[4], focused the thoughts of many executives and NPD professionals on the concept of disruption. According to Christensen, disruption occurs when an entity, generally a small "upstart" company, changes the playing field. In most cases the company introduces a product that is, initially at least, inferior to the incumbent by the standards generally believed at the time to be important to customers. However, it is lower in price and/or superior to the incumbent by standards valued by a new population of potential customers.

In its infancy, digital photography was a poor substitute for film. Resolution was poor, resulting in sub-standard photographs. Many dismissed digital photography as inconsequential. The results, nonetheless, speak for themselves; Kodak and Polaroid, once giants, are shadows of their former selves.

Lest we think that disruption and the indifference or contempt that people have for disruptive products is something new, consider the Western Union internal memo which said in 1876, "This 'telephone' has too many shortcomings to be seriously considered as a means of communication. The device is inherently of no value to us.[5]" Or consider the words of Marechal Ferdinand Foch, Professor of Strategy at France's Ecole Supérieure de Guerre, who is reported to have said "Airplanes are interesting toys but of no military value.[6]"

Even the disruptors themselves can undervalue the significance of their own innovations. Though Kodak had, themselves, introduced the world's first digital camera in 1975, their own chairman, George Fisher, said in 1997, "Electronic imaging will not cannibalize film."[7] To my mind, this last statement exemplifies one of the most striking examples of this myopia; Kodak's failure to recognize the opportunity (or from a more pessimistic viewpoint, threat) presented by digital technology. How can a company, having recognized the new technology and even having developed the first product to exploit it, fail to follow through in its capitalization? The roots, I believe, are in their desire to preserve the past. Consider that Kodak followed a "razor blade" strategy of making its money on consumables rather than cameras. Cameras were sold primarily as a tool for increasing the sale of film.[8] While Kodak is still clinging to its Picture Kiosks, most of us, having abandoned our film cameras for digital ones, take thousands of photos while using no consumables at all. In the meantime, what has happened to the once-great company? In 1997, ironically the same year in which Fisher made his optimistic but fateful statement about cannibalization, Kodak's stock-market value hit its peak of $30 Billion. From then on, it's been a ride toward oblivion.

Now, setting aside our universal ability to correctly call all of Sunday afternoon's plays at the water cooler on Monday morning, if you had led an extraordinarily successful company that had had the sale of consumables as a cornerstone for a century, how eager would you have been to abandon that strategy and the infrastructure you had created to manufacture those profitable consumables? If we are honest with ourselves, I'm guessing many of us would have to admit that we would have made the same mistakes.

So, should disruption concern us only if we sell a physical product? Quite the contrary. Let's say that our product is the delivery of home video entertainment. Though they were once omnipresent, when is the last time you saw a Blockbuster store? Netflix began its business by offering essentially the same service (read "product") as Blockbuster but with some twists. First, they were quick to recognize the potential of DVDs and offered only them while Blockbuster clung to its inventory of VHS tapes. Netflix delivered the media by mail rather than rely on the customer's willingness to visit a store while Blockbuster clung to its thousands of retail outlets. Netflix also developed a software engine that created a profile for each customer and then recommended films that he or she might like. There were more differences but they are not particularly relevant here.

While all these things helped Netflix to gain on Blockbuster, the death blow was Netflix's success in VOD, Video on Demand. Netflix recognized the VOD threat or, as they saw it, opportunity early on. While industry observers saw the potential emergence of VOD as a threat to Netflix, the company, recognizing that their mission was delivering the best home video experience rather than renting DVDs, saw it as an opportunity. At the top of the video rental business in 2000, Blockbuster apparently misjudged the seriousness of the threat. In fact, when Netflix founder and CEO Reed Hastings made a cross-marketing proposal to Blockbuster CEO John Antioco and his team, he was reportedly laughed out of the office.[9] Hubris built on success is dangerous indeed; ten years later; Blockbuster filed for bankruptcy.

Certainly, Netflix didn't do things perfectly, either. Their split of the DVD and VOD businesses alienated many customers and took a toll on their stock price. However, they were on the right track overall. Once we found ourselves in a world where anyone with a satellite, cable or Internet connection could immediately download and watch any of a virtually unlimited selection of movies, is there any question as to what happened to Blockbuster and its bricks and mortar stores?[10]

Ah, you say, disruption is caused only by high-tech companies whose technology makes the status quo obsolete. Not so. One of the examples that Christiansen used in his book *The Innovator's Solution* is old news now; the disruption of the big department stores by the likes of Kmart and Walmart way back in the sixties. This disruption was not based on new technology but simply on a different business model. The disruptors offered name brand hard goods with which customers were already familiar and which therefore didn't require a well-trained sales force. Consequently, they were able to cut their costs and offer the same products at a lower price, thereby attracting more customers and still generating a handsome return[11]. Does anyone truly doubt that this was, indeed, a serious disruption?

So, disruption is a real threat that could well result in the death, or at least near-death of an organization. One would think that executives everywhere would take the threat very seriously but that's not how it's played out. Perhaps it's because it's so hard to deal with. I'm not a psychologist but I hope you'll forgive me if I draw a parallel. In her 1969 book, *On Death and Dying*, Elisabeth Kubler-Ross proposed the five stages experienced by those approaching their own death; denial & isolation, anger, bargaining, depression and acceptance.[12] I submit that the threat to our business of a disruptive technology can affect us as does the threat of a terminal illness.

We can readily compile a list of the myriad reasons why a threat is not real; why the potentially disruptive product won't work or why customers won't accept it. By any other word, that is denial. Sadly, some companies move no further, thereby sealing their fate. Having not been inside Kodak, I cannot speak to the presence of anger but have little doubt that there was depression. Over the years, Kodak tried and failed at multiple attempts to combine digital technology with film-based photography but they would never simply let go of film. That sounds like bargaining to me. I will not prolong the parallel but you may find a little reflection along these lines worthwhile.

Such disruptions are startling and devastating for stakeholders but, fortunately for incumbents, they are relatively rare. Lest we take solace in the statistics, however, let us remember that companies are bested every day by competitive entries that make at least some of their products obsolete. While cataclysmic events may have doomed the dinosaurs, the slow march of evolution causes species, products and even companies to become extinct as well. Have you used a phone booth lately, or a pager? You might still have a fax machine at the office but I'm betting it's not used much and that it won't be there a whole lot longer.

Figure 1 - Well, at least the birds use it!

Wow, that was depressing but the flip side is quite exciting. We've established that one reason to innovate is to avoid obsolescence and extinction. Are there more positive reasons? Certainly. The most obvious is that you can be the disruptor! At least at this point in their lives Netflix and the digital camera folks feel pretty good about disruption! Wal-Mart may feel that way too, though I'm sure they're looking over their shoulders at Amazon et al. The disruptors, too, are vulnerable to disruption.

Even if you are not disrupting, the development of new products may well be the best way for you to grow sales, profits and shareholder value.

According to Forbes magazine's 2018 list of most innovative companies[13], the top slot belongs to ServiceNow, who enjoy a whopping 89.22% stock price premium based on innovation! That is, investors have bid up the stock price by over 89% above the value of the existing business simply because of their <u>expectations</u> of the results of the company's innovations! In fact, of the list's top 20 innovative companies, the <u>lowest</u> innovation premium is given by Forbes as being almost 60%. The lowest company on the top 100 list boasts a premium of over 30%! That clearly says that investors are willing to pay significantly more for a company's stock if they see the company as innovative.

There are other, less dramatic but more common, reasons to invest in the development of new products. Successful new product development pays off in sales and profits as well. According to Dr. Robert G. Cooper, NPD guru and coiner of the term "Stage-Gate®"[14], successful new products have an ROI of over 96%, have a payback period of less than 2.5 years and achieve market shares of almost 50%.[15]

Another benefit that is impossible to quantify but nonetheless meaningful is the power of leadership. People simply feel good about buying from a company they see as being on the leading edge. I once worked for a company whose most important product had been around for many, many years. Our problem was that the product was so good that neither we nor, thankfully, our competitors could come up with a better product at the same price point. We did, however, develop a wonderful new product that offered significant advantages but, sadly, at a higher cost. The new product fit a niche market and was very successful but, because of its cost, could not replace old faithful for the core of the market. Here's the interesting thing, however; though the patents on the old product had expired, its sales actually <u>increased</u> when the new product was introduced! Why? One reason stated by customers was that they wanted to buy from a company that they respected as a leader!

Whether you are inspired by the need to survive, a desire to reap significant financial rewards, the aspiration to be considered a leader in your industry or all the above, new product development offers one of the most reliable paths to success.

Chapter 2 - So Many Hurdles!

It must be considered that there is nothing more difficult to take in hand, more perilous to conduct, or more uncertain in its success, than to take the lead in the introduction of a new order of things. For the innovator has for enemies all those who profit by the old conditions, and lukewarm defenders in those who may do well under the new.[16]

— *Niccolò Machiavelli*

While Machiavelli was referring to changes in government leadership, his words apply remarkably well to the development of new products. Change may be exciting, it may be profitable, it may even be necessary for survival but, let's face it; change is a pain in the posterior!

On a day to day or even quarter to quarter basis, businesses are expected to be predictable. If a public company misses its numbers for a single quarter, investors get nervous and the stock takes a hit. If a private company falters, the bankers get nervous and that's never a good thing. To produce these predictable results, managers want their operations to be consistent. Henry Ford reflected the sentiment when he said customers could have their car in "Any color - so long as it's black." While it's unlikely that any business leader would take such an extreme position today, it is undeniably true that any change in the product line has the potential to disturb the "order of things" and can inspire resistance.

Even done well, the development and introduction of new products can be troublesome. Among the myriad potential issues are new suppliers, new materials, new processes, increases in inventory, lost time due to training… The list goes on and on. Given the issues that can arise even when it's done well, what happens when the NPD process is done poorly? Resources are wasted in resolving problems. Production is delayed or stopped. Orders are cancelled. Customer relations are strained and sometimes irrevocably damaged. Sales people spend their time fighting fires instead of getting new orders. The list here is longer than the previous one. Sadly, these results are far too common in today's organizations.

If you are still not convinced that things are not as they should be, here are some disturbing statistics. According to Dr. Robert Cooper, only a single commercially successful product results, on average, from 9 product concepts. Furthermore, 46% of the resources the average company spends on R&D go into ventures that fail.[17]

So, where do we fall short? Through my experience over decades, I have come to believe that the issues start at the top of the organization and work their way to the bottom.

Certainly, this list is not all encompassing and not every issue applies to every organization. However, I ask that you take an honest look at what follows to see where your organization may be falling short.

Absence of a Compelling Strategy

Every organization that is serious about new products must have a clear strategy to focus its efforts. To be meaningful, that strategy must first be founded upon a corporate strategy that clearly positions the development and introduction of innovative new products as critical to the company's success. Beyond that, the NPD strategy must clearly define the limits; the "bull's-eye" of products that are right for the organization. How far from that bull's-eye can or should we venture? How do we assure that we maintain focus yet have enough peripheral vision to assure we don't overlook a new bull's-eye (read: disruptive opportunity) that could redefine our business?

Lack of Commitment

It's one thing to say you want to do something; it's another to be committed to it. Organizational commitment starts with executive perspective. Let me get to know the people in any department or company and, without a word being said about the boss, I'll tell you a great deal about him or her. People reflect the attitudes displayed by their bosses' actions more than by their words. Whether or not there are some carefully-crafted words about innovation in the corporate strategy statement, unless the top executives wake up every morning thinking about how their product line is (or is not) evolving, the efforts of even the best people on the front lines will be frustrated.

As I've said, new product development is messy. There are many obstacles that will slow it down or stop it in its tracks. In the absence of executive leadership that will see that the obstacles are removed, the process, regardless of its quality or execution, will simply not be successful. Commitment is reflected in many ways and we'll discuss them in more detail as we proceed but among them are:

1. Resources - Funding, of course but also commitment of the time and attention of the executive team and many others throughout the organization.

2. Appointment for each project of a cross-functional team of committed and <u>empowered</u> individuals from all functional areas of the organization.

3. Assignment to each project of a qualified and committed product champion who will both lead the team and do whatever is necessary to remove obstacles to success.

4. Accountability of each team member, not just to his or her functional executive but to the welfare of the project and the organization.

If you are an executive who is not now and cannot be convinced that new product development is critical to your organization's success and you are not willing to commit yourself and your organization to it, stop reading now; you're wasting your time and your organizations money! If you are not (yet) an executive but are interested in working in a successful new product environment but find yourself working for the executive described above, change your career plans or find a new place to work! I know that sounds harsh but it is a fundamental truth. Sorry.

Alien Culture

Though it's harsh, I use the word "alien" deliberately. I'm not referring here to organizations that are simply bad places to work; those should be avoided in any case. I'm referring to those that are not <u>proactively</u> encouraging of the new product process. For new product development to succeed, the company's culture must be one that actively encourages people to take risks and to work collaboratively, putting the good of the enterprise above selfish personal or departmental goals. In the absence of such a culture, the process will be uncomfortable, frustrating, ineffective, or even detrimental.

For a culture to facilitate the new product process, it must be tolerant of and even encourage risk taking and the inevitable occasional failures, <u>even big ones</u>. It must encourage all involved in the process to put the organization's and the program's wellbeing ahead of their departments' and even their own. It must provide resources of people, money and time to get the job done and done properly. Its top executives must show by their decisions and actions as well as their words that new product development is a top priority. And it must show its commitment by measuring results and rewarding those <u>at all levels</u> responsible for success.

Lack of Discipline

A well-disciplined organization has established processes for its important activities and adheres to those processes. I will mention here that <u>blind</u> adherence can be problematic but will defer further treatment of that subject until a bit later. Even the best people, working without an effective process will, at best, struggle to deliver acceptable results. Yet, people who are "only good" can often deliver outstanding results when they work in an excellent process. Does that mean you should not seek excellent people? Of course not; excellent people working within an excellent process can move mountains and that should be your goal. Let's face it, though, some of our people are good to very good but not truly excellent. Assuming we still want them on the payroll, do we not want them to have the tools they need to perform at their very best? Of course we do.

So, what would we expect this process to do for us? Our process must maximize project value while at the same time managing the risk inherent to any product development activity. To maximize value, our process must assure that the resulting products are highly competitive & highly profitable. To minimize the risk at the same time, it must help the organization to filter out inferior projects and those that do not fit corporate strategy as soon as possible and then to focus the company's resources and attention on the best projects. And, it must do this while helping us to work quickly, efficiently and effectively. That last point is critical. Far too many companies have implemented processes that encumber the people with so much bureaucracy that little gets accomplished even when people put in extraordinary effort. We'll come back to this in much more detail later but for now I will simply say that the key element is a judicious alignment of process rigor with project risk.

Even the best process is subject to entropy, the tendency for any system to decay toward disorder. How often in the last five years have you either developed or had thrust upon you a new program or process? How many of them are still actively in use? Admittedly, some were ill-advised or were replaced by something even better. I'll bet, though, that many simply withered and died for lack of attention.

Here is where another aspect of discipline comes into play; the company must apply the process religiously (though not dogmatically!), project after project, year after year. For that to happen, there must be a champion of the process who sees that it is applied judiciously and that it is continually improved. Absent such a champion, the process is almost certain to wither and die.

Lack of Customer/Client Focus

Though I use both "Customer" and "Client" in the heading of this section, I see them as being the same in this context so I will use the words interchangeably.

Hear this; if your customer is not your central focus, it is unlikely that any product you develop will achieve great success. I'm not for one moment suggesting that you simply deliver what the customer asks you for. Almost anyone can do that and, in fact, we'll learn in chapter 5 that that is often precisely what you should NOT do! I am suggesting that you understand your customers even better than they understand themselves; that you know their lives or businesses so well that you can conceive of a product that will delight them before they can imagine it's even possible.

This customer intimacy thing is too important to be trusted entirely to sales or marketing or even to top management. Customer intimacy is the job of everyone in the company. Unless everyone in the company appreciates how important the customer is to the company and how his or her work impacts the customer's satisfaction, that satisfaction, and your company, will suffer. "Surely, you don't mean the janitor!" you say. Oh, but I do! Do you think a dirty rest room makes your company look good when a customer comes to call? Better to have the janitor appreciate how important it is that the job be done right than to browbeat him into doing his job well.

On a level much more closely tied to new product development, I'm appalled, though no longer surprised, when I talk to engineers or even marketers who have never even talked to a customer, much less visited a customer's facility. In my mind, this is pure folly. We'll come back to this topic in much greater detail in chapter 5.

Lack of Portfolio and Product Lifecycle Management

If you have an investment portfolio, you know that one of its key purposes is to manage the critical balance between risk and reward. Only the foolish blindly put all their money in high risk/high return or in low risk/low return investments. The wise develop a plan to divide their wealth among a variety of instruments to maintain a balance that is right for them at a given period in their lives. Then they shift funds periodically or as needed to maintain that balance. As their life conditions change, the plan is adjusted and balance reestablished. A product portfolio is directly analogous; a plan is developed to manage the risk/reward balance across the company's new project portfolio. A similar concept can be applied to the company's entire product line to minimize the danger created by having "too many eggs in one basket." Periodically, perhaps quarterly, the portfolio should be examined and project priorities adjusted to maintain the desired balance.

Product lifecycle management, on the other hand, is the process of continually monitoring each product's performance and making the adjustments needed to optimize the product's contribution to the company. It starts when the product is conceived and ends when sale of the product is discontinued or, in some cases, until there is no longer a need to provide after-sale service. Both processes are important, yet it is surprising how often they are neglected.

Chapter 3 - Strategy is the Foundation

What business strategy is all about; what distinguishes it from all other kinds of business planning - is, in a word, competitive advantage. Without competitors there would be no need for strategy, for the sole purpose of strategic planning is to enable the company to gain, as effectively as possible, a sustainable edge over its competitors.

— *Kenichi Ohnae*

There is nothing so useless as doing efficiently that which should not be done at all.

— *Peter F. Drucker*

In my early years as an adjunct instructor, my students were surprised when we began with chapter 7 of the primary text. The reason we did so was because the text's author delayed a discussion of strategy until that late in the book. With due respect to that author, I believe that an organization cannot even begin to consider new product development until it has an effective overall strategy as well as one for its new product initiative and until there is a shared understanding of both.

Organizational Vision and Strategy

Before we can address <u>new product</u> strategy, we must at least touch on <u>the organization's</u> strategy as the latter forms the foundation for the former. To get to bedrock, however, we will go one layer deeper; to vision.

Why are vision and strategy critical to our organization? Perhaps the most important reason is to focusing attention by providing a filter. Remember the old FedEx ad that had a guy repeatedly saying, "I can do that!" before looking startled and saying, "How am I going to do that?" Whether it's making a major acquisition, introducing a new product line or rearranging the office furniture, it's easy to say, "We can do that!" And, in fact maybe we <u>can</u> do any one or even a few of them. Perhaps every single one is backed by a compelling reason why it should or even "must" be done.

The problem is that we may not have the competency to do some and we rarely have the resources to do them all. In such cases, should we just take on the projects that are intriguing or that the CEO likes best? Or should we concentrate on those activities that have the greatest value to our company? And how can we know which have the greatest value to us unless we understand our company's vision and strategy?

A compelling, well-articulated and widely understood vision and strategy focus the entire organization's attention. They align all people and all programs towards the fulfillment of them. The power of this cannot be overstated and I'll present a powerful example shortly.

All in all, an organization without effective vision and strategy is a ship without a rudder; it may get where we want to go but the odds are certainly against it.

Before we continue, define terms. Over the years, I've participated in countless meetings dealing with these concepts and it must be said there has always been a fair amount of controversy over the semantics. In fact, the more books you read on the subject, the more conflict you will uncover. Therefore, while I freely acknowledging that there are different definitions, we'll avoid the debate here and proceed with the definitions to be used in this book.

For our purposes, we'll define vision as an image of where our organization will be at a specific point in time. You will remember that, in English, the future perfect tense takes us to the future and looks back at what has occurred; "I will have become...", "She will have been...", "They will have established..." and so on. Our organizational vision should take us to a specific point in the future and articulate what our organization has become. "In five years, we will have doubled sales and become the leading purveyor of kumquats in California" is a clear and compelling vision; one which both focuses attention and generates enthusiasm. (Of course, that assumes that it makes business sense and I am clueless about kumquat sales anywhere but I hope you get my point.)

That's a goal, right? Well, in a sense it is, but it's a goal on steroids. The most important distinction is that must have a scope that overarches the entire business and addresses what the organization will <u>be</u>, not what it will <u>do</u>. Simply attaining a specific level of sales by a certain year is a goal but hardly a vision.

To be meaningful, a vision must be aggressive. When President Kennedy said in 1961, "First, I believe that this nation should commit itself to achieving the goal, before this decade is out, of landing a man on the moon and returning him safely to the earth.[18]", what he called a goal was really a superb vision. How many people honestly thought it could be done much less envisioned how it might be accomplished? Experts at the time certainly questioned its attainability. Yet, it focused the entire nation on one of the most significant achievements of our time[19]. Imagine how the people in your organization would be galvanized to action in pursuit of such a compelling vision![20]

Once we know where we want to go, we need to develop a broad strategy for how to get there. We are not talking here of the plans or tactics necessary to <u>execute</u> the strategy but of the very broad outline of how we will achieve our vision. If our vision is, for example, to be recognized as a world leader in delivering aid to the most impoverished countries in Africa by the end of the decade, our strategy might include building a strong African distribution network while, at the same time, developing competence in fundraising.

For years, conventional wisdom has held that development of an organization's strategy must consider the organization's core competencies and its "Driving Force." Core competencies are the things that the organization does exceptionally well and that are key to its success. These core competencies might be such things as a particular technology, resonance with particular markets or customers, a unique distribution method and so on.

Though a company may have many core competencies, its driving force is the single one of those elements upon which its success is founded; the element upon which the corporate eye must be fixed above all others[21].

Let's look at the other side of the coin. It is just this heavy dependence upon core competencies and driving force that can make the organization particularly ripe for disruption and be the very seeds of its downfall! We have already discussed how Kodak's fixation on their competence in the production and development of film caused them to refuse to fully embrace digital technology. What an organization is especially good at or what element it sees as its driving force right now may, in fact, serve it well in the short run. In the long run, however, it could result in its death!

So, is the concept of driving force good or bad? Writer F. Scott Fitzgerald is reported to have said, "The test of a first-rate intelligence is the ability to hold two opposed ideas in the mind at the same time and still retain the ability to function." The way to address these two apparently conflicting realities is to consider strategy from polar opposite perspectives. On the one hand, an organization's strategy must leverage those things that have enabled its success in the past. On the other hand, it must continuously and actively consider that those very strengths may cause it to miss out on disruptive opportunities or even cause it to be disrupted into oblivion.

The organization's strategy must be focused enough to provide a useful filter and compelling enough to inspire its stakeholders. It must be the star which guides decisions and, while it should not be subject to frequent or ill-considered modification, the leadership team must not follow that star blindly. As disruptive opportunities or threats appear, the strategy and its interpretation must be challenged.

New Product Strategy

Having an excellent organizational strategy is essential but not enough. If the new product program is to be both effective and efficient, it must be guided by a well-crafted new product strategy. Again, without getting into a battle of semantics, I will suggest that the new product strategy is arguably a tactical element of the organizational strategy.

Just as the organization's strategy guides the organization, so does the new product strategy guide its NPD effort. To do so, it is naturally more focused and spells out exactly what is expected of the NPD endeavor. An effective NPD strategy sets both the expectations and the methods by which they will be met.

If the overall strategy does not clearly identify the organization's markets, technologies and product categories, its NPD strategy must do so. It must also identify the organization's approach to the development of new products.

It's especially important that the company's approach to new product development be clearly defined and articulated. Should the main thrust be to lead the marketplace by developing innovative new products? Alternatively, is the intention to wait for others to lead and then follow closely behind, executing more effectively by addressing the mistakes made by the leader? Or, does the organization believe it should maintain the product status quo, simply reacting defensively when competition forces it to do so? While each of these, and perhaps other, approaches have merit, one approach must be dominant and that governing strategy clearly communicated.

I would be remiss if I did not advocate strongly for the adoption of leadership as the principal element of both organizational and product development strategy. Some time ago I wrote a newsletter article entitled, "You Can't Lead by Following". In the article, I referred to a sailboat race. When my kids were young, Sunfish sailboat races were held every Memorial Day on the lake where we have a summer cottage. One of the races was for kids and, when my oldest son, Don, was eleven, he decided that he wanted to have a go at it.

At the time, he had zero knowledge of or experience in racing so he had to ask for my help. Worse, he announced his intentions only an hour or so before the race was to begin. Sailboat racing is all about strategy and, while I've been sailing all my life, I, too, was without racing experience. At the time, Don was still young enough to believe that Dad knew everything (this was before he became a teen and I became an idiot) so I was on the hook to do what I could to get him prepared to at least avoid embarrassment.

I gave him the only advice I could under the time constraint, "Watch for someone to establish a lead and then follow as closely as you can in his path, tacking (turning) where he does." It worked! Don was soon in second place and he maintained it for quite a while. Then disaster struck; he sailed past the guy in the lead! Suddenly, there was no one to follow and he found himself in the lead with no knowledge of what to do next! The crisis was short-lived; the former leader took advantage of the situation and retook the lead. Don wisely fell in behind him and finished in a very respectable second place. Second place is an excellent showing for an eleven-year-old boy in his first sailboat race and we were justly proud.

To some people, being part of an organization that is in second place is indeed acceptable and many companies have succeeded with that as their strategy but it means continuing to slug it out with competitors. To break out into the lead and hold it pays handsomely but requires discipline, resources and a unique set of skills.

While it's wise to establish and be guided by organizational and NPD strategies, blind adherence to them is foolish. I have no knowledge of the strategies that guided Kodak and Polaroid prior to 1975 but I'm willing to bet that the word "film" was featured prominently in both. Always remember to maintain the peripheral vision that is critical to identify and capitalize on disruptive opportunities.

Chapter 4 - Critical Climate and Culture

Just tasking a team to be creative won't get you to be innovative. It's having a corporate climate that gives people the space to experiment and take risks. Only then can you truly sustain it.

— Musician Steve Brown

To grow optimally, plants must have the right climate. In fact, some delicate species will die if the climate is not almost perfect. Product development is like a plant; in the absence of a climate that encourages its growth it will wither and, sometimes, die.

Commitment

As the adage about a breakfast of bacon and eggs goes, the hen is involved; the pig is committed. Commitment to new product development is not about lip service, it's about making the continual sacrifices necessary to assure success. As discussed earlier, new product development is messy. It's also risky, time-consuming, challenging, frustrating and expensive. Perhaps worst of all, its results are long-term; you make the investment now with the hope that you'll get a fitting return some time in a future that may be years away.

As a dyed-in-the-wool capitalist, it pains me to say it but Wall Street is a big part of the problem. Though Wall Street may pay a premium for companies who are known to be good at developing new products, in the short term they severely punish those who miss delivering the expected quarterly financial returns by even a trifling amount. Is it any wonder, then, that chief executives are reluctant to adequately fund activities that may deliver a reward sometime in an uncertain future? Is it any wonder that those activities are among the first to be sacrificed at the earliest sign of storm clouds on the economic horizon?

And it's not only publicly-traded companies that are affected by shortsighted vision; unless funded by visionary proprietors with a very healthy balance sheet or backed by an outstandingly enlightened bank or venture capitalist, the same reluctance to invest and readiness to slash will be evident in almost any organization.

I was fortunate to spend almost 2 decades of my career working for a company owned by a single individual, Richard Maslow, who was enlightened enough to invest heavily in new product development in good times and in bad. When, at one point, he carved out an NPD department separate from the rest of the organization, he said, "I don't care of you don't produce anything at all for a few years as long as you have an impact long-term." I was living in Camelot and I knew it. And, of course, we had an incredible impact and he was rewarded with a very handsome return.

It's an established fact that, while even excellent compensation fails to stimulate employees' performance, poor compensation demoralizes them. Likewise, while adequate financial support is a prerequisite of new product success, it alone is most definitely not a driver of it. Establishing the right culture takes a lot more than money.

Within most organizations, most of the people are busy "making the numbers" for the month or quarter. They are promoting the company and its product lines, closing sales, making and delivering products, providing product support, managing the financial accounts and a host of other activities. That's a good thing; these people must do those things and do them well if the company is to survive and thrive.

However, in many organizations, many of those same people are called on to also support the NPD program. Given the urgency to make the numbers, is it any surprise that those people are not eager to drop what they are doing to support new product development? While they may intellectually understand why the process is important, it's often seen as something that "those product development people" should do. So, when they are called on to support the process they are "too busy". Don't blame them, though; chances are that their bosses and even the company's performance management system are driving their behavior.

Many companies establish specific, weighted objectives for each of their employees with salary increases, bonuses and even continued employment dependent upon performance against them. For want of a better term, many organizations call them "MBO's" from the "Management by Objectives" method. At one point, concerned about the inadequate support I was getting from one department, I asked the department executive for a look at the MBOs for all his folks whose support I needed. What I saw explained the lack of support I'd been getting. The <u>maximum</u> weight for any person's objective relating to new product development was a paltry 5% and the MBO's for most of the people from whom we needed support did not mention new product development at all! Setting aside an employee's natural motivation to do those things that are likely to maximize his income, he is unlikely to put any significant effort into supporting new product development after the company has implicitly <u>told him</u> that it is of little or no importance!

It goes even beyond that. The chief executive and her entire staff must demonstrate through their own decisions and personal involvement that NPD is of critical importance to the organization. Yes, it means providing resources and saying all the right things but, more significantly, it means being personally involved; assuring that NPD initiatives are clearly aligned with organizational objectives, and establishing meaningful NPD metrics as part of the organization's balanced scorecard[22]. It means understanding and openly supporting at least the major initiatives and assuring that the measurable objectives of every employee apportion an appropriate weight to support of NPD. It means, at the very least, personally reviewing results on a periodic basis and, in all but the largest companies, it even means participating personally in the periodic reviews of significant projects that we will discuss in chapter 6.

All of that is a tall order and a difficult one to fulfill. Yet, an executive who is unable or unwilling to invest herself at that level must be prepared for lackluster results.

Customer Centricity

OK, I know that some of you are saying, "We don't really have customers." I assure you that you do. Depending on the nature of your organization, you may call them clients, patients, students, residents, constituents, or something else but, by whatever name, there is someone or something whom you serve. For simplicity here, we'll call those entities customers. You may even have several different levels of customers but we'll get back to that later. Suffice it to say that without that customer, your organization could not exist. To me, that makes the customer a pretty important entity!

It's generally accepted that executives and anyone whose job is to interact directly with customers must understand the critical nature of the customer relationship and to act accordingly. If your organization is to thrive, however, that understanding and behavior must extend to every person in the organization. Stew Leonard, founder of Stew Leonard's Farm Fresh Foods, a Connecticut-based dairy and grocery store, really understands that. A huge granite stone in front of each store's entrance is etched with the message, "Rule #1 -- The Customer is Always Right; Rule #2 - If the Customer is Ever Wrong, Re-Read Rule #1."[23] Azamara Cruise Lines gets it, too. Go on one of their cruises and you'll find that even the maintenance people will pause in their work to wish you a good day as you walk by.

Putting it in the more limited context of this book, consider this… If a product is developed solely as a showcase for the company's technical prowess, it will likely fail. On the other hand, if it is developed to improve the business or personal life of customers, it is much more likely to succeed. Success in new product development, then, demands that <u>all the people involved</u> in new product development have a full understanding of and appreciation for the customer's realities.

This customer intimacy thing is so important that we'll devote an entire chapter to it. Having set the stage, we'll move on for now.

Acceptance of Risk and Occasional Failure

Innovation involves risk. If an organization expects its people to be innovative, it cannot allow them to fear personal consequences of that risk. The organization must be tolerant of and even encourage risk taking and the inevitable occasional failures, even big ones. Anyone who has gambled in a casino (or the stock market!) knows that big rewards are accompanied by big risks. If you risk you sometimes loose. Why is it, then, that people who fail while taking a calculated risk are so often punished? Why is it that, in a culture that routinely punishes people who fail, executives are surprised that their people are unwilling to take risks? And why is it that, when they have no risk-takers, they cannot understand why they have little true innovation? I am certainly not implying that it's not necessary to sometimes take personnel actions against an employee who is clearly incompetent. I am saying, though, that those who take calculated risks and occasionally fail must not be punished! To do so is to undermine the entire innovation engine.

Let me tell you a story. I've been fortunate enough to work in some environments where we had very cordial relations with some of our fiercest competitors. There was one competitor who repeatedly, over a period of years, tried to entice me to defect to their side of the field. One day I noticed that my counterpart was not in the competitor's trade show booth and I enquired about him. What I was told is that he had made an expensive mistake and that the company didn't tolerate such things. Even if my ethics had not already precluded my changing sides, that little exchange would certainly have done so! Perhaps it was because of that competitor's risk aversion that they were never an innovation leader.

Conversely, I spent most of my career in a culture that never, ever punished risk-takers. The corporation's CEO even said, "If you are not failing once in a while, you're not taking enough risks!" I'm proud to say that, while I have occasionally had to fire people for repeatedly showing themselves unwilling to take risks, I have never punished one who occasionally took a calculated risk and failed. The result was that we were a leader in the development of successful, innovative products.

Collaboration

Culture goes beyond acceptance of occasional failures. I think my favorite word in this regard is "collaboration." Though I may not be supported by the etymology, to me the word "collaboration" has a more noble meaning than does mere "cooperation". Cooperation, according to the Encarta online dictionary, means "the act of working or acting together to achieve a common goal". In my mind, at least, that means I'll do my part towards the goal and you do yours. Lots of teams work that way and I believe that's one reason why their performance is sub-standard. I think that "collaboration" adds to "cooperation" the element of gestalt (the whole is greater than the sum of its parts). It means we'll not only each do our own part, but that we'll actively help the other guy do his! It means that the engineer doesn't tell the marketing guy why his request violates the laws of nature, she works actively with him to find something that will offer the customer similar functionality with a product that is technically feasible. It means that the manufacturing guy on the team will not just tell the design engineer why her design will cause production problems; he will offer concrete, positive suggestions as to how the design might be modified to facilitate production while still offering the same benefits to the customer. Mere cooperation involves compromise and when compromises are made, people walk away thinking, "Well, I guess I can live with that." When people collaborate as I interpret it, they walk away saying, "Wow, together we have really accomplished something; this is going to be great!"

I'm not talking about idealistic theory here; I've worked in both environments. It's frustrating and often infuriating to work in an environment that is merely cooperative and, most importantly, it leads to products that are less than they might be in many ways.

I spent several years when Vice-President of Marketing John Nackley and I, as Vice-president of Product Development, collaborated at a level that was extraordinary. John is a true visionary and the most competent marketer I've ever known. However, his appreciation of engineering practicalities is, understandably, limited. As a result, many of the very exciting product ideas he proposed ranged from impractical to impossible. The knee-jerk reaction of most engineers, myself included, would have been to simply explain why the idea wouldn't fly. He and I, however, took an entirely different approach. Often after biting my tongue, I'd start by digging more deeply into the request. Sometimes walking around the neighborhood, sometimes over lunch, sometimes just sitting on (not at) my desk, and once over a long weekend on my father's sailboat, we'd explore such issues as how the requested product would benefit the customer, why that was important and what else would offer similar or superior value. Then I'd say something like, "What if we could give you this…?" He'd reply, "Well, maybe that could work, but could you…?" or "Then, could you also…?" By going back and forth, sometimes over several sessions, we'd usually come up with a blockbuster product and, incidentally, have a great time doing it! Because, as I wrote earlier, people reflect the attitudes of their bosses, our behavior was emulated within our departments and the results during that period were spectacular.

Collaboration does not mean benign agreement. While personal conflict is counterproductive, differences of opinion and the candid sharing of them are to be actively encouraged. I've often shocked people by saying that church committees are among the most dishonest groups I've encountered. I say that, not because the members are immoral, but that they hold back what might be valuable insight in order to avoid causing offense or disharmony. Reflect on the number of times you have been in a meeting where everyone nodded in agreement only to complain about the outcome (and often the other attendees) after they left the room. Just as intense heat is needed to harden and temper steel, so is the heat of occasional conflict needed to reveal and address vulnerabilities.

I worked very closely for many years with a very capable man who was best described as confrontational. One rarely had a conversation with him, only an argument. His reaction to virtually any suggestion was a kneejerk, "No!" While I'll freely admit he was a challenge to deal with, he brought tremendous value to any team because his concerns were often valid ones and, by airing them openly, he helped the team to avoid problems. Having said that, I'm confident he would have been much more effective had he taken a collaborative, rather than a confrontational approach.

Collaboration means openly sharing conflicting views and working together towards a shared solution. The need for collaboration is not limited to the teams that develop the products but, rather, extends throughout the organization; upward as well as downward. It is of little value in a team's collaborating on a program only to have it fall victim to political intrigue in the executive suite or on the production floor!

Teamwork

In virtually all organizations, new product development is executed by cross-functional teams. Therefore, team dynamics are critical. For over two decades I had oversight responsibility for teams engaged in new product development. It has always frustrated me when people sometimes referred to these groups as committees. As I see it, committees and teams have very different objectives and methods of operation; they are different things entirely.

Think of any committee you've known. Chances are that it was created to exercise control over something. It's also likely that the membership was somewhat homogeneous and that all members had an equal voice on any given subject.

Now, think of a team. Whether to play a sport or for another purpose, I'm guessing the team was created to get something done! These two objectives are, in fact, often in direct conflict. The role of a project team is not to exert control, it's to get a job done quickly and effectively!

Semantics notwithstanding, the unfortunate reality is that many teams act like committees in that they vote or seek consensus on important issues, even when some members clearly have superior expertise in any given area.

Some years ago, I happened to be sitting in an airport waiting lounge as I was preparing a presentation on teamwork. I reflected on the flight crew and others who, I hoped, would work together to get me and my fellow passengers safely to our destination. How should such a group interact? Do I want it to operate by voting or consensus or do I want it to rely on its experts? Should the baggage handling crew make the weather predictions? Should the flight attendant decide whether a forecast thunderstorm presents a serious safety threat? Sure, it's perfectly OK for the flight attendant to opine, "Gee, those clouds look scary!" but then he's out of it; someone more qualified in that area needs to make the go/no-go decision. A product development team is no different. While anyone can and should offer an opinion on any subject, it's critical that the subject expert make the final call!

Team leadership is critical. I know there are proponents of leaderless teams but I cannot agree; there must be some**one** who is ultimately responsible for results. There was a time when I was one of only two directors reporting to our vice president. Occasionally the

VP would say, "I want you and Joe to work together to do such and such." Though Joe and I did, in fact, work very well together, without one of us holding himself personally accountable, each would tend to wait for the other to take the lead. Often, nothing would get done. After a while, my response to the boss became, "Please assign the task to either of us and ask the other to assist."

Based in some bad experiences, we had a sign hanging in our conference room that read:

WHOSE JOB IS IT?

This is a story about four people. Their names were Everybody, Somebody, Anybody and Nobody.

- There was an important job to be done and Everybody was asked to do it.
- Everybody was sure that Somebody would do it.
- Anybody could have done it but Nobody did it.
- Somebody got angry about that because it was Everybody's responsibility.
- Everybody thought Anybody could do it but Nobody realized that Everybody would wait for Somebody to do it.
- In the end, Everybody blamed Somebody when Nobody did what Anybody could have done!

Figure 2 - Whose Job is It?

While I don't agree that just Anybody can be a team leader, unless Somebody is ultimately responsible, Everybody is going to be disappointed when Nobody carries the ball.

If focused responsibility is expected of a team's leader, it follows that for every task, a single person must have ultimate responsibility for its completion no matter how many people must collaborate on to get the job done. It is essential that everyone on the team know who has ultimate responsibility for each task and who and to what degree each person is involved in that task. A good way to illustrate this and, in fact, a good way to manage it for each phase of each project is the example "Responsibilities Matrix" illustrated by Figure 3.

PRE-GATE 2		Project Mgmt.	Sales	Marketing	R&D	Industrial Design	Des. Eng'g	M'f'g Eng'g	Prod
Responsible PERSON ->		C. Jones	J. Bezos	A. Ries	T. Edison	R. Loewy	W. Carrier	H. Ford	S. Walton
Action steps	Status								
OVERALL responsibility for this phase (Indicate lead ONLY!)		Lead							
Define project scope	Complete	Support		Lead	Support	Support	Primary support		S...
Review strategic alignment	Complete	Primary support		Lead					
Review/update addressable market	Complete		Primary support	Lead	Review	Review	Review		
Complete competitive analysis	In process		Primary support	Lead	Review	Review	Support		
Complete initial customer research	In process	Support		Lead		Primary support	Support		
Identify potential service issues/opportunities	In process			Support			Support		
Identify potential quality issues/opportunities				Support			Support		
Identify potential ...urement ...ities	Complete						Support		Lea.

Figure 3 - Responsibilities Matrix

The matrix lists the various departments as column headings and individual tasks as row labels. There is also a column to record the status of each task. As an aid in determining where attention is needed, conditional formatting can be applied so that completed tasks are shown in green, those in progress in yellow and those not yet started in red. Because of my strong feeling that a specific <u>person</u> must hold responsibility for each task, a row is provided for that purpose. Within each cell is entered the role each person plays in the completion of each task. In the example, those roles are "Lead", "Primary Support", "Support" and "Review". Because it's important that one and only one person have ultimate responsibility for the task's completion, there can only be one "Lead" and a well-designed spreadsheet will show an error if no lead or more than one lead is specified for a given task.

My recommendation is that a set of such templates, one for each phase, be established for the organization but that each individual project team be empowered to add, delete, or redefine tasks as appropriate for their project.

Given the number of books and other materials devoted to team performance, I'll leave the subject now with the admonition that a highly functional team is critical to the successful new product.

Chapter 5 - Customer-Centric Design

Get closer than ever to your customers. So close that you tell them what they need before they realize it themselves.

— Steve Jobs, Founder of Apple

"All too often, the product is designed in a vacuum, the pipedream of engineers who love the technology but may never have seen living, breathing customers use their companies' products."

— Thomas J. Peters and Robert H. Waterman, Jr, "In Search of Excellence"[24]

Some would entitle this chapter "Voice of the Customer" but I have a problem with that highly popular term. I don't for a moment doubt that what the customer says is important but the term can be easily misinterpreted. If it's interpreted in the context of "give the customer what he asks for", it can do more harm than good. The fact is that, while customers may know what they <u>want</u>, they can rarely envision the products that will most <u>delight</u> them.

I will admit that the idea of jumping on a customer's suggestion and immediately starting a design project is compelling. The pressure to develop new products as quickly as possible makes it especially enticing, especially if the concept appears easy to commercialize. If the customer is a valued one, our confidence in their knowledge and our desire to make them happy adds to our eagerness to begin. Some would go so far as to call such an opportunity a "no brainer." Having been down that road too often, I strongly urge you to avoid such a temptation.

Following a customer's suggestion, or even asking many customers for their suggestions is highly unlikely to lead you to the discovery of successful, breakthrough products. In my experience, customer suggestions are most often for incremental enhancements to existing products or straightforward extensions to the current product line. It is true that some such enhancements and extensions may be needed to keep your product offering fresh, and it is sometimes appropriate to address them. However, the lure of such opportunities is such that you may well find your time consumed by them, leaving no resources to develop the major advancements needed for your organization to thrive.

Furthermore, something that is very important for a single customer my not hold any interest whatsoever for others. I concede that if you've vetted the idea sufficiently with a customer you may succeed in pleasing <u>that</u> customer. If that is your only goal and the customer is important enough to you, it may be the right thing to do from time to time but you cannot build your NPD program on that approach.

Finally, even in the unlikely event that the suggestion is a clue towards a breakthrough, that clue must be seen only as a place to <u>begin</u> the research that makes up the balance of this chapter.

Although the need to periodically enhance or extend the product line and to occasionally customize products for important customers is a real one, those things cannot be the core of your NPD program.

Here's a little mental exercise as an illustration. Imagine you are living in the early 1930's. One of the most significant items in your living room is a radio. In fact, it's the focus of the family's attention on most evenings. In addition to music and news there are many comedy and drama series such as "Fibber McGee and Molly", "The Life of Reilly" and "The Shadow". More likely than not, your radio is an attractive and rather imposing piece of furniture prominently located in the living room both for convenience and so visitors can see and appreciate it. The radio band, of course, is only AM. Reception and sound quality are poor and stations may be limited.

Now imagine that a representative of RCA, the Radio Corporation of America, comes to your town and invites you and your neighbors to a meeting at the local community center. Once everyone has gathered, the leader explains that the company is vitally interested in developing the next generation product. This will be a brainstorming session to collect the "voice of the customer" to assure that the new product will meet your "unmet needs." Normal brainstorming rules apply; no idea is a bad one, no criticism allowed and so on. What responses might be expected?

I've tried this exercise in my university classes and, even though my students were living in the 21st century, their responses were almost universally those that might have been expected 80 years ago...

- Better reception
- Better sound quality
- More stations
- Easier tuning
- More attractive cabinet design
- Different wood species
- Etc., etc. etc.

Only <u>once</u> in all my classes did any of my students say they wanted a picture on the front so they could see what was happening! And, of course, unlike our fictitious panel of the 1930's, my students knew about television!

Before they were introduced, who among us would have suggested the development of the television, the laptop computer, the smart phone, the DVR or any of the other ubiquitous products around which our lives revolve?

My message is this... If your idea of collecting the "voice of the customer" is asking folks what they want, it's highly unlikely that you'll get anything more than incremental improvements to what already exists. Granted, those improvements may be necessary to keep your current offering viable in the face of competition but it is unlikely to do more than that. Much more is needed if you wish to propel your company to the next level. To do that takes an entirely different approach.

Now, what if the RCA interviewer's questions had included questions like...

- "So, tell me, why do you listen to the radio?"

- "Ah, for entertainment. What else to you do for entertainment?"
- "Oh, the movies? Why do you go to the movies?"
- *[A series of probing and follow- up questions would be asked here and then, perhaps...]*
- "Well, if you could somehow see the action on your 'radio', would that have value for you?"

The example is simplistic but can you see how such questions might reveal totally new possibilities, perhaps even planting the seeds of disruptive innovation?

To develop truly innovative, commercially successful products, you must interpret the term "Voice of the Customer" more broadly. It must be aimed at learning about the customer's life. What is important to her? How does she use the types of products that you sell? What frustrations does he have with the product? How has he modified the product to better serve his purposes? The list goes on but hopefully you grasp the idea; if you understand the customer, you can often discover a "need" that she did not even know she had! When you fill that need, your customers will be delighted and both you and they will benefit.

Discovering Needs, Part 1 - Preparation

You are about to embark on perhaps the most critical part of the NPD journey, discovering what will make your customers rush to you with their money and walk away happy. Clearly, preparation is critical so let's consider some critical factors.

You may believe you have a full understanding of the markets you serve and of your customers and their needs. In fact, if you've served the same market and customer group for a long time and especially if you are the market leader, you may be very secure in your "knowledge." Such confidence will, however, blind you to many opportunities. Your prime objective at this point, then, is to forget everything you know and explore the marketplace with a totally open mind.

You will need to collect a lot of data, some of which may seem irrelevant as you collect it. Nevertheless, the better you understand your customers and the problems they face, the better prepared you'll be to help them address those problems so, when in doubt, record it.

Remember, people do not want your products, they want the results that your products deliver. As economist and Harvard Business School professor Theodore Levitt said, "People don't want quarter-inch drills. They want quarter-inch holes." In this case, the holes are the objective; the drills are simply a means for achieving it. As you do your research, concentrate on your customers' objectives. What is it that they want to accomplish? At the same time, what obstacles must be overcome and with what constraints must the user contend?

Types of Customers

The first step in customer research is the compilation of a list of customers whose input would be valuable. Resist the urge to rush out and visit your best customers. Instead, carefully consider the possibilities.

Some people interpret the word "customer" to mean the entity (person or organization) that places the order and from whom they collect their money. Others interpret it to mean the end-user of the product or service. In fact, the term applies to both of those entities and more. It must include every entity that plays a part in or can influence the purchase decision, everyone in the distribution chain and everyone who uses or is impacted by the use of the product. Since each of these can influence the sale or purchase, each must embrace the product if it is to be successful.

In some cases, the end user (some prefer the word "consumer" here) exercises uncommon influence over her employer. Executive chefs are an example. These prima donnas can, in many cases, dictate what kitchen equipment is to be available to them lest they take their name and skills elsewhere.

Let's look at the other end of the influence spectrum. You might say, "If McDonald's corporation decides to buy a fryer from Ajax Manufacturing Company, it doesn't matter whether the kids making the fries like it or not." In the short run, you'd be correct. On the other hand, if a lot of those kids find the fryer difficult to understand or use, their output will be substandard. McDonald's will eventually uncover the product's shortcomings and Ajax will be out and the manufacturer of a more user-friendly fryer will be in.

An end user who likes your product will make both it and you look good; one who hates it will do the opposite. Remember, though he may be far down in the organization's pecking order, it is the end user who is the ultimate customer!

In many industries, consultants can exert tremendous influence. Architects and interior decorators, for example, though not customers in a literal sense, often specify what materials and furnishings will go into a building. As such, they must be treated as customers even though they may not be part of the purchase transaction. In fact, they are often the primary target of the marketing campaigns of the companies that sell consultant-specified products.

Dealers, distributors and others in the distribution chain must be considered as well, though their interest is a bit different. In many cases, they can sell a variety of products from a variety of companies. Your job is to get them to spend their time pushing your company and your product! If they are to do that they must first believe in your product or, at the very least, believe that they can make their customer believe in it. Furthermore, if they are going to spend time selling your product rather than something else in their bag, they must see your product as one that is easy to sell. That means more than simply being attractive to the buyer. It means that it is easy to understand and to explain. Understanding the needs of the folks in the distribution chain is a key ingredient to success.

After you've compiled your initial customer list, you will likely find that it contains exclusively or at least primarily the names of your best customers; those with whom you have a good relationship. Of course, when we seek advice we naturally turn first to our "friends"; those whom we trust and whose opinions we value. And, indeed, we should talk to those folks. Remember, however, that the information you gather from your best customers will be biased because they are already happy with you and your products. Furthermore, if they value the relationship they may avoid saying something that could cause offence.

Your target list must contain the names of former customers and non-customers. These are the folks who will tell you what's wrong with you and your products. Admittedly, it's much more difficult to get appointments with these folks but it's most definitely worth the effort. As Microsoft founder Bill Gates said, "Your most unhappy customers are your greatest source of learning."

The Research Team

What registers in our brains is not necessarily what we hear and see. Rather, it is information filtered by our education, experience, biases and blind spots. To minimize the damage caused by those filters, customer visits must be done by a cross functional team of at least two, and preferably three, people.

In an interview, questions must be asked, non-verbal responses must be observed and copious, accurate notes must be taken. That's just too much for one person to do adequately. An interviewer, of course, initiates and maintains the dialog with the customer. She may certainly make brief notes herself but her primary job is to manage the interview. While she is concentrating on that, a dedicated notetaker documents the interview, recording the input received. A third person, if available, can act as an observer to spot and record non-verbal cues. He can also monitor the process itself so that it might be further refined[25].

When the team members come from different functions, they are more likely to see things differently. I liken this effect to binocular vision. When we see though only one eye, we cannot properly perceive depth. (If you doubt this, put a salt shaker on the table in front of you, close one eye, then quickly reach out and put a vertical finger down on top of the shaker.) Our ability to perceive depth comes from the fact that each of our eyes sees the same thing from a slightly different perspective. Likewise, when two or more people see the same sights or hear the same words, each will do so from his or her own perspective and, if they later discuss their observations, a new dimension will emerge; one which could not have been perceived by either person alone. The cross-functional requirement accentuates the difference in perspectives and optimizes the effect.

In the middle years of my career, I did a lot of customer research with a colleague who is an industrial designer. I'll have more to say about industrial designers very shortly but, for now, let me just say that these folks are very right-brain dominant while we engineers are left-brain dominant. He and I typically came away from customer interactions with very different observations but our <u>combined</u> experience was invaluable.

The Role of Industrial Design

OK, having just introduced the topic of industrial design, allow me to go off on a little tangent to explain how that profession fits into the picture.

Industrial Design is a profession about which most people know little or nothing, yet I believe the use of good industrial design professionals can significantly improve NPD results. If you have heard of (or even used) industrial designers, you may think of them as product stylists; the folks that make products attractive. Indeed, many companies cheat themselves and their customers by using them solely in that way. While styling is, indeed, one of their capabilities, they are capable of much more.

I've already alluded to the role industrial designers can play in customer research. In fact, their education, training and, generally, their personality makes them well suited to gathering information from customers. The fact that their education is more closely aligned to the arts than to the sciences tends to make them comfortable asking questions that, to engineers, might seem pointless of even foolish.

They can also play a pivotal role in identifying opportunities, developing product concepts and working collaboratively with engineers on the final product design.

In my view, an industrial designer is to a product what an architecture is to a building. While it's the architect who generally determines the look of the building, that is only a part of her job. Whereas engineers assure that the structure is sound and that all the systems work flawlessly, architects address the way that we humans interact with the building. If the building is a courthouse, it must look imposing; if it's a hospital or senior living center, it must look welcoming and non-threatening. Equally important, such factors as the flow of people through the hallways, the convenience of rest facilities and countless other considerations are under the purview of the architect. If, after you spend some time in a building, you find that you feel comfortable, the architect has done her job well; if the building just doesn't feel right, she might have fallen short.

In a like manner, an industrial designer's responsibilities should encompass the entire human interaction with your product. If a tool is well balanced, the grip feels like it was molded to your hands and your fingers fall on the controls naturally, the industrial designer has done his job well. If it's hard to use or just doesn't feel right, he has fallen short in his performance.

Just as the architect must have an intimate knowledge of all aspects of how the building is to be used and of the people who will use it, an industrial designer must be intimately involved with the same factors as applied to a product.

When the products are electronic devices or software, a similar profession comes into play but, in that case, it's called "interaction design". When addressing the role of industrial designers, I stated that some companies shortchange themselves by using them solely as stylists. Likewise, interaction designers are sometimes tasked only with interface design. Author Alan Cooper referred to this as 'putting an Armani suit on Attila the Hun."[26] If you've used a program that was simple to learn and use and where the actions you needed to take were intuitive, chances are an interaction designer was involved. I have two DVRs. One is a joy to use and the other makes me swear at it every time I touch it. I'd bet a lot of money on which was developed with the help of an interaction designer!

To be clear, if you make hand tools, you need an industrial designer. If you make software, you need an interaction designer. If you make technical products like smart TVs or DVRs, you need both. I don't use the word "need" lightly here; I feel strongly that these professionals are essential to a vital product development program.

If your current practice is to bring in an industrial designer to make an established design "pretty" or to use an interaction designer simply to make your screens attractive, think again; you are doing it backwards. Get these folks involved on the discovery phase, then let them lead the concept development and provide support during the design phase.

For more information on industrial design, turn to IDSA, the Industrial Design Society of America.[27] For more information on interaction design, turn to the Interaction Design Foundation.[28]

Involvement of All Team Members

I firmly believe that, while most customer interactions may be executed by team members from such disciplines as marketing, industrial and/or interaction design and design engineering, all members of the core team must develop an understanding of customers' realities that they cannot attain while sitting in their offices. It is one thing to "know" things because you have been told; it's quite another to have the visceral understanding that can only come from customer interaction and personal observation. Such involvement will create the empathy that is needed when it comes time to overcome overwhelming obstacles to deliver what the customer truly needs. Therefore, all core team members must actively participate in at least a few customer interactions.

The Role of Sales Professionals

It's now time to address the very delicate issue of the involvement of your organization's sales force in the needs discovery process. Let me first go on record by saying that, while many engineers stay away from the sales guys, I love them. At a trade show or convention, I could always be found with them, not other engineers. I also deeply respect the role which they play and the competence with which most professionals play it. I also admit that, given their roles in the distribution chain, they are key to the success of every product.

Having said that, I must caution you about their role in the process of discovering customer needs. New product opportunities are only occasionally found by simply asking the salesforce what they'd like to see or why sales have been lost. Given the pressure under which these folks normally operate, it's only natural for them to look for ways to make their jobs easier and to fabricate simple excuses for every lost sale. "Our price was too high." (In my experience, that's number one on the hit parade.) "Our deliveries time are too long." And then there's one that can lead you down a false path, "We do not have this or that feature that the competitor has." While that last reason may <u>occasionally</u> have merit, I know from experience it is often simply an excuse. I do not for a moment suggest you ignore such comments but you should take them with several pounds of salt; it's vital that you vet such comments extensively though direct communication with customers in the manner that I'll explain shortly.

I also caution you about having sales people accompany you on visits to "their" customers. Think about it; whenever the customer sees the sales person, he is directly or indirectly trying to sell her something. When he shows up with you, she will assume it is just another selling situation in disguise, even if you say otherwise. Under those conditions, the exchange will not be as open as it could be.

Expect the sale person to "insist" that she be along. Recognize that he has good reason for concern; people who do not have the right experience or training may well say something that will cause problems with the customer relationship. Given their nervousness, I've seen salespeople interfere with the process to its detriment. Consequently, it's essential that you educate and train all members of the visitation team and that, if sales folks are in attendance, they be admonished to introduce you and then act as flies on the wall.

Geography

I hope we all understand that a product that will be a hit in one country may not sell at all in another. However, you may be surprised to learn that there can be large and sometimes inexplicable differences between what is accepted by the same types of customers from one state to another. And no, I'm not referring to the clothing in Hawaii vs. Montana; I'm referring to, for example, hospital equipment in Boston vs. San Francisco. Why does this occur? Truthfully, I haven't a clue! Having been burned by assuming the research done in one US region applies uniformly across the nation, however, I strongly advise that, even if economics dictates that you do most of the research close to home, you do enough remote research to assure yourself that what you've learned close to home applies to your entire target market.

Discovering Needs, Part 2 - General Guidelines

Whatever you do, <u>do not</u> use these customer visits as a veiled sales tool. In fact, make your motives abundantly clear by your words, actions and attitude. Yes, there is a possibility that a new or renewed sales relationship will develop but that must be taken as a serendipitous consequence, not even a secondary objective.

If you've done your homework correctly, you'll be visiting many people in many places. As you progress from site to site, build on the knowledge you've collected, observing and skillfully asking questions of others to determine whether what you've learned at one place rings true at others; whether the "gold" you have discovered is a part of a vein or merely a random flake.

Though it should go without saying, I'll say it anyway; avoid closed and leading questions at this point in the process. While it may be appropriate to ask, "Do you prefer red or green?" near the end of the entire project as you are finalizing details, now is most definitely not the time for it. Here you are working on a higher plane entirely.

The notetaker must take copious, <u>detailed</u> notes throughout the process and <u>do so in an open and obvious manner</u>. There are two important reasons for doing so.

The first reason is obvious; to preserve the data. Recollections can fade or become distorted over time. Even the "brilliant insights" that you are confident that you'll remember will merge into the morass as you perform interview after interview over a period of weeks or months. In addition, once you forget where you learned what, it will be impossible to go back for follow-up information. The more detailed your notes, the better you will be prepared when it comes down to consolidating your research and creating product concepts. To avoid ambiguity, try to use actual quotes for key points whenever possible.

The second reason for taking the notes is to demonstrate to the interviewee that you highly value her input. Because people love to share their wisdom when properly motivated, meticulous notetaking will increase both the volume and the quality of the information you collect.

Be aware that some of the feedback you'll receive may not apply at all to your mission. You may hear responses like, "Your prices are too high!", "Your deliveries are always late!", or even, "That salesman of yours stinks; he's forever making appointments and then failing to show!" Whatever you do, don't brush such comments aside. Rather, express genuine interest, ask follow-up questions to gain a full understanding of the complaint, take copious notes and, when you get back to the office, pass the information on to those who can address the issue. In so doing, you will both demonstrate your concern for the customer and provide your organization with information that could enhance, or even save, the relationship. I say again, though, do not fall into selling mode as doing so will greatly compromise your primary mission.

Discovering needs, Part 3 - Asking

"Cleansing" Questions

Referring to my hypothetical RCA example, I am not suggesting you refrain from asking customers the typical questions such as "What features would you like to see in our next model?" In fact, it is essential that you do so for three reasons. First, the interviewees expect you to ask such questions. They may have anticipated them and will be disappointed if you do not. In fact, if they have been forewarned of your visit, it's likely that they've come armed with some requests. To appear disinterested is a bad way to start. Second, even if the suggestions you receive at this point are mundane, they may still have value for enhancement of the current product line. Note and report them because, remember, continual updating of the product line, while perhaps less exiting than great leaps forward, is nonetheless a critical part of product line management. If you ignore such suggestions while your competitors heed them, you'll find yourself playing catch-up; hardly the role of a leader! And third, though it may be slim, there is always the chance that a truly innovative suggestion will be made and you most certainly cannot afford to miss it!

At this stage, these "cleansing questions" would be something like...

- Why do you use or need this item?
- What do you do with it?
- How well has this product been working for you?
- Did you consider other products? What did you like/dislike?
- What would you like to see in a new product?

Again, the objectives here are to demonstrate sincere interest in the opinions of the interviewee and to gather insight into possible product improvements and line extensions. If you get something more, consider that a windfall.

Digging More Deeply

The next line of questioning is where you are somewhat more likely to strike gold. Your objective is to understand the issues faced by your subject in the environment in which you are interested. For example, let's say your company makes or wants to start making tools for professional plumbers. To simplify this discussion, let's assume you have a working knowledge of plumbing. Some questions that might get things going might include...

- What kinds of jobs to you really enjoy doing?
- What types of jobs do you dread?
- What tasks are particularly taxing?
- On which types of jobs do you make the most/least money?

This is, of course, a short list but hopefully you grasp the idea. The answers to those questions, in any case, are not enough. In six sigma training, we are taught about the "five whys". Like a young child, keep asking questions until you have a deep understanding. There is a caveat here; excessive use of the word "why" can sometimes make it sound like you are challenging the interviewee. Beware of your tone and vary your approach with such phrases as "tell me more", "help me to understand" and so on.

Listen carefully and make notes even if the interviewee gives you information for which you did not ask. This is exactly where you are likely to get the most helpful insight.

A question I always liked to fit in somewhere was, "What aspect of your professional life keeps you up at night?" In one industry in which I worked, the answer often came back, 'Employee turnover." We might have quickly moved on. After all, why would such a response have any impact on an equipment manufacturer? Fortunately, we did not because digging more deeply over a series of interviews revealed the fact that the ergonomics of existing equipment left a lot to be desired. Therefore, the work was often backbreaking and, after a while, employees simply quit! Voila; a product line was born! Had we dismissed the response as irrelevant, we'd have missed the opportunity entirely!

The adage says, "There is no such thing as a stupid question." As it turns out, asking so-called "stupid questions" is a valuable technique when used intelligently. (Yes, I know that sounds like an oxymoron.) The most skilled person I know when it comes to understanding customers' latent needs is Bob Cohn, now owner of "Product Solutions", an industrial design firm. Bob and I worked together for many years and did a lot of customer research together. Bob was fearless at posing questions that made me cringe. They seemed terribly naïve and, quite candidly, I feared they made him look like an idiot. Idiot he most definitely is not and his seemingly stupid questions served two critically important purposes. First, the responses were sometimes very different from what one might have anticipated and provided unique insights. Secondly, they put the respondent into "teaching mode" where they would drop their guards and go to great lengths to share their wisdom with him. I confess that my own ego is too weak to pull this off but Bob used the technique very successfully.

Regardless of whether you can pull off the "dumb question" technique, <u>do not under any circumstance</u> try to impress the interviewee with your own (or your company's) expertise! Doing so puts <u>you</u> in the role of expert and that is highly likely to cause him to clam up. It's critical that he understand that you are here to learn because you see <u>him</u> as the expert.

Though I have provided a few example questions here, resist the urge to develop and work from a questionnaire. While using such a crutch (and I use that word quite deliberately) can simplify the tasks of asking questions and processing responses, it will also severely limit the value of the information gathered. It's OK to compile a short list of high level topics you want to cover but use it discretely and let the interview flow like a conversation, not an interrogation. In so doing, you will find that the interviewer opens up much more and you will find yourself asking follow-up questions which you had not anticipated. Again, this is where gold is to be found.

Discovering needs, Part 4 - Watching

Ethnographic Research

I confess that I had engaged in the activity for decades before I ever heard the term but the process I'm about to describe is called Ethnographic Research. If a picture is worth a thousand words, what is the worth of emersion into the life of your customer?

What is said during an interview often does not reflect reality. I am not suggesting that an interviewee would lie to you; I'm saying that what you hear is what the interviewee thinks is true or wants to believe is true, not what is true. When you ask about a procedure, you will often hear what is supposed to happen or what happens under ideal conditions. You may even get a digest of the pertinent parts of the organization's ISO 9000 manual.

Things are not always as they should be. Some people simply cut corners, shortcutting established procedures for their own purposes. Even the most dedicated people sometimes deviate from the established way of doing thing if they think their own way is better. Supplies sometimes arrive late or do not meet specs. Equipment does not always work as it should. The weather does not always cooperate. When such things happen, people make adjustments to get the job done as best they can. For these and many other reasons, what you see "in the field" often deviates significantly from what you'd heard in the office.

In order to discover how you might delight your customers, you must gain a full understanding of what happens in the real world. To do that, you must see people at work under actual conditions. That means getting into the thick of things. Here is a roadmap for your trip:

1. Ethnographic research does not replace the series of interviews; it supplements them in a meaningful way. Use the interviews to develop an understanding that will put your observations into context.

2. Realize that those who know you're watching may not work as they would when alone. When possible, use your peripheral vision to observe others as well.

3. Observe all <u>activities</u> that involve the product category under consideration. Be sure to observe adjacent or related activities, looking for additional product opportunities.

4. Observe all <u>tasks</u> related to accomplishing the activity. Are these tasks necessary and appropriate or are there better ways to accomplish the same result?

5. Observe products (equipment, tools, software...) used to perform the tasks. How well suited are the existing products to the accomplishment of the tasks? With what issues are the users forced to cope? How have the users modified the products to better suit them to the purpose? This last point is critical; it's amazing to what extent people will go, using cardboard, string, duct tape and so on to modify their equipment to serve them better. Whenever you see that, embrace it as a cry for help!

6. Note and record the physical and emotional environment. What is the condition of lighting, floors, housekeeping and so forth? What physical factors must be considered while designing the product? How much pressure are users under; are people hurried, harassed, nervous? With what negative emotional factors must our users contend and how might we mitigate them?

7. Ask questions to better understand the user's realities and to distinguish the <u>theory</u> of activities from their <u>actuality</u>. Probe until you get to core issues rather than superficial responses.

8. Despite my admonitions above, don't be afraid to ask end users for their suggestions for new products or product improvements; they are often the most knowledgeable about

what is needed. As discussed earlier, it is not terribly likely that you will get world-changing suggestions but user input is almost always valuable to one degree or another and they will appreciate your honest interest in their opinions.

What if we can't watch?

I could have addressed this topic under the heading of "asking" but I've delayed presenting it because this technique is a poor substitute for ethnographic research and should be used only when observation is impossible because of security regulations, geography or some other unavoidable factor. When observation is impossible or impractical, we can turn to a technique developed by our friends in Human Resources for conducting employment interviews.

The technique is called Behavioral Event Interviewing (BEI) and it is based on the reality that, if you ask people what they would do under a given set of circumstances, they will often tell you what they believe they should do. On the other hand, if you ask them to remember a situation in which they found themselves and then ask them what they did do, you will get a more valid response. HR professionals use this technique with the confidence that past actions will predict future ones. We use it to get to the reality of the workplace rather than a fantasy of what should be.

Each BEI must be done with an actual end user, not a supervisor or other surrogate. The methodology is this:

1. Ask the user to recall a particularly difficult or frustrating day on the job. This must be a real occasion, not a hypothetical one.

2. Ask her to describe it to you in detail.

3. Remember, you are trying to simulate an observation so, based on the event described, probe with additional questions to form a picture in your mind of what you might have observed had you been present.

4. Ask follow-up questions as you would have done during actual ethnographic research.

5. If the occasion warrants it, follow the same process for one or more additional occasions.

6. If possible, repeat the exercise with other users at the same facility.

Just as the use of this methodology for employment interviews is a poor substitute for following a candidate around on his job, the technique is far less effective than ethnographic research. It is, however, better than dealing with hypotheticals. The biggest problem is that people are often not conscious of the obstacles they face every day. Once we've driven around a pothole in the road long enough, we do it without any conscious effort. Someone asking us about our daily drive may never hear a word about the pothole. Despite its limitations, a behavioral event interview may be the best alternative when we cannot observe.

Discovering needs, Part 5 - Deciphering the Data

Having done exhaustive research (if you are not yet exhausted, you've probably not done enough), and having gained a visceral as well as an intellectual understanding of the lives of your customers, it's time to develop concepts for a product for which they will, indeed, beat a path to your door.

Your problem now should be that you have a lot of data. It is also likely that you have some pet ideas for knockout products or "killer apps". If so, it's terribly tempting to latch onto one or more of those ideas and start designing. **Don't do it!** Jumping on that "no brainer" may well keep you from discovering the true gold. Even though top management may be spurring you on, I cannot stress strongly enough the need to pause and carefully consider all possibilities.

Affinity Diagramming

It's probable that the data you have is widely scattered and the task of organizing such a mess is daunting. My favorite approach to this is affinity diagramming; it is effective, it builds consensus among team members and it's fun. Here's how to do it:

1. Buy a big supply of sticky notes and markers.

2. Get the whole team involved; the more the merrier. The results will be better and, at least as importantly, you will have a shared vision of the path forward.

3. Meet in a room where you have a large, unobstructed wall surface onto which you can affix the sticky notes.

4. Distribute the pages of notes from your interviews and ethnographic events among the team members and have them transpose the individual comments, observations and other tidbits onto the sticky notes, one "factoid" to each sticky note. In the corner (or on the back) of each note, put a reference code that will allow you to trace it back to its source as needed.

5. Stick all the notes on the wall <u>at random</u>.

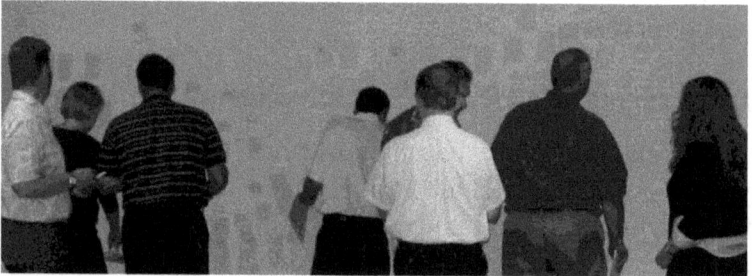

Figure 4 - Affinity Diagramming

6. Now the fun begins... With everyone working at the same time, <u>silently</u> rearrange the notes so that like items are together. It's a good idea to stick related notes together like shingles but be sure all text is visible. Anyone can move any note or group of notes as he/she desires and anyone else can later move it somewhere else. If someone believes that a note needs to be in more than one place, it's OK to make a copy but use that ability sparingly. There must be <u>no communication!</u> That is, no one can explain his/her logic. Someone needs to police this as the temptation to explain one's reasoning can be overwhelming!

7. It's worth saying that you can perform this activity during a single session or you can initiate it and then leave it for days, allowing people to rearrange things as inspiration hits them.

8. At some point, the activity will slow to a virtual stop. At that point it's OK to talk about the groupings and to rearrange the notes as needed.

9. Create a heading for each group, either by selecting one of the notes from it or by creating a new one. Put that note on top and mark it in some way to identify it as the header.

10. Before you remove the notes from the wall, have someone record everything so you have a record for use in future deliberations. In some cases, a series of photos will do the job.

You may be surprised to discover how effectively you'll have consolidated the information. Some information will be trivial and may be discarded. <u>However</u>, at this point, do not reject anything because it's impractical; reject it only if it's inconsequential. A fine line there, I know.

Developing Winning Product Concepts

Features & Benefits

It's all too common to come away from our research saying our customers want our products to be "more efficient", "more economical", "more aesthetically pleasing" or "easier to use". Such generalities are simply not actionable; more specificity is necessary.

Among of the terms you hear frequently in this regard are "features and benefits". The words are often run together to the point that it sounds like a single entity or that there is a one-to-one relationship between the two. In fact, features and benefits are two very different things and, while they are <u>sometimes</u> related, often, sadly, they are not. It is critical that you understand the fundamental differences between the two.

Think of it this way. A feature is something which, more often than not, costs you money. That cost may be occurred during the development process, during the production of each item or both but it's rare that there is not a cost connected to a feature. A benefit, on the other hand, is something in which the customer finds value and for which he will pay. Remember this above all else: **customers don't pay for <u>features</u>, they pay for <u>benefits</u>!**

Since your goal should be to optimize the value proposition of your product, you must ignore each and every feature that does not deliver significant benefit to the customer (read: customer value) no matter how sexy it may seem to you. At the same time, you must maximize the benefits that are the most important to your customer. As management guru Peter Drucker has said, *"Customers pay only for what is of use to them and gives them value."*[29]

The Kano Model

In the '80's, quality guru Noriaki Kano developed a model for evaluating the effect of various product attributes on customer (in this case, read "user") satisfaction.[30] The Kano model looks something like this:

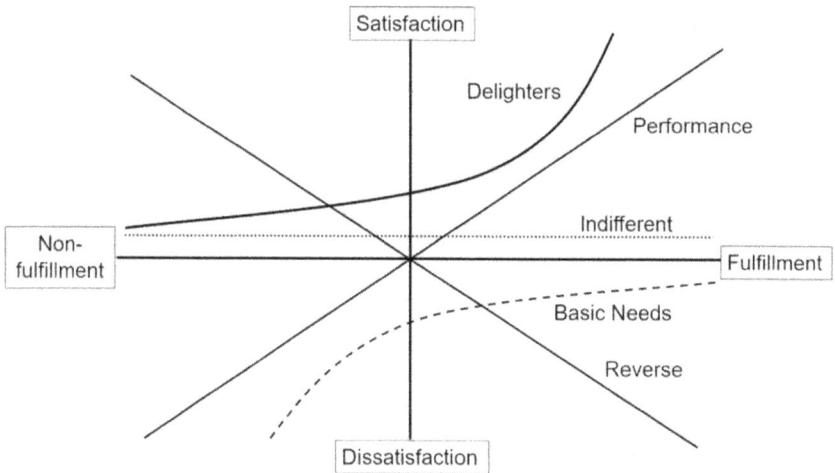

Figure 5 - The Classical Kano Model

Let's look at each of the categories of product attributes. As you reflect on the following paragraphs, keep in mind that these comments pertain to users in general and generalizations can be misleading. We'll shortly address how avatars can help us understand the nuances, but for now, we'll generalize.

There are certain attributes that just must be there; they are simply the cost of entry. Without them, you have no saleable product at all but, beyond that, you get no "extra credit" for them. I'll bet your car has a means to steer it and that you wouldn't have bought it otherwise. Steering comes under the category called "Basic Needs" or "Must Haves" as do the engine, brakes and so on.

The "Performance" category is also sometimes called the "One-dimensional" category but I eschew that label for reasons that will become clear shortly. In general, peoples' satisfaction with the product rises with the performance of attributes in this category. Again, using automobiles as an example, miles per gallon is a performance attribute; the higher the better.

I am convinced, however, that the performance curve is more complex than the linear one shown above. The following, I think, better reflects reality.

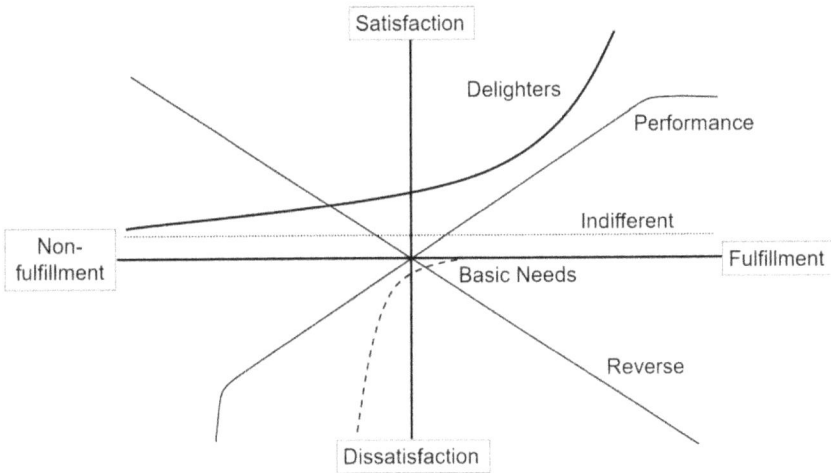

Figure 6 - Updated Kano Model

Even when "more is better", there are often limits. I happen to like to drive a bit faster than some people so let's take maximum speed as an automobile attribute. To avoid the sticky issue of speed limits, let's assume we are driving on one of the autobahns in Germany. Should the curve of satisfaction as a function of maximum speed be a straight line? If the car's maximum speed was 20 MPH, would there simply be low satisfaction or would there be no satisfaction at all? I think none at all. Would a car with a maximum speed of 500 MPH provide more satisfaction than one that topped out at 250? I think not. My revised performance curve shown in Figure 6 reflects the fact that performance attributes may have a minimum below which they simply cannot fall and a maximum above which an increase in performance provides little or no additional value.

"Reverse" attributes are not simply the reciprocals of performance attributes. In other words, we're not referring to "fuel burn" (fuel burned per mile) as a reverse attribute because it is the inverse of the more logical MPG.

Before my son took pity and bought me a universal remote (an exceptionally good one from an interaction design standpoint, by the way) I had on the table next to my easy chair no fewer than 7 remote controls related to my entertainment center. At one point I counted the buttons. Without considering that many buttons had multiple functions depending on what other button you pushed first, there were 277 physical buttons on that table! My wife felt much more strongly than I did that number of buttons is most definitely a reverse attribute!

"Indifferent" attributes are those about which, as the label implies, are of little or no value to the user. That certainly begs the question of why they are there in the first place! It may be because they are a hold-over from a past when they did have value, because, some engineer or executive thought they'd be "nifty", or because someone in sales or marketing requested them "because the competitor has it." In any case, if users are indifferent to an attribute, little or no money should be spent in providing it.

"Delighters" are the holy grail of product development. They will, if carefully considered and well executed, separate your product from the pack and almost assure its success. Delighters are attributes that, if they are absent, are not missed but, if present, are embraced enthusiastically. The term generally applies to new attributes that had not even been envisioned earlier.

Over time, however, attributes that were once delighters can find themselves downgraded to performance or even basic needs. Believe it or not, when I was a child, car heaters were considered a luxury (and therefore delighters) even in Pennsylvania where it can snow from October until May! They were not standard equipment; they had to be ordered as options or installed as aftermarket items.

More recently, when I bought my first car that provided Bluetooth connectivity to my mobile phone, I was delighted. Now I would not consider buying a car without it. Therefore, capitalize quickly on any delighters you implement but, unless you can protect them by patents or otherwise, be prepared to accept them as the cost of doing business as time goes on.

There is another important caveat concerning delighters. **A delighter poorly executed becomes a dissatisfier!** When they were first introduced, a car's moon roof was a delighter. However, if that moon roof leaked, you'd better believe it would be a very strong dissatisfier!

The curves provided, of course, are intended only to illustrate the concepts. While it is doubtful that you could formulate mathematically accurate curves for each product attribute, an understanding of the nature of each attribute is essential.

Furthermore, I noted earlier that the curves relate to users in general and all customers are not created equal. If you make software for drug stores, it would be unwise to assume that what's good for one of the large chains is applicable to a mom and pop operation. (Yes, there are still a few around.) Therefore, it is critical that you understand the nature of the market. If your target market is not totally homogeneous (and it is probably not) you must consider its entire breadth and depth. It may well be that for your product, one segment of the market sees a given attribute as a delighter while another sees it as a basic need and yet another as a reverse attribute. Assuming the market has more than one segment, you must understand those segments, select the one or ones you wish to serve and then fully research each of them. Each of the selected segments becomes, in essence, a distinct target market and each may necessitate the development of options or even entirely different products. Therefore, before you establish product attributes, firmly identify the **target market(s)** you wish to reach!

Avatars[31] Make It Real

As we've said earlier, all users are not alike. To homogenize them is dangerous; if we refer simply to the needs of "the user" we refer to an amorphous being that does not even exist. Therefore, we must look at the disparate user roles independently.

A useful tool for understanding the needs of disparate roles is the concept of avatars. While the term avatar originated in Hinduism and later became popular in the world of computer gaming, we will use it here to refer to personifications of each user role. By creating an avatar for each role, we can make each more distinct and definitive. Perhaps more importantly, we can connect with each on a more personal level.

Let's say our product is a production machine such as a lathe. Using avatars, each person who interacts directly or indirectly with the machine gets a personality. The lathe operator becomes "Joe", the supervisor "Mary", the set-up technician "Allen" and the maintenance worker "Jeff".

To maximize the effectiveness of the avatars, it's helpful make them as specific as possible. Based on your extensive research, you will be able to construct each avatar with its critical characteristics, with emphasis on its objectives, jobs and constraints as described in the next section.

To make them more effective, furnish each with not only a name but some fictitious but believable personal characteristics. While avoiding offensive stereotypes, don't be afraid to apply characteristics that are typical to the role. Though I will be criticized for doing so, I recommend that you forget political correctness here. Your objective is to make each avatar memorable so that team members can relate each to its respective role. In our example, our lathe operator's avatar could be a statuesque, thirty-year-old blond who went to Harvard and drives a Porsche. While politically correct, it is unlikely to serve the purpose of being easily related to the role. As an alternative, consider tattooed, forty-five-year-old Joe. He attended a trade school for two years before a stint in the army. After his discharge he worked at two other companies before joining his present employer ten years ago. He has a wife and two grown children, drives a seven-year-old pickup truck and likes to stop for a beer with his friends on the way home from work. If we also include a picture, perhaps taken from a public domain website, Joe becomes both believable and memorable. As we discuss what might be important to Joe rather than to "a lathe operator", his avatar provides understanding and focus.

After you've created an avatar for each of the users who are affected by your product, your team can totally abandon fruitless discussion of the needs of the non-existent homogenous "user" and concentrate on the distinct needs of "Joe", "Mary", "Allen" and "Jeff".

Results, Tasks, & Constraints

In his excellent book, "What Customers Want", Anthony Ulwick, suggests we look at Jobs, Objectives and Constraints[32]. What follows is an amalgamation of his thoughts and those based on my own knowledge and experience.

Results

Remember, people don't buy products, they buy the results that the products deliver. To get those results, they buy products to do jobs for them. One does not buy a saw because he wants a saw; he buys it because he needs to cut wood. He doesn't get a credit card for the sake of having a credit card but rather to facilitate the task of making purchases. It's critical to remember that, while we are focused on our products, our customers, consciously or unconsciously, view them merely as vehicles for delivering the results they need. Our challenge is to focus first, not on the product, but on the desired result. Is it quarter-inch holes, quickly-delivered hamburgers, accurately prepared tax returns, or even to be regarded as attractive or prosperous? Done correctly, our research will reveal the results that are important to our customers.

Tasks

Having identified the desired results, the next step is to identify the tasks that must be performed in order to deliver them.

Let's look at even a simple result, a quarter-inch hole. To deliver that result (i.e. drill the hole), we must:

- Determine where the hole is to be made.
- Perhaps mark the location in some way.

- Get a device capable of cutting the material (e.g. a drill bit).
- Possibly attach the cutting device to some sort of tool that facilitates making the hole (e.g. an electric drill).
- Position and activate the tool and cutting device.
- Create the hole.
- Put the device(s) away and clean up.
- Possibly perform periodic maintenance.

More complex results may require multiple levels of tasks. The first level of tasks is broader. If the result is quickly-delivered hamburgers, the first-level tasks might be procuring and storing materials (meat, buns, etc.), taking orders, collecting payment, gathering ingredients at a workstation, cooking the burgers and so on. Then, each of <u>these</u> tasks can get broken down further as we did with the holes.

Is that a lot of work? You bet! But consider that **each of these miniscule tasks, many or even most of which may be taken for granted, may offer an opportunity for creating value if looked at in a new light!**

Constraints

The next step is to consider the obstacles or constraints that make completion of each task difficult or impossible. Our ingenuity as humans allows us to overcome constraints daily, often doing so almost automatically. An obvious example is finding an alternate route when a highway is closed. We do it so often and under so many circumstances that we often take such flexibility for granted. The alternate way of doing things can, after a time, become the norm and the constraint that necessitated it becomes forgotten.

Let me give you an example involving a terribly low-tech product. When you attend a large banquet, you can be confident that your rubber chicken was not freshly prepared. So that all attendees could be served relatively quickly, the food was cooked long before you sat down to eat, then stored in a heated cabinet to maintain its temperature. The preparation process includes the steps of arranging the food on each plate and placing a cover over it. A half dozen or so of these "assemblies" is stacked and the stack is carried to the cabinet with the intention of placing the plates inside. Here's where the constraint comes in; the cabinet door is closed to keep in the heat! While still holding a stack of hot plates, the worker now must somehow get the door open. That is done by a dance such as unlatching the door with a little finger and then opening it with one foot while balancing on the other. If the worker leaves the door ajar as she leaves to simplify the procedure the next time around, a supervisor sometimes notices the open door and closes it to avoid heat loss. Then the dance begins again. You may laugh, but these

Figure 7 - The Banquet Dance

behaviors were observed and this photo taken during an actual ethnographic study! The point of the story, though, is that these heated cabinets had been used and the silly dance practiced <u>for decades.</u> The practice came to be considered normal and, until that ethnographical study was done, no one saw anything wrong with it! Only through ethnographic research with an eye towards constraints was it corrected with a simple foot device that unlatched and opened the door. When the product was introduced, everyone was amazed! In retrospect, the solution seems obvious; but you can't create a solution until you first recognize the problem! A focus on constraints can offer incredible opportunities.

Underserved and Overserved Needs

Mr. Ulwick's book also addresses the critical concept of overserved and underserved needs.[33]

If a leading product is rich in a particular feature and if its success can be attributed to that richness, it's tempting to believe that more and more of that feature will result in still more success. That concept was discussed earlier when we explored Kano theory. You will remember that, in Figure 6, I took the liberty of "tweaking" the Kano model's performance curve to indicate that above a certain point further improvement adds no value. To address that phenomenon, Mr. Ulwick uses the term "Overserved needs". Having spent most of my career in new product development, I have experienced the phenomenon all too often. I would hate to account for the thousands of hours that I've seen squandered on improving products in areas that were already overserved.

Equally wasteful are time and money spent on features that Kano labeled as "indifferent", that is the ones that deliver no compelling benefit and therefor offer no value.

At the other end of the scale are the underserved needs; those that, <u>while important to the user,</u> are not addressed at all or which, like the banquet cart door, are not even recognized. Clearly, this is a diamond mine.

This concept deserves far more attention than can be devoted here and I strongly recommend Mr. Ulwick's book.

The Ersatz Catalog

Once you've identified a package of benefits for a proposed product (or product line), it's difficult to know whether those benefits will, in fact, be embraced by the marketplace. A simple device that I've seen used effectively is the "ersatz catalog"

When you believe you know what the product might be like, create very rudimentary prototype marketing collateral to promote it. If the project is a single product, the collateral might be a simple "cut sheet". A full product line calls for something more comprehensive, perhaps a rudimentary catalog outlining the breadth of the line as well as the salient features of the individual products. Don't spend a lot of effort making it "pretty"; your primary focus should be the content. The key is the creation of the "bullet points" that will inspire adoption of the product.

It's amazing how this simple device highlights the strengths and weaknesses of your proposal for, if you can't create inspiring collateral based on the benefits offered by your product, it's time to back up and redefine the project.

Product Platforms

A product platform is, essentially, a set of underlying elements that can be shared among a wide range of products. By sharing common elements, the platform makes it possible to introduce an entire product line in a shorter time and at a much lower cost than would be possible if each product in the line were created as a separate project. As we will see, the approach has other advantages as well.

For many of us, the concept of product platforms came into our consciousness in the early 1980's when, facing a financial disaster, Chrysler introduced the "K-car". The platform in this case involved the chassis, drive train and so on. In 1981, with much fanfare, Chrysler introduced the first cars based on the K-car platform; the Plymouth Reliant and Dodge Aries. Throughout the 80's, additional versions were introduced but the game changer came in 1984 when, using the same platform, Chrysler was able to introduce the first minivans, the Dodge Caravan and Plymouth Voyager[34].

Having allowed Chrysler not only to survive but to survive, the platform approach has been shown to be a powerful concept that has broad application. If the platform is well envisioned initially, the ability to share major components and technologies across a wide range of related products will deliver several distinct advantages.

First, the overall cost of the development program will be reduced since the underlying platform components (e.g. in the case of a vehicle, the motor, transmission, chassis, etc.) need only be designed once and then applied across the product line. Likewise, the use of common manufacturing systems will result in lower costs for them as well.

Second, time to market for the entire product line will be shorter than it would be if the products and the systems to produce them were developed independently.

Third, manufacturing and purchasing of common components in larger volume will result in lower cost of goods sold.

Fourth, once a robust platform has been developed, it can often be applied even to products that were not envisioned when the platform was conceived.

Nothing is without its disadvantages, however. Because of the greater care needed for the design of the underlying components, development cost and time to market for the initial offering can be greater when using the platform approach.

Also, though I am a strong proponent of the use of product platforms, I have often been frustrated by the difficulties that sometimes arise when a revision to one of the basic elements is necessary. Suppose products A, B, C, etc. are based on platform Mercury. Now suppose a desired change in product A requires a change in core component alpha. If alpha was used only on A, the change might be straightforward. However, suppose it turns out that the change to alpha will cause a major problem when it is used in Product C. Modifying the proposed change in alpha so that it avoids the problem with product C could cause issues for product N. And so on. Not only must the proposed change be vetted against the entire product line, in some cases finding a compromise is difficult or impossible. The issues created by this interconnectedness can be frustrating but, on balance, the advantages of product platforms far outweigh the disadvantages.

I qualified the advantages listed above with the words, "If the platform is well envisioned initially." A useful tool for envisioning the platform is the product roadmap.

Product Roadmaps

Whether or not your product offering will be platform-based, it is likely that will involve more than one SKU (Stock Keeping Unit). Given the understandable desire to achieve increased sales as quickly as possible, there will always be pressure for the offering to be as broad as possible. Often, there will be pressure to introduce everything at once both to make a "big bang" in the marketplace and to maximize sales potential. There are several reasons, however, to spread introductions over time.

- The larger the scope of the initial project, the longer it will take and the greater the risk. Conversely, limiting the scope <u>of the initial offering</u> will reduce both risk and time to initial introduction.

- Though sales of a more limited initial offering will be more modest, they will come much sooner than they would if you were to delay introduction until "everything" is ready. As a result, the earlier positive cash flow will help to fund ongoing development.

- Earlier introduction provides earlier feedback, which can be used to refine future offerings.

- While a "big bang" introduction may have great impact, spacing the introduction over time provides an ongoing opportunity to keep customers engaged through "New from..." messages. In addition, it sometimes gives the salesforce justification for additional sales calls.

Limiting the scope of the initial introduction must be done judiciously, however; the range of products offered must have the "critical mass" needed to have a significant impact on the market. This is an important point that cannot be overemphasized.

While it is indeed possible to have the product line evolve naturally, it is wise to have a plan for how that evolution might progress. Graphically, the anticipated evolution can be depicted in a Product Roadmap such as the one shown in Figure 8.

The vertical axis here represents the feature richness of the

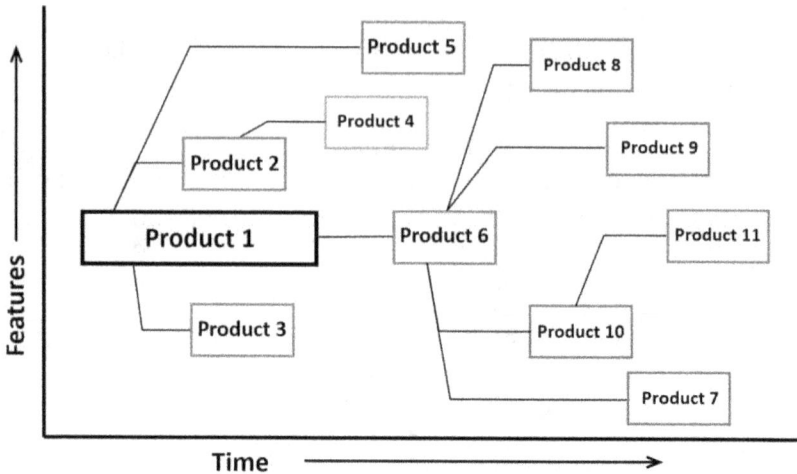

Figure 8 - Product Roadmap

product. In more basic terms, the "better" products are nearer the top of the chart. Admittedly, though, such distinctions are often arbitrary and, in some cases, vertical position becomes one of graphical convenience. The horizontal axis represents time.

In the example, Product 1 represents the core product. Products 2, 3, 5 and 6 are derivations of or accessories for product 1. Product 4 is an offshoot of product 2 and so on.

If such a roadmap is created during the initial planning stages and updated over time, there will be, from the beginning and throughout the product's life, an appreciation for how the product line will develop over time. Such an understanding can reduce the pressure for the initial offering to be overly complex.

Chapter 6 - The Development Process

"We get brilliant results from average people managing brilliant processes, while our competitors get average or worse results from brilliant people managing broken processes."

— *Fujio Cho, Former President Toyota Motor Corporation*

Good is the enemy of great.

— *Jim Collins*

If you've ever been saddled with a new process simply to satisfy ISO or some other regulatory or standards requirement, the word "process" can bring back memories of endless paperwork that, while satisfying the standard or regulation, did nothing for the organization other than to slow it down and frustrate the people who were trying to get a job done. Sadly, such ineffective, inefficient processes are all too common and sometimes originate, not from some uncaring, external agency but from within our very own organizations.

While a poorly conceived process is likely to do more harm than good, a well-designed and intelligently executed one will enhance results while saving time and reducing risk, effort and frustration. Even the best people, working without an effective process will, at best, struggle to deliver acceptable results while people who are only "good", working within an excellent process can often deliver excellent results.

Our goal here is to institute a process that is not just good but excellent. But wait; that's just the kind of generality we warned about in the last chapter! Just as we would not begin designing a product until we know exactly what benefits it must deliver, neither can we begin designing a process in similar ignorance. So, let's start by discovering the benefits our process must deliver.

NPD Process Deliverables

Focus

Too many companies squander time and money on NPD projects which, even if they were to be executed flawlessly, would be unlikely to have substantial positive results. Some projects are ill-fated because they are not in alignment with the organization's corporate or new product strategies. Some are aimed at markets for which the company does not have and cannot readily develop distribution channels. Others have addressable markets that are so small that, even with a large market share, would deliver only meager returns.

I wrote earlier that NPD guru Dr. Robert Cooper contends that only one out of every 9 <u>concepts</u> results in a successful new product. He also contends that it takes 100 <u>ideas</u> to get that single project[35]! Therefore, one of the fundamental benefits expected from our process is the ability to maximize the organization's return on its new product program by focusing resources on those projects having the greatest potential. You can't focus on everything. Therefore, our process must help us to cull out not only bad projects but also the good (or even very good) ones that are simply not as good as the excellent ones that have the greatest value. Ignoring the less worthy projects to focus on the excellent ones, while sometimes controversial, is the surest way of optimizing results. As Dr. Cooper says, "You've got to drown some puppies!"

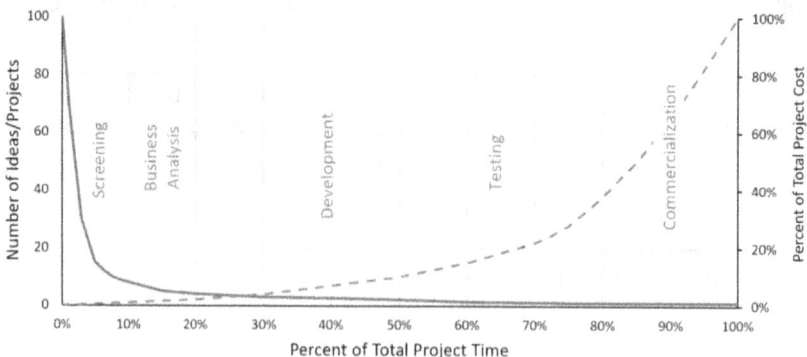

Figure 9 - Project Attrition

The best way to assure focus is to not only cull less-worthy projects but to do it as quickly as possible. While the data used for Figure 9 are simply illustrative, the dashed-line represents the way costs increase during the life of a typical project. Initially, costs are low but increase dramatically through development, testing and commercialization.

Our goal should be to cull projects early in their life before significant resources are expended as illustrated by the solid curve. A kill near the end of a project means that you have not only wasted a lot of time and money, you have also missed the opportunity to work on a worthier one.

The final step in maintaining focus is to prioritize the projects remaining so that the worthiest receive the attention they deserve, even at the cost of starving those less worthwhile.

High Quality Execution

Another of the major expectations of our process is that it will assure that we do the right things, that we do them correctly and that we do them in the right sequence. Quality of execution means that market and customer research is done effectively. It means that that research is used to develop concepts that will delight customers with benefits that are truly important to them. It means that products or services are designed and tested in such a way that they deliver the benefits at a price that is both attractive to the customer and profitable to the company. It means that the products can be produced in a timely manner and with acceptable levels of disruption to operations. And of course, it means that the company receives an excellent return on its investment.

If the project team is not executing each and every one of these things well, we should expect the process to force a correction or the cancellation of the project.

Risk Management

Management of risk is a major objective. We've already established that new product development is inherently risky and that risk is not something that companies swallow eagerly. While we cannot eliminate the inherent risk without abandoning all efforts towards new products, by instituting specific protocols along the way, we can keep them in balance with the anticipated rewards.

Speed

Based on prior experiences with processes, this one may be a bit of a surprise. One of the most frequently expressed concerns about use of a formalized process is that, "It will slow us down." In fact, the concern is a valid one; a poorly conceived or poorly executed process <u>will</u> quite likely slow things down. I've experienced exactly that and I'll bet you have, too!

A properly designed and intelligently executed process, on the other hand, will help you to succeed more quickly. You will notice that I used the term "succeed more quickly." I did not say, "will help you get any product, no matter how flawed, to market more quickly." It is quite possible that, ignoring the process, you can throw something together and get it out quickly, but our objective should never be to get "something" to market. Rather, it should be to develop and introduce a product that, from the day it is introduced, is eagerly embraced by the marketplace and has a powerful, positive effect on the organization.

The cliché asks, "If you don't have time to do it right, how will you find time to do it over?" Our goal here is to implement a process to do it as quickly as we can while still doing it well.

Product Excellence

Whether we offer the best product on the market or simply the best for the price should be based on our corporate strategy. By any measure, however, our products must offer value greater than those of our competitors. Our aim is not to establish a level playing field; it is to tilt the field in our favor!

Obviously, a product cannot be considered excellent unless it, above all, effectively addresses needs that have been previously underserved. Our process should assure that we develop products that have excellent quality <u>relative to selling price</u>. In other words, they must deliver excellent <u>value</u>. Hyundai, at least at this point in their evolution, cannot be expected to compete on overall quality against the likes of Mercedes, <u>nor should they even try</u>! However, many feel that their value relative to their price is actually superior.

Quality targets for each project must be established in light of both the product's target market and the organization's corporate and New Product strategies. Our process must assure that we meet or exceed those targets.

Alignment

Just as the success of an athletic team depends on all team members working together, the success of NPD projects is highly dependent on the collaboration of all parts of the organization. NPD is not just the responsibility of marketing. Or sales. Or technology. While overall responsibility must lie with top management, all departments have a very real responsibility to not only tolerate but to proactively support the program for the overall good of the organization, <u>even when their provincial interests are compromised</u>.

Our process must assure inter-departmental alignment at all levels, from corporate department heads to project team members.

Profitability

We must never lose sight of the fact that, at least in most cases, the purpose of all of this is to make a profit for our organization! Generally, we would expect our new products to offer profitability at least as great as any they replace and as the company's overall profit.

To also assure a favorable payback from the project investment, our process must provide for periodic reviews of all financials; proposed pricing, project costs, production costs, selling and distribution costs, net present value and so on.

The Phase-Gate Concept

As its name implies, the phase-gate process is based upon the concept of dividing a project into a series of phases separated by control points or "gates". The concept is not at all new; it has been around for decades. I was, in fact, introduced to it in early 1979 by the late Jacque Edwards[36].

Put simply, the Phase-Gate process accomplishes the objectives just cited by reviewing critical variables at significant decision points such as when the project is initiated, when engineering is about to begin, when capital equipment is about to be purchased and so forth. These milestones, or "gates", divide the project into a series of phases. At each gate, a group of "gatekeepers", generally business unit executives, review the facts and determine whether the project is to continue into the next phase, be placed on hold, or be terminated to free resources for other opportunities.

To the best of my knowledge, no one has done more to promote the use of the process than Dr. Robert G. Cooper, who also coined and trademarked the popular term, "Stage-Gate$^{®}$"[37]. It is in deference to Dr. Cooper's trademark that I use the generic term "phase-gate". While my own work has been greatly influenced by Dr. Cooper, we have differences beyond semantics. My decades of experience working directly with such a process has led me to reposition some of the gates to points that I find are more conducive to smooth project flow.

Let me state here that I have heard and carefully considered the arguments against a phase-gate process. I agree with the proponents that it can be unnecessarily restrictive and that it can cause an organization to miss disruptive opportunities. However, those unfortunate results will occur only when the process is followed dogmatically. If it is intelligently applied as I will describe, the results will be those outlined above.

Process Structure

While many companies use a funnel to illustrate the product, I don't like the analogy. What comes out of a funnel? Everything that goes in! That is precisely what should NOT happen with our process; remember, one of our prime objectives is to filter out less-deserving projects. Therefore, I've concocted the diagram shown in Figure 10. While a bit more complex, it illustrates the process as what it is, a set of filters that purify the project stream by removing those projects that do not pass muster. The filters, of course, represent the gates and the sections of "pipe" between them the phases. It is significant that the pipeline narrows more aggressively and that the "wastebaskets" are larger during the early phases, indicating the importance of sifting out most inferior projects before significant resources have been expended on them.

The figure on the following page illustrates a full, 5-gate process intended for use on major projects. Lower-risk projects can employ simplified processes that will be addressed shortly.

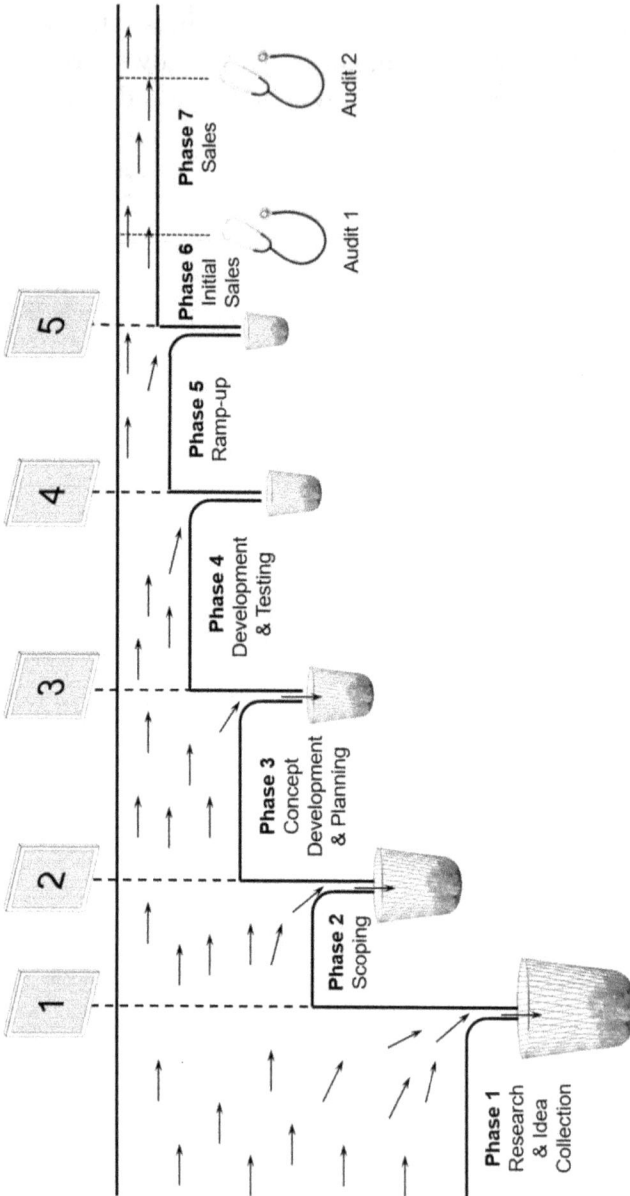

Figure 10 - The Phase/Gate Process

Phases and Gates in Detail

What follows is an outline of key activities that typically take place during each phase and the issues that are addressed at each gate of a "full-blown" project; that is, one with significant investment, complexity or risk. Simplified processes, better suited for simpler projects will omit some of the activities listed here.

Be forewarned that this is neither a comprehensive list nor is it necessarily entirely appropriate for your organization. In even the typical organization, there are tasks that do not appear here. Some that are listed may be inappropriate for you while others should be added in their stead. What follows is intended merely as an illustration of the nature of activities and questions.

Phase 1 - Research & Idea Collection

An important element here is volume; there must be a lot of grist for the mill if we expect enough quality grain after the chaff is removed! The organization must be constantly aware of changes in technology, the marketplace and elsewhere. Engineers, marketers and others must continuously monitor trade journals and the Internet as well as attend trade shows, seminars and conferences in a search for both opportunities and threats.

What changes are happening in the marketplace? With what new issues are our customers coping? What is happening in our customers' markets that might drive them to change the way they do business. In what ways will those changes affect their needs and wants? As we research customer needs for other products as discussed in chapter 5, what observations unrelated to that research reveal additional opportunities? What are our competitors doing or failing to do and what doors might that open for us?

What technological advances are being made? What new capabilities, materials or processes might open the way to the development of exciting, and perhaps even disruptive, new products? What material shortages or price increases will prompt changes in our business or the businesses of our customers? What new or revised laws, regulations or voluntary compliance standards will constrain our or our customers' businesses in ways that will compel or inspire change?

In addition to monitoring these and other factors and encouraging product ideas from employees directly involved in the NPD process, some companies actively or passively seek ideas from other employees and even from outside sources. There is an important caveat, however. As you collect suggestions, be conscious that, depending on the nature of the suggestion and other considerations, a person making a suggestion could have legal rights to the intellectual property surrounding resulting products. I strongly recommend input from legal counsel having expertise in intellectual property before reading or listening to suggestions from the outside. For greater detail, see "Outside Ideas" in appendix D.

Gate 1 – Idea Screen

If you have a robust process to discover opportunities, you will generate more than you can possibly resource. In fact, if you don't generate that volume, your front-end process needs work! The idea screen is intended to weed out, not only those ideas that are clearly inappropriate but also the good or very good ones that must be rejected to allow the organization to focus on the truly great ones.

The key questions to be addressed at this gate are:

- Does the opportunity fit our organization's overall and new product strategies?
- Does it fit a market that we serve or want to serve?
- Do we believe that the project's potential makes it worth considering?
- Do we have or can we create a channel to get the product to market?

At this gate we face two conflicting imperatives. First, we most likely need to screen out a high percentage of the ideas submitted. On the other hand, we most definitely don't want to reject those apparently crazy ideas that could result in a disruptive product!

Approval at Gate 1 signifies that the project is acceptable from a strategic standpoint. It authorizes and funds further limited investigation to gather more data. The word "<u>limited</u>" is important; resist the urge to expend huge amounts of time or money until the project passes through Gate 2.

Phase 2 – Project Scoping

Phase 2 does not require a full-fledged team; one or two marketing folks and one or two representing technology and perhaps production will generally be sufficient.

It is during this phase that we generate <u>initial</u> concepts that would <u>seem</u> to address the opportunity presented at Gate 1. Because in-depth research is not to be done at this point, the concepts will, by definition, be nothing more than preliminary ones. There are two important reasons to limit the development of the concepts during this phase. The first is, of course, that the whole point of this phase is to put a toe in the water without incurring a large expenditure of resources. The second is that people tend to fall in love with their ideas in proportion to the amount of effort they put into creating them. If the in-depth customer research that will be done in the next phase points in other directions, this emotional capital could hamper or preclude the necessary changes.

Beyond product concepts, the information to be compiled at this point includes <u>very</u> <u>preliminary</u> assessments of:

- The market. What opportunities exist? How big might the market be? Who is or would be our competition? What would we <u>guess</u> is the sales potential?

- Technical realities. In general, what technical competencies are required? Do we have or can we access those competencies? Are we likely to be successful from a technical standpoint or are there some unreasonably difficult obstacles?

- Regulatory requirements. Are there any regulatory or other standards that will be unreasonably difficult to meet? On the other hand, are there regulatory or other standards that would stimulate the sale of this product?

- Intellectual property. Are we aware of any patents that might restrict our ability to operate? Conversely, what are our initial thoughts about the likelihood of our obtaining patent protection on something we develop?

- A <u>very preliminary</u> Financial Analysis. **Please do not take this too seriously during this phase**; many a breakthrough and even disruptive project has been killed by applying financial rigor before the opportunity was fully understood!

I stress again the fact that the resources expended here, though greater than those expended during phase 1, should still be modest. If we can expect that a significant number of these ideas will meet an early demise, there is good reason to limit our expenditure of resources. Having said that, the work that we do perform must be done well. Most work required at this early stage can and should be done from the office in 40-60 hours of effort expended over a tight timeline. The Internet makes it possible to get a good feel for the landscape and a few phone calls and local visits to key customers and channel partners will generally be enough to put a bit more meat on the bones.

Gate 2 – Second Level Evaluation

Gate 2 represents a somewhat closer look, based on more information than was available at Gate 1. The key questions to be addressed at this gate are:

- How big is the addressable market? In other words, if we could capture 100% share, what would our sales be? Who are the main competitors and how strong are they? What market share might we reasonably attain? All things considered, does the project have sufficient sales and profit potential to be worthwhile?

- Do we feel there is an opportunity to develop a product offering with a sustainable advantage?

- Do we have the necessary capacity & technical competence?

- What are regulatory and IP restrictions and are they likely to be unreasonably burdensome?

- What regulatory issues offer opportunities and what IP opportunities exist?

- Does it appear this could be a good project financially?

Approval at Gate 2 authorizes <u>and approves funding</u> for much more detailed research into customer needs and the feasibility of the project as well as the development of concepts. Put another way, it authorizes and funds the building of the business case.

Phase 3 – Concept Development and Project Planning

The business case is established during Phase 3. This work includes a much deeper dive into issues previously studied as well as additional studies to establish targets, including a <u>detailed</u> set of specifications for the product(s) to be offered. While resources from additional departments are needed, it is still not necessary to charter a full-fledged, cross-functional team. Specifically, the work during Phase 3 encompasses:

- Rigorous customer needs research as explained in chapter 5.
- A thorough competitive analysis.
- Development of detailed product concepts and creation of means of communicating them, such as renderings, models (CAD or physical) and/or <u>crude</u> prototypes.
- Establishment of <u>complete</u> product specifications. It is crucial that these specifications be complete and accurate as they will serve as the basis for technical development.
- Evaluation of the concept(s) and product specifications by marketing, sales and trusted key customers and channel partners to assess acceptability and sales potential.
- Evaluation of the concept(s) and product specifications by operations, including procurement and production to identify and address any significant obstacles.
- Rigorous intellectual property analysis, including freedom to operate in view of pre-existing external patents and an assessment of the probability of obtaining patents that would prevent or discourage knock-offs.
- A sound sales forecast. (For more on the art of forecasting, see chapter 7.)
- A thorough financial analysis & justification.

- A detailed project plan, including timelines and resource availability and allocation.

Gate 3 – Go to Development

Gate 3 is sometimes referred to as a "money gate" because it represents authorization of a sharp increase in expenditure. The key questions to be addressed at this gate are:

- Is the proposed product one that we want to offer? Will it reflect favorably on the company; will we be proud to offer it?

- Will it provide a distinct, sustainable advantage? Is it differentiated from competitive products in ways that are meaningful to the customer? Can we protect it from competitive assault through patents or other means?

- Do we have or can we access the necessary competency and capacity to design, produce, market, sell and distribute it effectively?

- Are we satisfied with this project as an investment? Is the projected return favorable? Are we willing and able to authorize the necessary funds to carry the project to completion? A comment here is appropriate. I've seen cases where, even though the capital requirements were clearly presented at Gate 3 and approval to proceed was granted, when the design was completed and it was time to "pony up", the capital investment was denied and the project cancelled! What a tragic waste of resources!

- What is this project's attractiveness and priority against other projects? Even if this is an excellent project, are there others that are more favorable and which should therefore be resourced instead? While choices among competing worthy projects are best addressed through portfolio management (see chapter 8), it makes little sense to approve funding at a gate and then, after additional expenses are incurred, set the project aside in preference for another. If there are serious concerns, it might be appropriate to put the project on a very short hold pending portfolio review. Project priority is a key question and a difficult one to address. Nevertheless, failing to do so will result in a logjam of products, each one lacking the resources necessary to bring it to fruition.

- Do we believe in the team? Even an excellent project is likely to fail if the team is not competent, motivated and aligned. I've attended too many gate meetings where a team member made a statement and another said something like, "Wait, I never agreed to that!" or "No, that's not at all the way I remember that discussion!" Wow; that is the time for the gatekeepers to send the team away and move on to discussion of the next project!

Approval at Gate 3 authorizes <u>and funds</u> design and testing of the proposed product based on the specifications presented. Also authorized and funded are planning for production. Funding for capital investment is <u>tentatively</u> approved as well.

Phase 4 – Design and Testing

I must mention that many implementations of the phase gate process incorporate a gate between development and testing. I've tried it that way and was continuously frustrated by a simple fact; testing often reveals the need for design revisions! Under that structure, let's say a design is presented for a gate review and approved. The approval authorizes the team to proceed to testing. Too often, testing reveals that the design is fundamentally unsound; major design changes must be made that affect features, cost, or whatever. As a result, the design (with its associated advantages) that was approved by the gatekeepers <u>is no longer on the table</u>. Do we then have to <u>go back</u> to that gate and get approval for the revised design? Those of us who have lived the day to day realities of product development understand the sad reality that this can happen multiple times in a single project! This means either a repeated loop in the process or "cheating" by doing a certain amount of testing before it's been authorized.

How much better it is to acknowledge the reality and combine the two activities into a single phase as recommended here! There is a caveat, however; if testing is terribly expensive or prolonged, then approval of the design prior to testing is appropriate even with its drawbacks. In that case, the process can be modified by inserting a gate.

In my preferred process, however, Phase 4 is when the design and testing (or "technical development" if that term better applies to your organization) are carried out. For any significant project, it will generally require a significant investment of time, personnel and other resources. This is the time to charter a full cross-functional team of competent individuals, <u>each fully empowered to speak for his or her department</u>.

The work performed during Phase 4 is extensive and involves, to one degree or another, most facets of the organization. It includes:

- Product design, of course. This is the core activity and all others revolve around it. This does not involve design engineers alone; while they have primary responsibility, all functions must collaborate towards the design that serves the company best.

  The production department (by whatever name) must play a proactive role, not only providing yes/no feedback on proposed designs but, more importantly, providing suggestions for how the design might be modified to better fit the realities faced before they are available for sale. For example, procurement is responsible, initially to warn of any materials that are difficult to obtain, later to facilitate collaborative interaction between suppliers and designers and finally to identify and select suppliers. Manufacturing engineering (or similar function) must address design aspects that are potentially troublesome to produce, making positive suggestions for revisions. Similarly, quality assurance is called upon to identify potential QC issues and make suggestions to assure the production of high-quality products.

- Prototyping & testing. While I'm addressing these activities separately from design, all three are interrelated and iterative. Prototyping and testing should be begun early and repeated often. Initial prototypes might be of a single component or sub-system and the associated tests of limited scope. However, delaying testing until the entire design is complete can be terribly inefficient if earlier limited testing would have revealed component or subsystem design flaws in a timelier manner.

It should go without saying that both alpha and beta testing is often required. Alpha or lab testing is valuable and even essential, of course. In addition to appropriate standardized tests, ad hoc ones that help to predict field performance can also be helpful. This, however, should normally be supplemented with beta testing by end users in the real world.

- Production planning. As the design evolves, production must begin to make plans for commercialization. For example, procurement must know how and from whom materials will be obtained. Manufacturing engineering must determine exactly where and how the product will be made and what facilities, equipment and personnel are required. Quality assurance must identify production testing requirements and develop plans for implementation. As the design nears completion, this information and more must be rolled up into a comprehensive plan to assure that high quality products can be produced in the forecast quantities at or below the target cost.

- Feedback from trusted key customers and channel partners (dealers, distributers and so on). This is to be sought, not only after design is complete but frequently during the design process. From my perspective, nothing is as frustrating as completing the design of a product that functions perfectly from a technical perspective but is not embraced by customers. In addition to verifying that the design is on the right track (or prompting you to revise it if it is not) this activity allows marketing and sales to verify or update their sales forecast; a critical activity. Admittedly, this will expose you to the risk of competitors becoming aware of what you are doing and appropriate steps must be taken to mitigate the risk. Is it not riskier, though, to introduce a product that falls flat in the marketplace?

- Updated intellectual property analysis. As the design evolves, what had been preliminary analyses can and must be replaced with more realistic ones. The patent landscape must be examined to see if patents not owned by the company might be infringed. If so, design changes to avoid infringement must be instituted or licenses obtained. On a more positive note, opportunities for patents are identified. Patent searches are done and, if there is potential for meaningful patents, applications are filed to protect the IP even if the company decides not to introduce the proposed product.

- Analysis of product safety and compliance with regulations and voluntary compliance standards. Product safety as well as compliance with regulations and voluntary compliance standards must be reviewed as the design evolves and appropriate design changes made as needed.

- Preliminary marketing plan development. As the design proceeds, marketing should begin to identify marketing activities and evaluate their impact on sales. A sometimes-forgotten issue here is the potential cost of promotional activities. It is not uncommon for a company to base its forecast on a given marketing program, then neglect to implement the program and wonder why sales have fallen short of forecast!

- Financial update. As implementation costs, sales forecasts and production cost estimates solidify, the financial analysis must be updated to reflect the new realities.

- Iteration on all the above. It would be wonderful if these elements could be addressed sequentially in a single pass. Sadly, the entire process is iterative and, in most cases, the design and other plans will evolve as additional information becomes available.

Gate 4 – Prepare for Production

If Gate 3 is a money gate, Gate 4 is, at least potentially, a money gate on steroids! In some cases, the proposed product can be made with existing facilities, equipment and tooling and, consequently, at limited expense. On the other hand, the passing of this gate could mean the expenditure of millions of capital dollars for equipment and even facilities. In either case, there is a lot of work to be done during Phase 5 so approval here should never be taken lightly. The key questions to be addressed at this gate are:

- Do we still believe in the team? As stressed earlier, the competency, alignment and commitment of the team are critical to success. Before proceeding, the company must be confident that the team is up to the task.

- Are we completely comfortable with the product to be offered? Does it offer benefits that will be compelling in the marketplace and will the proposed selling price be acceptable in view of the value offered? Is the product sufficiently differentiated from competitive offerings? Are the competitive advantages sustainable by patent protection or other means?

- Was our alpha and beta testing sufficient? Have the results convinced us that the product will function as expected and that customers will embrace the product and buy it in sufficient quantities to fulfill the forecast?

- Are we comfortable that our product will be safe and in compliance with statutory regulations and applicable voluntary compliance standards?

- Do the proposed procurement, production and QC plans give us confidence that we can consistently produce a quality product at the cost, in the quantities and at the rate required by the forecast?

- Are we confident in the financial aspects of the project? Do we believe the figures? Are we satisfied with the forecast sales and profits and the project's return on investment? Do we have the resources and willingness to fund it according to the plan?

Approval at Gate 4 authorizes <u>and funds</u> ramp up to production, including the procurement of all needed facilities, equipment, tooling and/or personnel. It also authorizes and funds the preparation of a detailed marketing plan.

Phase 5 – Ramp-up

Phase 5 is where everything is made ready for full-scale production. If authorized, limited inventory may also be built near the end of this phase. Specifically:

- If required, facilities are acquired and commissioned. Necessary machinery, tooling and all other necessary equipment is procured and installed.
- Production personnel are assigned and trained.
- Pilot production is performed to verify the efficacy of methods and training. If authorized, some inventory may be created.
- A detailed marketing plan is created and prepared for implementation.
- If desired, test marketing is performed and the marketing program adjusted as required.

In summary, during Phase 5 everything is put in place for commercial launch of the product.

Gate 5 – Go to Launch

Gate 5 authorizes commercial launch of the project. The story goes that Dr. Albert Einstein was challenged by a student who claimed that the questions on an examination were the same as on the previous year's. Dr. Einstein allegedly said, "The questions are the same; the answers are different."[38] Such is the case with Gate 5; the questions to be addressed are essentially the same as those asked at Gate 4. The reason that we have Gate 5 at all is that the passage of time may have resulted in different answers to the earlier questions. There may be cases where the actual ramp up happens so quickly and with so few changes that Gates 4 and 5 can be combined. The only truly new questions introduced here are:

- Have we established well-reasoned pricing? Is it based on product value and other market realities rather than costs? In other words, are we getting paid in full for the value we are offering? On the other hand, will the target price enable us to achieve the forecast sales? Will it generate at least the financial return previously approved and, if not, is the return nonetheless acceptable?

Approval at Gate 5 authorizes introduction and sale of the new product. One might conclude that the project has been completed at this point but it most definitely is not.

Phases 6 & 7 - Launch & Full Production

At this point, production, marketing and sales are in full swing. If all goes according to plan, customers are purchasing the product and it is shipping and performing according to plan. While the team may be freed somewhat to work on other projects, their work is not finished. It is essential that product performance and quality, sales levels and production costs be monitored and swift action taken to address any shortfalls.

Audit 1 – Process Audit

Within a few months after product launch, an audit is performed for two purposes.

First and most important is an analysis of the NPD process as it applied to this project. The focus here must not be on finding fault or assigning blame, it must be on identifying opportunities for process improvement. The key questions are:

- What went particularly well?
- What could have been done better?
- What, if any, additional education or training should have been provided?
- How might the process itself be refined?

The second purpose is to do a <u>preliminary</u> assessment of production activities, product performance and quality, sales levels and production costs. Product quality cannot be compromised, even early on. News of substandard product quality will spread throughout the salesforce and customer base amazingly quickly. <u>Any</u> issues here must be dealt with quickly and decisively. Be careful, though, to avoid overreacting to modest shortfalls in sales or profits as they are not at all unusual at this early stage. For more information, see "Adoption and Diffusion" in chapter 7.

Audit 2 – Results Audit

A results audit is called when conditions have somewhat stabilized but certainly not more than a year or so after launch. The emphasis of this audit is an analysis of results against plan. The key questions are:

- Is product functionality and quality everything that we promised?
- Were capital expenditures and project costs within budget?
- Are sales and profits at the levels we expected them to be at this point?

Here again, the focus must not be on blame and punishment; excuses are largely irrelevant. The focus, rather, must be on:

- What must be done now to correct deficiencies so that we can deliver what we promised?
- How can we further improve the NPD process to avoid similar issues with subsequent projects?

Simpler Processes for Simpler Projects

We've stressed earlier that it is important to balance rigor against risk, applying no more rigor than is necessary in light of the risk inherent in each project. To do otherwise is to encumber the process with useless red tape. Just as you wouldn't apply the same level of analysis to the selection of a candy bar as you would to the purchase of a house, neither should you burden the organization with excessive rigor in the absence of significant project risk.

What we described in detail in the previous section applies to the full-blown, 5-gate process. That process is appropriate for major projects; those that:

- Require large investments of time or money.
- Involve technologies that are new to the company or to the world.
- Are expected to have a major impact on the company's image.
- Will require a new distribution system or extensive salesforce training. Or…

- In any other way involve significant risk.

Simpler projects call for a simpler process. For many years, my normal practice was to work with the project manager at the beginning of each project to customize the process in light of that project's risk and other factors. Working together, we'd delete requirements, sometimes combine phases and sometimes even skip a phase or two entirely. For whatever reason, perhaps complacency, I continued to do this even after Dr. Cooper introduced his "Express" and "Lite" processes[39].

Eventually, Dr. Cooper convinced me that I was making way too much work for myself and, as a result, I adopted the concept (if not precisely his process details). I readily confess that life got a lot simpler for me! The simplified processes are shown in Figure 11.

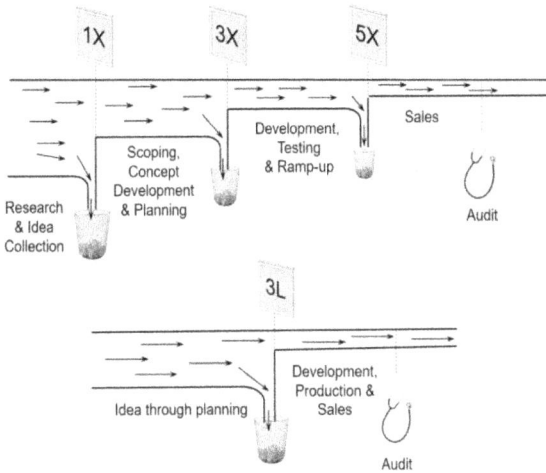

Figure 11 - Processes for Lower-Risk Projects

While the 5-gate process used is for the most complex projects, the 1-gate process is obviously for the other end of spectrum; the projects sometimes referred to as no-brainers. By the way, although I'm using it here, I hate that term. I've been bitten in the posterior so frequently by so-called no brainers that I sometimes think of them as decisions made by people with no brain.

"Why would we need a formal process at all for a so-called no brainer?", you ask. We all know from experience that nothing is ever as simple as it appears at first. Let's say the proposed new product is nothing more than an existing product in a new color. Wow, what's the big deal; no brainer, right? Well, maybe so. But wait a minute. Will we have to buy and inventory a new paint? Will production have to schedule an additional run from time to time? Will we incur lost production and production delays because of the color change? Will we have to inventory a new finished product SKU or will every order for the new product involve a separate production run? Will the catalog have to be updated? The list is potentially a lot longer. Certainly, the answer <u>may</u> clearly be that we should introduce that new color but there are, nevertheless, factors that should <u>at least be considered</u> before we go rushing in! The answer is a simple process with a single decision point (Gate) where such questions are asked and answered.

Between the two extremes lies the 3-gate process as illustrated in figure 11.

	1-Gate		3-Gate		5-Gate	
Strategic Fit	Perfect	☐	Perfect	☐	A stretch	☐
Competitors	Existing	☐	Existing	☐	New	☐
Distribution Channels	Existing	☐	Existing	☐	Expanded or New	☐
Resource requirements	Small	☐	Modest	☐	Substantial	☐
Capital Investment	Negligible	☐	Small	☐	Substantial	☐
Project Expense	Small	☐	Modest	☐	Substantial	☐
Technology	Existing within company	☐	Simple and well known	☐	New	☐
Customer Needs	Well understood	☐	Requires modest research	☐	Requires substantial research	☐
IP and regulatory issues	Well understood	☐	Well understood	☐	Unknown	☐
Operational fit	Perfect	☐	Very good; little change needed	☐	There are substantial issues	☐
Overall project risk	Negligible	☐	Modest	☐	Substantial	☐

Figure 12 - Process Selection Matrix

Figure 12 is an example of a simple matrix intended to <u>aid in</u> the selection of the appropriate process. Don't be deceived by the matrix, though; there is no science here. In the end, it's a subjective decision but the factors in the matrix will provide some guidance. The aim is to choose the simplest process that addresses the project's risk; the matrix simply helps you to evaluate that risk.

Simple projects do not only justify the use of fewer gates; the rigor at each gate can often be reduced as well. Notice in Figure 12 that the 1-and 3-gate processes apply for, example, to projects involving existing competitors and distribution channels. That being the case, little or no study is required in those areas. The same reasoning applies to other issues as well.

Process Execution

The best process in the world is of no value at all if it is executed poorly. Only excellent execution of an excellent process will yield the excellent results that you deserve. To assure excellent execution, keep in mind the following factors:

Commitment and Discipline

Make no mistake about it, blind, intransigent adherence to a formal process is counter-productive when some flexibility would clearly improve the outcome. In fact, it is exactly such rigidity that has given the phase/gate process a bad reputation in many quarters. Let me say this another way; regardless of how efficient and effective your new process looks on paper, if you follow it blindly, it is likely to fail!

I said back in chapter 3 that, for the process to work, the entire organization, from the top down, must be committed to it. That commitment must be demonstrated in intelligent process discipline. If gatekeepers don't take their roles seriously, if gate approval is given even when a team shows up for a meeting without having met the gate criteria, if projects are carried on outside of the process, if projects keep running in the background (even "on the back burner") after they've been killed at a gate, the organization will conclude, correctly, that the organization is not committed. At that point, the process has failed.

Intelligent balance is critical. Dogged adherence to process requirements when they are clearly irrelevant wastes time and resources while frustrating those earnestly working to get the job done. Excessive flexibility, on the other hand, will result in anarchy and the loss of the many benefits the process was intended to provide.

Consistency

For gate meetings to be both efficient and effective, both the project teams and the gatekeepers must understand exactly what information is to be presented at each gate. Therefore, a standard list of deliverables, including the issues and the precision expected at each gate, is essential. For example, a sales forecast would be expected for each gate but, while an educated guess might be appropriate at Gate 1, the forecasts presented at the later gates would be expected to be based on thorough analyses. Since simpler projects require less rigor, they will justify the use of modified lists. While creating the lists requires a fair amount of deliberation, their use reduces the possibility of wasting effort gathering superfluous information as well as of failing to provide information required by the gatekeepers.

Likewise, a consistent presentation format has significant advantages that will be discussed later in this chapter.

Simultaneous Loose/Tight Controls[40]

I borrowed that term from Tom Peters and Robert Waterman's "In Search of Excellence". Applied here, however, it means that, regardless of which of the three processes we are using, it is <u>normally</u> appropriate to expect all requirements to be fully complied with. Yet, intelligent people must have flexibility to modify the requirements for individual circumstances. Remember, we do not want to apply more rigor than a project's risk justifies. For example, if we've completed a competitive analysis for a certain product line three months ago, do we really have to do another now that we're introducing a very similar product? It's imperative, however, that the team seek any dispensations <u>in advance</u>. If, instead, they make an erroneous assumption and omit something they think is not needed and the gatekeepers disagree, they'll end up without the approval they seek and the project will be set back or terminated.

Gate Meetings

<u>*Yet another meeting???*</u>

I am among the many people who believe we have far too many meetings in our lives. I've often joked that we go to meetings to explain why we're late on a project; the excuse being that we've been busy going to meetings! Consequently, I completely understand the natural objection to yet more meetings, this time to review projects and to decide whether they should proceed to the next phase. I get it; I really do.

Unfortunately, I can see only two alternatives. One is to forget the phase/gate process entirely. The other is to replace the gate meetings with the circulation of a document containing the deliverables, asking each gatekeeper approve or disapprove.

I assume that if you've read this much of the book, I've convinced you that the first alternative is a bad one.

The second alternative, that of passing a document around for signature, is one against which I would argue vehemently. I contend that, if the results are to be meaningful, circulating a document will take more time than a well-organized and well-executed meeting (more on meetings shortly). If they do more than scan and rubber stamp the documents, many reviewers will have questions or will wish to seek clarification. How, then, will the resulting answers and clarifications be circulated and what new questions will result from that exchange? If, on the other hand, clarification is not sought and delivered or questions are not asked and answered, can we expect the gatekeepers to reach intelligent conclusions?

The most serious drawback, however, is the lack of collaborative <u>dialogue</u>! The most important advantage of having a properly run gate meeting is that it facilitates a shared understanding of the facts, a free (if sometimes volatile!) exchange of opinions and a shared ownership of the final decision. I've seen the pass-the-document-around process at work and the results are abominable.

Meeting imperatives

So, having eliminated the alternatives we're faced with the task of making gate meetings as efficient as possible. Based on my own experiences, I feel safe in assuming that most meetings you attend are largely a waste of time. It is possible, however, to have an efficient meeting if it has the following characteristics:

- An agenda, prepared in cooperation with interested parties, is distributed well in advance of the meeting. That agenda lists not only the topics to be discussed but <u>the time to be allotted to each</u>. While it may sometimes be appropriate to depart from the schedule, doing so must be done with the appreciation of its impact on subsequent projects. (More on that below under meeting tools.)

- Requirements for gate approval are pre-established and fully understood by both gatekeepers and team members.

- Each project is presented in a standard format using templates created to minimize effort and to assure that the requirements have been met.

- Copies of all presentations are delivered to all gatekeepers by a specified time well in advance of the meeting. (I recommend 2 to 3 working days).

- Each gatekeeper carefully reads all documents and comes to each meeting prepared for discussion. If there are questions or controversy, the gatekeeper seeks clarification in advance of the meeting.

- Every gatekeeper is present at each meeting or is represented by a fully authorized representative with full "Power of Attorney" to act on his/her behalf. Things fall apart completely if, after a decision, someone demands a "recount" because of his or her absence, so any gatekeeper who is absent and is not represented by a "Power of Attorney" implicitly agrees to abide by all decisions made. If the gatekeeper is a truly critical one (e.g. the CEO) who is unwilling to empower a representative, the alternatives are to reschedule the meeting or to agree in advance that he/she will abide by the group's decisions.

- Based on the shared preparation, presenters NEVER go through the slides line by line or even slide by slide! Don't you hate it when a presenter thinks you can't read, even when you haven't seen the material in advance? Hands down, the best gate presentation I've ever witnessed was one where the presenter put up the title slide and said, "OK, you've reviewed all the material; any questions?" Admittedly, it's rarely that simple. Something relevant might have happened in the days between document distribution and meeting time. There may be a point of conflict that needs to be highlighted and addressed by the group. There might be something of major importance that needs a bit of additional emphasis. (Do you really want to gloss over the need for a multi-million-dollar capital investment?)

- The inevitable tangential issues are tabled for a separate session and someone is assigned to address each.

- Gatekeepers and others are <u>expected</u> to challenge data, assumptions, facts and recommendations to assess their accuracy <u>and the team's commitment and confidence</u>. At one gate meeting I chaired, a team made a compelling argument for the development of a product line that would have been new to the company. They had conducted thorough customer research and developed promising concepts. In his very authoritarian voice, the company president, who has a strong background in marketing, asked the team why they thought we'd have any success at all against the very strong market leader in that category. The team folded almost immediately, saying that his point was valid and they were wrong in asking for approval. The project was killed. In private after the meeting, the president told me that he was disappointed that the team had folded so easily, saying he thought the project was a good one. Was he wrong in allowing the project to die? Not at all. If the team had such little confidence in their work and their commitment to the project was that weak, the project would have failed upon meeting its first, inevitable obstacle. The project was already terminal, the president simply removed life support. If it was confident in its data and recommendations, the team should have fought vigorously, not yielded so readily to authority.

- The meeting is focused on collaboration. Being challenging does not mean being antagonistic! Discussion must be focused solely on issues, not people. I've harped earlier on the importance of collaboration. I'll not beat it to death here but I believe that word is perhaps the most powerful in the NPD lexicon. When people collaborate, they may argue, even passionately, but they do it respectfully and with their only goal that of reaching the best decision for the organization as a whole.

- Discussion and decisions are focused on the relevant facts. Intelligent use of a scoring model such as the one presented in appendix B can help assure that focus.

- When discussion has concluded, a decision is made on the status of the project. While some organizations send the team members from the room while the gatekeepers have further discussion and reach a decision, I strongly oppose that idea. Team members should be shown the respect of an open discussion and should be encouraged to participate in it. Witnessing and participating in the entire process will not only make the team members feel respected, it may lead to a better decision and, in any case, better prepare them for their next presentation. The decision must, of course, be reached and communicated promptly.

With respect to the project status decision, let me say that the team's role is not necessarily to argue for approval of a project! I was mentoring a client's young project manager as she prepared for the first presentation of the company's first-ever gate meeting. Her problem was that project she had been assigned was a pet project of the company's owner, yet she did not believe it fit the company's strategy. I counselled her that she had been hired as a professional and, as such, was expected to collect and study the data and make her recommendation accordingly. With a lump in her throat, she came to the meeting with a "Kill" recommendation. If you don't think that was a volatile discussion, it's because you don't know that company's owner. He was livid! He put up a series of passionate arguments, but she and her team shot them all down. In the end, the gatekeepers collectively killed the project and the owner stormed out of the room, slamming the door. As owner, he had every right to carry on with the project anyway, but he was wise enough to trust the group decision. I will say that, had he done otherwise, the company's entire phase/gate process would have been stillborn.

Meeting outcomes
It is important that the decision reached be strictly limited to one of the following options:

1. **Approval (AKA "Go")** – The project is approved to enter the next phase and all funds and other resources for that phase are allocated.

2. **Conditional Approval (AKA "Conditional Go")** – This can occur when only a minor unresolved issue is preventing

approval and the likelihood is that it will be favorably and quickly resolved. Imagine that Frank, the manufacturing engineer, reports that he believes the injection mold will cost no more than $25,000 but that he won't have confirmation until next Tuesday. The gatekeepers are naturally reluctant to grant approval without knowledge that the $25,000 figure is accurate yet are also unwilling to wait for an update at the next meeting, resulting in a delay of a month or more. If Frank's track record is a good one, the gatekeepers could choose this option to grant tentative approval (along with funding and resources) conditioned upon Frank's confirming a defined, acceptable cost by, say, Wednesday morning. It is crucial that the conditions be fully documented and enforced! In the spirit of full disclosure, (or perhaps just to "vent my spleen") I will say that I worked for a corporation that absolutely forbid conditional approvals under any circumstance. I still cannot comprehend why it would be better to wait for another meeting to discuss such a trivial issue but that may just be me.

3. **Recycle** – This occurs when key information is missing or the data presented is unacceptable. While the project has not been killed, specific actions or information are required before approval can be given. Under this outcome, the team must give an updated presentation within a specified, relatively short (i.e. 1 or 2 month) time period. The short timeframe is important because, otherwise, it's likely that other, previously acceptable data could become obsolete. A greater delay would require a new, complete gate presentation.

4. **Hold** – This occurs when the project is worthy of approval but, due to priorities, cannot be resourced immediately. Since approval automatically grants resourcing, it cannot, therefore, be approved. Here again, the hold should be only of a short duration. After a few months, the accuracy of the data is questionable and a new presentation must be made.

5. **Kill** – The project has been disapproved and <u>no further effort or resources are to be expended on it.</u> As NPD guru Bob Cooper says it, "we too often wound projects, we don't kill them'"[41] Don't fall into that trap; wounded projects sap

resources from the company and energy from your people. When a project has been killed, let it rest in peace!

I've listed the possible outcomes in an order that I felt made them easy to explain but, considering the undisputed fact that far too few projects are ever killed, I <u>strongly</u> urge you to reach your decisions in reverse order. That is, to first consider whether the project should be killed. Only if it should not be killed should it be considered for hold. Only if it should not be held should it be considered for recycle, etc. Approval should be granted only after each of the other four options has been discarded. Put another way, a project is guilty until proven innocent. The sample templates I provide my clients present the alternatives in that order.

A last word on gate meetings

I know of at least one company that schedules a dedicated gate meeting whenever a team is ready for a gate. In an organization with a vital new product program, that makes for a LOT of meetings and a lot of scheduling hassles! Given the typical difficulty of gathering high-powered people for even a single meeting, I recommend periodic (perhaps monthly) meetings at each of which several projects are presented for gate approval. Given the time and effort of scheduling, gathering, getting coffee, etc., it's much more logical to do it that way. Of course, how often you do it will depend on your own realities. I also suggest that you schedule your meetings many months in advance and expect people to arrange to be there. Naturally, there will be crises that call away key gatekeepers; if a key customer wants the CEO <u>right now</u>, that goes to the top of the priority list. However, if NPD is important to the company, responsible people will try to comply with the schedule whenever possible.

Gatekeepers - Roles & Expectations

If the gates are a critical part of the process (and I would argue fervently that they are), then it follows that the gatekeepers play a critical role. It is my considered opinion that the role of the gatekeepers is so important that responsibility should rest with the business unit's top officers. While some would argue that that those people are too busy, I would ask in turn, "What is more important than the future of the company?" There is a valid argument, I suppose, for the position that lower-level managers might serve as gatekeepers for Gate 1 and perhaps even for Gate 2 but, purist that I am, I prefer to see top executives even at those early stages of the process. To do otherwise raises the possibility that potentially disruptive products are killed prematurely based on strict guidelines when those guidelines might be set aside by daring and visionary executives.

From a functional perspective, gatekeepers should represent, at minimum, the chief executive and the department heads of all departments involved in the process. While department titles may change, perhaps considerably, from one organization to another, examples include the CEO and/or president as well as the vice presidents of marketing, sales, research, engineering, manufacturing, procurement, distribution, finance, etc. Yep, that's a lot of horsepower and a considerable investment. However, since these are the folks that will be providing the resources, enduring the pain and, hopefully, enjoying the gain, who would you leave out? The inclusion of these important people serves first to assure that their viewpoints are considered and second, to gain their emotional commitment to every project that passes a gate.

While it should go without saying, I must stress that each of those department heads is not present to serve the provincial interests of his or her department but rather to assure that the right decisions are made for the organization. Yes, I know that's almost a cliché but you and I both know how it often works!

Above all, it is critical that every one of the gatekeepers takes his or her role seriously. I'm sorry to say that I have seen gatekeepers with their eyes on their laptops or phones during a meeting, participate little or not at all, then go along with a gate approval and later undermine or at least fail to enthusiastically support an approved project. There is simply no excuse for that; every gatekeeper must be fully engaged.

I'm sorry to say I have seen gatekeepers who felt it was their job to trip up the presenter, perhaps to demonstrate their knowledge or authority. Tough, collegial challenges aimed at gaining an understanding of the facts or an assessment of the qualifications, commitment or alignment of the team are both appropriate and expected. Mean-spirited comments and questions that belittle or badger presenters are not!

Just as any good leader fills many roles, so do the gatekeepers. From the title, we might correctly assume they are judges, deciding what projects are appropriate for the company and which are not. From a slightly different perspective, they serve as venture capitalists, deciding which projects are deserving of funding. In another, more positive, role they are coaches, both guiding and challenging the team members to accomplish great things. They are sometimes even cheerleaders encouraging the team to persevere when things are going wrong. Good gatekeepers enthusiastically embrace all those roles.

Templates & Tools

If people are going to enthusiastically embrace a process, they must accept it as the easiest, most efficient way of doing things. A Saturday's home project is much easier when the right tools are available. The same concept applies here; providing the teams with the right tools will enable them to get superior results in much less time and with much less effort. And think of this... When they discover the right way to do the project is the easy way, what do you think they'll do? There are many tools you can employ but I've found these to be among the most effective:

Presentation templates

There was a time in my career when our phase/gate process had relatively well-defined phases and gates but no clearly defined deliverables for each. Nor did we have a format for presentations. The result was that each team came prepared to present what they thought the gatekeepers wanted to see. Invariably, some of what was presented was of no interest to the gatekeepers and therefore a waste of time and effort. Worse, the teams often neglected to present material that was critical to intelligent decision making and which therefore resulted in the need for a do-over and the consequent delay. Was this the fault of the teams? I don't think so; the company had failed to clearly define the requirements.

Furthermore, team members spent a lot of time figuring out how to present their findings and designing the graphics for their presentations.

Templates rectify that problems by clearly indicating what information is required and, just as important, what is not. Properly prepared, they also establish in what order and in what format it is to be presented. This consistency eliminates the "creative" effort required to build every presentation from scratch and allows gatekeepers to focus on the information itself rather than on how it is presented.

If they are created in such a way that tables and graphs can be copied from a spreadsheet, the templates can be created quickly and easily. I recommend that you use "sticky notes" and slide presentation notes to clarify requirements.

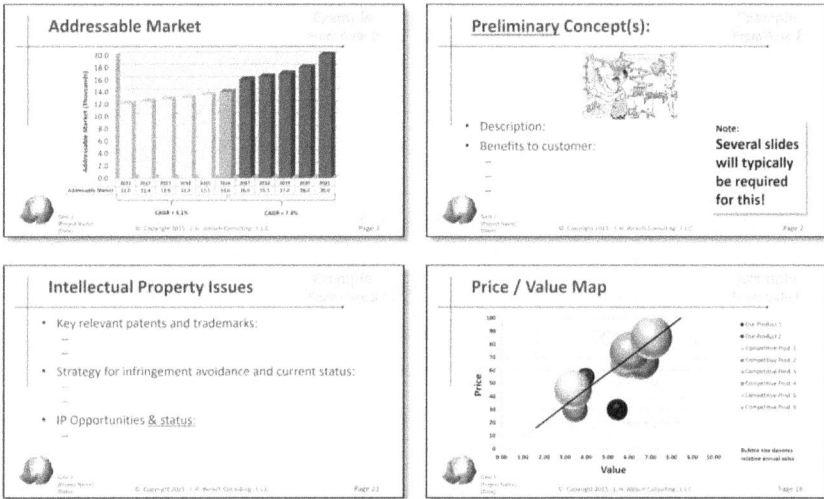

Figure 13 - Example Presentation Templates

Spreadsheet templates

Spreadsheet templates greatly reduce the amount of time it takes a team to arrange and format data tables and charts for meaningful, professional presentations. Would you rather create a chart from the ground up, deciding which chart type to use, what data to include and even what colors to employ? Would you like to "play around" with 3D effects, shading and all the "nifty" things you could do? Or would you prefer to plug the data into an already-prepared table and have the chart created automatically. Admittedly, the former may be more fun but the latter will get the job done more quickly and easily and perhaps even get you home in time for dinner.

Equally important, spreadsheet templates provide clarity. Think of the last spreadsheet you've seen at a meeting. Unless it was very simple or one which had been shown many times before, chances are that someone asked something like, "Does that cost include overhead?" or "Is that the list price, the net price or the price after rebates?" When tables and charts are consistent from project to project, the answers to those questions are already known.

Checklists

It's embarrassing to admit but one of the persistent problems I faced when I was chairing gate meetings was that required slides would "mysteriously" disappear from presentation templates. For some reason, the missing slides would have contained data that the team was having trouble gathering or that would have shown the project in a less favorable light. Far be it from me to conclude that the deletion of a troublesome slide was anything but accidental but there is that possibility. However, it's hard to notice what's NOT there and easy for a presentation to conclude without anyone picking up on the deficiency. As a result, we sometimes found ourselves in the awkward position of having approved passage of a gate without having considered all the facts. Later, when someone said, "Well, how did we envision the addressable market at Gate 3?" we were embarrassed to find that the data had never been presented!

A proper checklist should list defined deliverables in parallel with the presentation templates. Using such a checklist at every gate meeting will highlight any omissions and, consequently, improve the quality of decisions made.

As we learned earlier, the process must be flexible enough to allow teams to omit specific data in some cases. That flexibility sometimes means that a team is granted permission to exclude certain information. However, it is critical that such permission be granted with discretion and in advance. Recording that permission on the checklist along with the reasoning behind it can be invaluable during a subsequent project audit.

Meeting tools

I'm almost embarrassed to list these as their use should be absolutely required for every meeting. I'm referring to agendas and minutes.

An agenda must not only spell out the subjects to be discussed (in this case the projects to be reviewed for gate approval) but also the time allocated to each. While circumstances may dictate that discussion of a project may be extended, that must be done with the knowledge that either another project will suffer or the meeting will run into overtime. My template has a row for each project and columns for subject, presenter(s), duration, start time and end time. Since it is Excel-based and has meeting start time listed near the top, only subject, presenter(s) and duration need be inserted for each project; start time and end time appear automatically. And, of course, if you adjust the time for a project, you can see how the result flows through the schedule. Can you see what I mean about letting the template do the work?

Minutes must be written and distributed within a few days of the meeting. Coupled with discipline, a template for minutes will assure that they are focused on pertinent facts rather than containing a rambling account of protracted discussion. A well-designed template would provide for the following pertinent facts for each project:

- Very high-level treatment of any points of disagreement along with their resolution. For example, "While there was heated debate, we agreed to limit the offering to the 7 SKUs recommended by the team."

- Documentation of agreement on items of singular importance. For example, "It is recognized that commercialization of the project will cost $1,250,000."

- Documentation of assignments of responsibility. For example, "George will provide Mary with a detailed list of mold requirements by Monday, July 1."

- Final decision on the project's status, accompanied by qualifying details when required. For example, "Project Alpha was conditionally approved. Full approval is contingent upon Frank's informing the committee by noon on 5/7 that the mold cost is no greater than $27,000. Absent that full approval, the project is recycled until the next gate meeting."

Education & Training

I cannot overemphasize the need for effective education and training; the former to explain the "why" and the latter to explain the "how." It's probably best to hold several sessions with different groups of people, each with different objectives.

Introductory executive session

The first session is one with top executives and other key associates. It can be relatively short and is aimed, first, at reviewing the benefits expected from the new process along with its concepts and terminology and second, at establishing collective commitment to the program and path forward. It is perfectly acceptable to handle this as an agenda item at a regular executive staff meeting so long as it is not seen as a trivial topic shoehorned in among the "important" ones. Because the executives must be recognized as solidly in support of the new process, any reservations or concerns must be resolved here or at future executive meetings, not at educational or other meetings with a wider audience.

General session

The purpose of the general session is to introduce concepts and the workings of the process to a broad audience encompassing the executive staff, department heads, middle managers and the professionals from all departments who will be even peripherally involved in the new NPD process. While this represents a substantial commitment of manpower, it will pay dividends in understanding and commitment.

It is critically important that the chief executive of the business unit and the entire executive staff be present and visibly involved throughout the session to deliver the message that the process is fully endorsed by the executive staff and that they will be participants as well. In fact, the first agenda item should be the chief executive's declaration of commitment to growth through new product development and an explanation of why this new process is the best way to achieve it. Here I must echo something I said in chapter 4; if deep commitment cannot be expressed earnestly, the organization should not have arrived at this point because the process is almost certain to fail! I suggest that you have a chat with each of the executives before this meeting, asking that they show solid support, reserving any serious concerns for private, executive-level discussion.

The business leader's comments would be followed by...

- ...an outline of the benefits that the process will deliver to all stakeholders.
- ...an overview of the process, including a high-level explanation of phases and gates. A slide with a graphic such as that shown as Figure 10 would be appropriate.
- ...an overview (only) of the roles and responsibilities of a development team.
- ...a brief description of the work to be done during each phase and the nature of the issues to be addressed at each gate.
- ...introduction of the gatekeepers and a description of their roles in the process.
- ...a declaration of the critical importance of the gates as control points and an explanation of the rigid expectations for each (i.e. clearly defined deliverables, clear, unambiguous criteria and a defined output).
- ...an explanation of the nature of gate meetings and of what is to be expected at each one. It should be stressed that gate meetings are <u>intended</u> to be challenging; that the gatekeepers will not approve a project just because they like an idea or the person(s) promoting it. As W. Edwards Deming said, "In God we trust; all others bring data!" Also, it must be made clear that team members and others are expected to respectfully share their candid beliefs even if they are contrary to what those in power believe.
- ...the definition of the five possible outcomes from the presentation of each gate (i.e. Kill, Recycle, Hold, Conditional Go and Go).
- ...emphasis of the critical importance of post-launch audits of each project to refine the NPD process as well as to identify and take all corrective actions needed to assure that each project delivers the results promised.

Admittedly, that's a lot of material to cover and the number of attendees will be large. Consequently, the organization will be making a significant investment in such a meeting. While there may be a few executives who will not be personally involved in the process and can therefore be excused after they "fly the flag". All others must fully understand the process and their roles in it. Properly educating and training is, therefore, well worth the investment.

Gatekeeper session

The final 2 types of training can occur in either order but I'll arbitrarily start with the one for gatekeepers. At this session, the nature of gate meetings and the roles and responsibilities of the gatekeepers are explained in greater detail. Specifically, the issues to be addressed are...

- ...the need for the gatekeepers to consistently show support for the process by their actions as well as their words.
- ...the need for each gatekeeper to be present at each gate meeting and to become deeply involved in each discussion.
- ...the fact that, if they must miss a gate meeting, gatekeepers must send a fully empowered proxy to speak in their stead or agree in advance to abide by all decisions of those gatekeepers in attendance.
- ...the nature of the work to be done during each phase and the information to be presented at each gate.
- ...exactly what will be approved (or otherwise) at each gate (e.g. approval of Gate 3 authorizes and funds complete product design).
- ...exactly what is meant by the five possible outcomes at each gate (i.e. Kill, Recycle, Hold, Conditional Go and Go).
- ...the fact that the gatekeepers serve as[42]...

    Bankers, to make go/kill decisions on projects and the funding of them. (It's important to stress here that a "Go" gate decision must always be accompanied by allocation of people, funding and all other resources needed for completion of the next phase!)

    Enforcers, to instill & enforce process discipline.

> **Quality Assurers**, to assure that projects are executed in a quality fashion.
>
> **Mentors**, to provide advice and share wisdom.
>
> **Godfathers**, to help remove obstacles, including unnecessary red tape.

- ...the value and nature of monthly or bimonthly project update meetings at which the status of all active projects is reviewed to identify and remove or mitigate any obstacles faced by the teams. (More on that shortly.)

- ...the importance and nature of quarterly or biannual reviews of the organization's NPD project portfolio to assure that efforts expended are aligned with organizational strategy and priorities. (More on that in Chapter 8.)

- ...the need to discuss key NPD metrics at executive meetings no less often than quarterly and to take decisive action as needed. (More in Appendix F.)

You may want to also address details such as the timing and location of meetings, agendas, minutes and so forth.

For more detail, refer to the sections, "Gate meetings" and "Gatekeepers - Roles & Expectations" earlier in this chapter, "Status Updates" in the next section as well as chapter 8 and appendix F.

Team member session(s)

While gatekeepers have overall control of the process, it is the team members who will bring new products to life. As they have the most comprehensive responsibility, their training will be the most extensive and complex. It will almost certainly involve multiple sessions both because of the sheer volume of material and because some training will apply to some members but not others. For example, while all must have a general understanding of customer research and all should participate in it to some degree, those who will be intimately involved in most of that research must have a greater understanding of the mechanics. Likewise, leadership and related training may be appropriate for those who will manage projects. Among the other important topics are...

- ...a deep dive into the phases and gates including a detailed review of what topics are addressed and with what rigor they will be studied during each phase. The deep dive must also address the deliverables required at each gate.

- ...definition of the roles and responsibilities of each of the development team members.

- ...the nature of and need for collaboration.

- ...the nature of an NPD team and the fact that, while all are expected to share their opinions and insights, it is the experts on any subject who make the final decisions. Grossly oversimplifying, that means that, in the end, marketers will define the target feature set while engineers will specify the engine.

- ...the fact that each team is expected to resolve all internal conflict in advance of gate meetings and to present their case in a united front unless, after exhausting all alternatives, they must ask the gatekeepers to act as mediators.

- ...the nature of gate meetings, including how to prepare, what to expect of the meeting and gatekeepers, and the five possible outcomes. Team members must be made to understand that collegial debate is a vital part of the process and that they are expected to respectfully defend a position they hold even if it is unpopular.

- ...a detailed explanation of the tools and templates provided to facilitate the collection and analysis of data and for its presentation at gate meetings; their application and how they are to be used. It may well be appropriate to have breakout sessions as there is a lot of material to cover and different functions will be using different tools and templates.

Ongoing training

These efforts are not something to be done once and forgotten. As new gatekeepers and team members are appointed, they need to receive the same level of education and training as did those who were present at the outset. Periodic follow-up sessions should be held both as reminders and to communicate information concerning revisions.

Facilitation

To be successful, the process must be continuously facilitated by a process owner, a single person who has responsibility for the its correct application and continuous improvement. It is the NPD process facilitator who...

- ...in cooperation with top management, formalizes and implements the process that best suits the organization.

- ...provides (or arranges for other competent personnel to provide) initial and ongoing education and training to assure that everyone, from executives, through gatekeepers, to team members and auxiliary personnel, fully understands both the "why" and the "how".

- ...attends (and possibly chairs) gate meetings to assure that the process is being followed intelligently (i.e. conscientiously but not pedantically). This means assuring that all participants come to each meeting fully prepared and that the suggestions for effective gate meetings listed earlier are carried out at every meeting. Among the challenges is keeping the agenda relatively on track even when powerful executives want to dwell on tangential issues.

- ...continually tracks (or has an assistant track) progress of all projects in the portfolio, sending reminders as necessary to assure that projects are proceeding according to plan.

- ...continually monitors the health of the process and improves both the process itself and the way it is implemented within the organization.

- ...when requested, meets with team leaders at the beginning of each stage to determine whether, based on project risk, certain requirements can be eliminated or their rigor reduced, then issues dispensations as appropriate.

- ...when requested, reviews draft presentations to provide feedback before the presentations are posted.

- ...as soon as possible after presentations are posted, reviews them and notifies the team leader of erroneous or missing information. When some information might be met with strong resistance, counsels the team leader be to either reconsider it or prepare adequate support to overcome objections.

Status updates

When a project is in its early phases or when it is an especially simple one, the gates may come in quick succession. In other cases, as during the development phase of a project that breaks new ground, or the ramp-up phase of a project that requires the procurement and commissioning of equipment or facilities, the time between gates may be many months. During such periods, it's not uncommon for projects to drift off course or to languish due to lack of attention.

Periodic, formal status update reviews serve the dual purposes of keeping executives apprised of progress (or lack thereof) and stimulating team members to keep the project on schedule.

Such reviews should be held on a monthly or bi-monthly, schedule, and should address major, if not all, projects. These meetings need not be protracted; only 5 to 10 minutes need be spent on each project unless it is experiencing serious difficulties. The questions that need to be answered for each project are:

- Is the project on budget and schedule and will it deliver the results promised when the most recent gate was approved?
- What have been the major accomplishments since the last review?
- What slippages or other disappointments have occurred since the last review?
- What are the major hurdles being faced or anticipated?
- And most importantly, what does the team need from the organization to stay or get back on track?

I recommend that each team present for each project a single page "dashboard" that gives a high-level picture of what the team sees as the ultimate timeframe, sales, investment and so forth in comparison to that which was approved at the previous gate. The example dashboard template shown as Figure 14 would be used between gates 2 and 3. In it, you will notice that sales and profits are shown for both the "Project" and the "Product". The difference between the two is that the latter apply to the proposed new product (or product line) alone while the former include the effects of cannibalization and synergistic sales; in other words, the effect of the entire project on the company's revenues and gross profit.

Sales & Profits		2016	2017	2018	2019	2020	TOTAL
Gate 2 Forecast	Sales of New Product	$ -	$ 300.0	$ 1,150.0	$ 1,410.0	$ 1,580.0	$ 4,440
	Net Sales from Project	$ -	$ 290.0	$ 1,127.5	$ 1,379.0	$ 1,538.0	$ 4,335
	GP% of New Product	0.0%	24.2%	31.3%	33.3%	34.3%	
	Net GP% from Project	0.0%	24.1%	31.4%	33.4%	34.6%	
	Net GP$ From Project ($K)	$ -	$ 69.8	$ 354.4	$ 461.2	$ 532.5	$ 1,418
Current Forecast	Sales of New Product	$ -	$ 325.0	$ 1,250.0	$ 1,530.0	$ 1,740.0	$ 4,845
	Net Sales from Project	$ -	$ 315.0	$ 1,227.5	$ 1,499.0	$ 1,698.0	$ 4,740
	GP% of New Product	0.0%	22.3%	28.8%	30.7%	31.2%	
	Net GP% from Project	0.0%	22.2%	28.9%	30.8%	31.4%	
	Net GP$ From Project ($K)	$ -	$ 69.8	$ 354.4	$ 461.2	$ 532.5	$ 1,418

Investment & Return		Gate 2 Plan	Expected Finish
Expense	Engineering	$ 164.0	$ 171.0
	Manufacturing	$ 66.5	$ 76.5
	Marketing	$ 269.0	$ 271.0
	Other	$ 30.0	$ 30.0
	TOTAL($K)	$ 529.5	$ 548.5
Capital	Building	$ -	$ -
	Machinery	$ 80.0	$ 80.0
	Tooling	$ 30.0	$ 30.0
	Other	$ -	$ -
	TOTAL($K)	$ 110.0	$ 110.0

Timeline	Gate 2 Plan	Actual	Currently Expected	Comment
Gate 1	1/7/16	1/7/16		
Gate 2	1/30/16	2/1/16		
Gate 3	4/3/16		4/3/16	
Gate 4	7/14/16		7/14/16	
Gate 5	11/5/16		11/5/16	
Commercial Availability	1/10/17		1/10/17	
First Post-launch Audit	5/7/17		5/7/17	
Second Post-launch Audit	10/18/17		10/18/17	

		Gate 2 Plan	Expected Finish
IRR	3-Year IRR (%)	18.5%	20.3%
	5-Year IRR (%)	42.2%	40.0%
NPV @	3-Year NPV ($K)	($184.7)	($195.8)
25%	5-Year NPV ($K)	$149.8	$134.6
General Comments:			

Slippages are highlighted thus.

Figure 14- Project Dashboard

A Word about Project Management

Properly designed and implemented, the phase/gate process is an excellent one for doing what it was designed to do; to examine the validity of projects at critical points in their development in order to filter out the unworthy ones and assure the success of the worthy.

What it is NOT designed to do in and of itself (at least in any implementation I've seen) is to manage the thousands of issues that must be resolved before a product can be successfully launched. To do that, we turn to the discipline of project management.

While project management is a critically important topic, it is much too broad to address adequately here. Rather than gloss over such an important topic, I refer you to the countless volumes that have been written on the subject as well as to the readily available software. I will, however share a couple of thoughts...

The Project Manager

In this book, I've used the terms "Project Manager" and "Team Leader" interchangeably but, by whatever name, a project needs such a person if it is to be successful. The project manager must have her finger on the project's pulse, planning days, weeks and sometimes months ahead and anticipating and addressing every need. That's a huge job and not one to be taken lightly. Sadly, I've witnessed projects where the project manager had no training in the role whatever. I've even seen projects that had no clearly-defined project manager whatsoever!

If possible, a single person should fill the role of product manager throughout the project's duration. For several years, I worked in an environment where project managers were changed as a project passed from phase to phase. At the time, it seemed logical to assign the role to the team member who had the most "skin in the game" during a given phase; a marketer during the "idea phase", an engineer during the "design phase" and so on. That was a complete disaster! In the first place, the very person who had the most technical responsibility during a phase was the one also burdened with the project's overhead. This had two negative consequences. First, the most critical resource for each phase was overtaxed. Second, her position could hardly be impartial. As one project manager put it. "If I am the industrial designer as well as project manager and the industrial design work is falling behind schedule, I'll be a lot more forgiving than I would be if someone else is falling behind!"

Furthermore, managed this way, the project resembled a relay race with one runner picking up the baton from the previous one. Trust me, the baton was dropped often and, predictably, each person typically blamed the other for the missed handoff. As I look back, I'm embarrassed both that we implemented such a system at all and that we held onto it for so long! Please don't make the same mistake!

The Urgency Paradox

If we are to get our excellent product to market in the shortest possible time without compromising quality, we need to start vigorously and maintain a brisk pace until we reach the finish line. I'm not implying that we can afford to move like a tortoise but, thinking back to the children's tale of the hare and the tortoise, it's more important to maintain the pace than to loaf along and then sprint for the finish line.

In his business novel, "Critical Chain[43]", the late Eliyahu Goldratt introduced the concept of the "student syndrome". He reminded us that, regardless of how much time they are given, students will typically not even begin work on an assignment until shortly before it is due. Then they work day and night to complete it.

Apparently, such habits follow us into our business life. In their excellent book, "Developing Products in Half the Time"[44], Preston Smith and Donald Reinertsen describe behavior that is all too common and that I'm sure each of us has displayed. Think back to a time when you were at the very early stages of a long-term project. The deadline (in our case, product introduction) was far in the future. You had a million other "more pressing" issues so, day after day, you pushed the new project file to the side of your desk. Or you were trying to schedule a meeting with those responsible to plan the project, and the responses you got to a request for a meeting "as soon as possible" were something like, "Well, I'm pretty tied up; how about 3 weeks from Thursday?" Admit it, you accepted the loss of three weeks without protest because you were busy, too.

Now, jump forward to the point when found yourself behind schedule a month before the deadline. What would you have paid to get those three weeks back? Near the end of a project, we've all paid for overtime, overnight shipments and many other things to gain even a few days. Yet, at the beginning of a project, we think nothing about squandering weeks or even months!

Don't fall into that trap; when a project is initiated, think about what you'll be willing to do near the end of the project. Then, apply the same sense of urgency immediately and throughout the project's duration.

Chapter 7 - Introducing the Product

"People are in such a hurry to launch their product or business that they seldom look at marketing from a bird's eye view and they don't create a systematic plan."

— *Dave Ramsey*

As we've seen, marketing plays a crucial role from the very beginning and throughout any NPD project. Their expertise and insights are essential to the establishment of organizational and new product strategies. They are the prime players in analysis of the marketplace, in selection of target markets and, as we have seen, in the identification of product opportunities. As the design develops, they provide input based on their own knowledge and experience and seek feedback from trusted customers and channel partners. And, long before completion of development, they begin to plan the market launch so that, when the product is available, the market is eagerly awaiting it.

Ralph Waldo Emerson allegedly said, "Build a better mousetrap, and the world will beat a path to your door." Whether that is an accurate quote is academic; it expresses a sentiment that is often accepted. It is also so very wrong! In their thought-provoking book, "Why Johnny Can't Brand", Bill Schley & Carl Nichols suggest that a more accurate statement might be, "If you build a better mousetrap, absolutely no one gives a s--t.[45]"

For a product to sell, it must not merely be sold, it must be marketed. As we slave for months over a new product, its alleged advantages become so "apparent" to ourselves that we cannot help but expect customers to beat down our doors to get at it the moment it becomes available. While we've been doing all that slaving, however, those prospective customers have been, in most cases, muddling along, blissfully ignorant of their "need" for our new widget. Unless a prospect is actively dissatisfied with a product he has been using, expecting him to take time from his busy live to evaluate and try ours is asking a lot. As we'll see shortly, the more novel a product is, the more evaluation is necessary and perhaps paradoxically, the greater the need for effective marketing!

As this is not a marketing book, I'm not going to go into a great deal of detail on the subject but, since it does no good to develop a product unless it is marketed effectively, I feel it's important to provide an overview of some of the concepts that apply directly to new product development.

Product Differentiation

This should go without saying but is worth saying anyway; your new product must stand out from your those of your competitors or customers will have little reason to risk a change from the status quo. Hopefully by the time you get to this point in the book, you will appreciate the merit of addressing customers' needs in a way that has thus far been ignored. The difference, though, can in be many things beyond the product itself; price, quality, availability, brand image and so on.

It's essential that you clearly differentiate your new product, not only from those of your competitors, but from your own products as well. If the new product will replace an old one, a "New and Improved" tag will sometimes breathe new life into a tired product even if the "improvements" are minor. That, however, is an approach likely to have short term results at best.

If the new product offers distinct advantages over your current one(s), it may be that some customers will migrate to the new while others, perhaps those with different needs, remain loyal to the old.

I spent most of my career working for a company that is best known as a manufacturer of commercial shelving. As boring as the product sounds, the company has remained the market leader by making substantial innovations and introducing new alternatives for over half a century. It's interesting to note, though, that they still sell a fair amount of a product that was introduced in 1955 and that a product line that was introduced in 1969 is still one of the mainstays of their business. How can this be? Because each product line, including that ancient one, is clearly differentiated from the others by being targeted at a distinct set of customer needs.

So, you might ask, "Why not design one product that addresses all of those disparate needs?" One answer, of course, is price. Even if you <u>could</u> make a nice profit by offering a car loaded with leather seats, navigation system and so forth at the price of a basic, stripped down one, would it not make more sense to offer two cars, one for the economy buyers and another for those willing to pay a much higher price?

Another answer is that the compromising, "one size fits all" approach usually results in products that don't fit anyone particularly well. A wise man once told me, "Show me a person whom everyone likes and I will show you a mediocre person." I contend that a similar sentiment applies to products; a product intended for everyone is unlikely to be spectacular for anyone.

Finally, the differences in needs may make suitable products mutually exclusive. Some people want an audio system that gives them a lot of control over the sound. Others, like my wife, don't want to deal with the complexity that such a system entails; they want to turn the system on and perhaps change the music source and adjust the volume. If your current audio product is one my wife would like, there might be ample justification for introducing a different one for the audiophile. It would be essential, then, to market the two products in such a way to attract both types of customers <u>and</u> to make it clear to each which one they should buy.

Some companies offer an astonishing array of closely related products without presenting a clear differentiation message. I recently set out to buy a device that was supposed to capture the mosquitoes that make life miserable at our lake cottage in Pennsylvania. When I went to the website of a company recommended by a friend, I was overwhelmed by the choices. OK, there were some for inside use and others for use outside; I get that. There were some that claimed to protect a larger area than others. I get that, too. However, there were many with identical descriptions, yet which carried different prices. In many cases, I could find no reason to buy one over the other. There MAY have been clear differentiators but I certainly couldn't find them!

It may be useful to review chapter 5 for a refresher on how different groups of customers may have different needs and desires.

If your customers can be divided into such groups, you may be wise to offer them different choices. If you do that, be sure to clearly communicate the differences between the products in ways meaningful to your them.

The words, "in ways meaningful to them" in the last sentence are important. Simply offering a comparison of specifications is often insufficient. Many websites allow you to select several models of a product, a laptop computer for example, and click a button to see a comparison of specifications. That's great for someone who can understand what the specs mean, but how does that help someone with more limited technical knowledge? While it is most definitely advantageous to clearly communicate the difference in technical specifications, be sure to <u>also</u> convey the differentiation message in ways understandable to non-technical customers.

A tangential thought... With electronics products, it is sometimes possible to design an offering in which one physical product can be adapted to address different customer groups simply by moving a jumper, flashing the software or entering an "unlock" code. Years ago, I bought a portable GPS that displayed US maps only. When I wanted to take it to Europe, though, I only had to go to the manufacturer's website, pay a (rather substantial) fee and retrieve a code to be entered into the device. Viola; the GPS offered European as well as US maps! The manufacturer shipped one product but addressed two (and perhaps more) different customer groups at very different prices.

Positioning

The subject of product differentiation leads directly to this one. In my not-so-humble opinion, one of the most powerful marketing concepts is that of positioning, introduced by Al Ries and Jack Trout and outlined in their book, "*Positioning: The Battle for Your Mind.*" The book has been around a while, but the concept is as valid now as ever. In their definition, the authors write:

> *Positioning starts with a product, a piece of merchandise, a service, a company, an institution, a person. Perhaps yourself.*

But positioning is not what you do to a product. Positioning is what you do in the mind of the prospect. That is, you position the product in the mind of the prospect.

So, it's incorrect to call the concept "product positioning." You're not really doing something to the product itself.[46]

Despite Reis & Trout's distinction, the term "Product Positioning" is common, and I freely admit that I sometimes use it myself.

If you have followed the guidance offered in chapter 5, you will design your new product, not only with features that differentiate it from those of your competitors, but with tangible benefits that are meaningful to your customers. Your task then will be to communicate those benefits to prospects in a concise, yet compelling, way.

When Reis and Trout wrote their book, they wrote of the difficulty of having a message heard in light of the "Assault on the Mind" by an overabundance of advertising and other information[47]. That was written in 1981, well before the Internet was made public! Wow! If the word "assault" was appropriate then, I don't know what we'd call it now! In a world with seemingly infinite choices, positioning is a way of separating your message from the noise, of distinguishing your product from those already crowding the marketplace.

When asked about their positioning strategy, I've heard unenlightened marketers answer, "Low Price", "Easy to Use" or "High Quality." Given the multitudes that can make the same claims, are those terms truly distinctive? Are they something that will resonate in the mind of a prospect?

To have value, your position must be meaningful, and your positioning statement must clearly and meaningfully set you apart from competition. It must be, above all, simple. Forget the long explanations of everything your product does; no one will remember that. Boil it down to the very essence, a short phrase or sentence that is both impactful and memorable.

While many advertising slogans have nothing whatever to do with positioning, some have been carefully crafted to reflect a product's or even the company's position. Well-known examples in history are:

- "Melts in your mouth, not in your hands" – Mars, Inc.'s way of communicating the benefit of their hard coating.

- "The un-cola" – 7up's clear differentiation from the colas.

- "When it absolutely, positively, has to be there overnight" – An especially effective message in the early days when Fred Smith's FedEx service was virtually the only way to get that done.

- "Have it your way" –Burger King's way of differentiating its willingness to custom-build a burger from the standardization offered by McDonald's.

- "We try harder" – Avis's way of making hay out of their #2 position by implying that Hertz was lazily coasting on their leadership position. Personally, I think, that, if it truly reflected how they ran their business, it was brilliant.

In contrast, consider, "I'm Lovin' It", "Just Do It!", or even "Don't leave home without it." They may be memorable, but they do not differentiate the companies or their products from the pack at all. After 50 years of using the incredibly distinctive "We Try Harder", Avis dropped it in 2012 in favor of "It's Your Space"[48]. What the heck does THAT mean?

The establishment of a strong position and then communicating it with an impactful positioning statement is not only important for promotional purposes, it also helps the organization to determine whether the new product is meaningfully different. If you can't clearly position your offering, perhaps you don't know the market as well as you should.

The Importance of Leadership

In chapter 3 we discussed the power of leadership. Leaders have the inside track when it comes to capturing the minds of customers. Name a fast-food hamburger joint. McDonald's, right? Online shopping? Amazon. Facial tissue? Kleenex. Cotton swaps?

Q-Tips. Are those the best companies or products? Maybe and maybe not but that doesn't really matter, does it? To paraphrase another advertising slogan, leadership has its privileges.

If you are the leader, yours is the first name that comes to mind when one thinks of the product category. All other products are compared to yours and, if your value proposition has remained strong, your product becomes the default choice. What's more, you can often increase sales, not only by promoting your brand, but by simply promoting the <u>category</u>. Many of us remember a very popular ad campaign of the 1980's that used the message, "Soup is good food." While they naturally mentioned their own name, Campbells aimed the ads at promoting soup as a category, knowing that they would be the primary beneficiaries of increased soup sales.

The Power of Being First

In any race, the first to cross the starting line is the de facto leader, if only momentarily. Likewise, the first into the market gains the leadership position by default. Note that you don't have to <u>really</u> be first, you simply need to overshadow the trailblazer to the point where everyone forgets who was <u>actually</u> first across the starting line. Those who've never heard of brothers Charles and Frank Duryea's Duryea Motor Wagon Company might well assume that Henry Ford was the first manufacturer of gasoline-powered automobiles.

The first mover advantage is easily lost, though. Wilbur and Orville Wright were the first to succeed at powered flight but, rather than actively marketing their invention, their fear of potential competition caused them to keep the product itself a secret. If ever there was an example of someone giving up first-mover advantage, this was it.

What can you do if you're too late to be first? Can you be first in a category? FedEx was most definitely not the first delivery service, but they were the first to offer nation-wide overnight delivery. Yes, UPS quickly caught on, but it's the FedEx name that has become a verb; "I'll FedEx it to you". Likewise, Xerox was not the first to make a copier, but they did make the first plain paper copier, and the company's name has become almost synonymous with both the noun and the verb, "copy". If you can't be first, see if you can identify an important category, then be first in it and promote that fact heavily.

Positioning is relatively easy to explain, yet difficult to do effectively. Though it's an old one, I still strongly recommend Ries & Trout's book, "Positioning, the Battle for Your Mind."

Branding

I don't really want to get into this except to make a few points.

First, a strong brand name can be worth much more than the organization's physical assets. It carries that value because it motivates customers to buy the organization's products, often at higher prices. Go into a convenience store and compare the cost of Fiji or Evian water with that of a generic. Do you really think there's a significant difference beyond the label?

Second, while an extravagant marketing program might help to create a brand that will allow you to sell a me-too product at an inflated price, the best way to create a strong brand is to base it on a product or service that offers clear, meaningful, distinguish benefits. My guess is that Fred Smith didn't have a terribly difficult time getting folks to see the value of getting things delivered overnight.

Third, tie the brand to the position gained through the innovative offering. Fred Smith did it through both the name of the company, FedEx and his early slogan, "When it absolutely, positively has to be there overnight." Brilliant!

Pricing

If you are offering a product that provides clear benefits beyond those offered by your competitors, you owe it to yourself and to your stakeholders to be paid accordingly. Although that may seem painfully obvious, many organizations fail to enjoy the price their product deserves.

Cost-based vs. Value-based Pricing

I have seen far too many situations in which pricing decisions started with product cost. Frequently, companies see pricing as simply mathematical; start with product cost; factor in overhead expenses and profit objectives and, voila, a price pops out. The formula is simply:

$$Price = Cost / (1 + GM)$$

...where GM is the expected percentage gross margin, expressed as a decimal). This approach is easy, efficient and <u>wrong</u>! The cost-based approach establishes the floor; the lowest price the company can accept. Do you really want to get the <u>lowest</u> price possible?

Value-based pricing, on the other hand, establishes the ceiling; the highest price acceptable to the customer. By basing it on the product's value as perceived by the customer, we can secure the optimal price. Certainly, a floor cannot be higher than the ceiling so cost and margin requirements cannot be ignored. Therefore, target product price must be established as one of the product requirements during the planning phase, and the product must be designed so that its cost will deliver <u>at least</u> the minimally acceptable gross margin.

By the way, it's perfectly OK to get even an <u>incredibly</u> high margin if the price is acceptable to your customers and generates the sales level you seek! It's been reported that, during their heyday, Polaroid enjoyed a 90% margin on film. They didn't seem to mind at all! A caveat is in order, however. High potential margins are powerful inducements to competition, so be sure you have strong intellectual property or other defenses in place before you get too greedy.

Intangible Value Elements

Remember, product value is established, not in your own mind, but in the mind of the customer. We've discussed value in detail earlier so those points need not be repeated. When it comes to setting prices, however, it's important to remember that customers' perception of value extends beyond the physical product.

Think of your offering as an egg. The yoke represents the physical product, its features and the benefits they bestow; the product's durability, quality, aesthetic design, option set and so on. These are the tangible elements.

That yoke is surrounded by intangible elements that also influence what customers are willing to pay. High on the list is your brand name. The name Lexus commands a price premium over a Toyota that is well above what might be justified by the physical differences. Additional elements include such things as company reputation, product availability, warrantees, customer support, return policies and so forth.

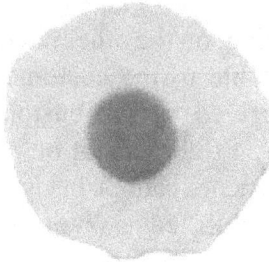

Figure 15 - An Egg is More than the Yoke

Pre-sale consulting services can be especially significant in establishing value. My wife and I were recently faced with the need to furnish a room, the shape of which was troublesome. Visiting a well-known furniture retailer, we were offered, at no cost, the services of a professional interior designer who came to our home, asked questions about how the room would be used and then worked with us on a floor layout as well as selection of the furniture, including fabrics, finishes, etc.

Could we have bought similar furniture more cheaply elsewhere? Of course. Did we actually pay for the services indirectly? Certainly we did. Were we nonetheless satisfied with the price based on the total value we received? You bet we were! When you consider the value of your product, do not forget the non-tangible elements. They will affect what customers are willing to pay!

I've frequently heard sales people say, "We need a better product at a lower price." With apologies to my friends in sales, that's a cop-out. Sure, it makes selling easy; so easy, in fact, that my response was frequently, "If we did that, why would we need you at all?" If your product is worth more to your customers, be sure to charge for the value the product delivers!

The Price/Value Map

A good way to visualize how your proposed price stacks up with those of your other products as well as those of your competitors is through a price/value map.

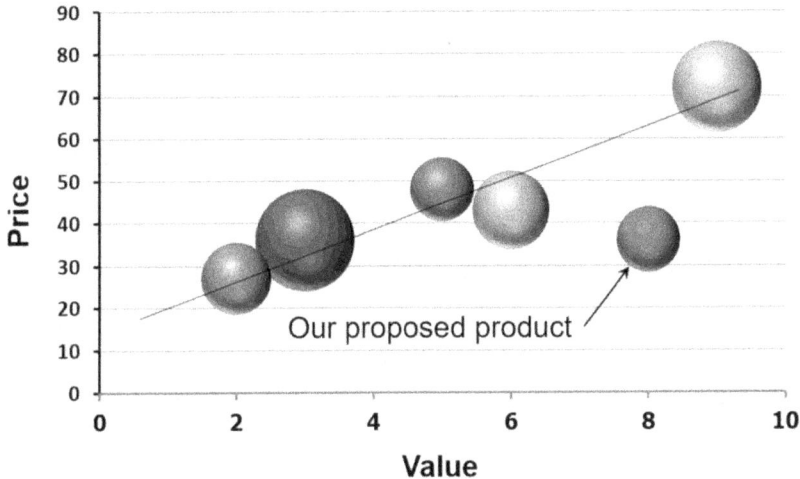

Figure 16 - Price/Value Map

A chart such as that shown in the figure is created by completing a price value spreadsheet from which a bubble chart is generated. Price is shown on the Y axis and "value" on the X. We'll discuss how value is determined in a moment. The bubbles represent the products under consideration; potentially your own as well as your those of your competitors. The size of each bubble represents sales volume of that product.

While price is easy to determine, putting a number on value is somewhat more difficult and inaccurate. I recommend that you go through the valuation exercise with the help of a group of people who are knowledgeable and, to the extent possible, unbiased. First, identify the parameters that are most important to customers in determining value for the products in the category under consideration. Those parameters might be capacity, acceleration, efficiency, quality and so on. The list need not include all parameters but must include the most important ones, not forgetting the intangibles. Next, assign a weight to each parameter as a percentage, such that the weights for all parameters add up to 100%. Then, for each product, enter your best guess as to how <u>customers</u> would value the product under each of the parameters on a scale of 1 to 10. So, product A might get a score of 8 for capacity but only 3 for efficiency while product B gets a score of only 4 for capacity but 9 for efficiency. Yes, I'm fully aware that this approach depends the manipulation of a series of guesses, but I think it's better than making a single, undirected guesstimate of total value. The exercise will result in a column of values. Finally, add columns for price and sales volume and create the bubble chart.

I freely admit that the source of the data means that the chart is, by definition, inaccurate. However, if you've made reasonably good evaluations, it will be enough to give a general picture.

In the example shown as Figure 16, we see that the proposed product is grossly underpriced based on its value. The initially determined price would have resulted in lost profits and something else as well...

We tend to link price and value in our minds. A candy bar that costs $2.00 must certainly be better than one that costs only $1.00, right? If you set your price below that of your competitors, your customers will have trouble believing that your product is, in fact, better.

Furthermore, if the price is initially set too low, it's difficult to increase it quickly or significantly. If it's set too high, on the other hand, it's relatively easy to reduce it through promotional or other discounts. In fact, establishing both a high list price and an introductory promotional discount is an excellent way of establishing the value while driving initial sales.

Pricing Strategies

Throughout this book, we have concentrated mainly on the development of high-value products that generally command premium prices. Before we leave the subject of pricing, though, let's put that into the context of other alternatives. This is not an exhaustive list nor am I presenting a comprehensive treatment of each; this is intended solely as a brief introduction of some alternatives.

Premium Pricing

We've stated again and again that products that have a substantial competitive advantage normally command a higher price. In fact, setting too low a price may dilute the "high value" message. To warrant premium pricing, it is essential first, that your product deliver value commensurate with that price and, second, that you effectively communicate its distinct value to your customers. Remember also, you must protect your advantageous position with patents, with continued innovation or, preferably, with both.

Price Skimming

Think of price skimming as premium pricing on steroids. If, when you introduce your product, there is significant pent up demand, it may be possible to price the new product at a point above that which would be indicated by the price/value map. This strategy must be applied and managed carefully, though, because high prices are likely to lure competitors into copying your offering. In the absence of fundamental patent protection, you must carefully manage your costs and be prepared to lower your price quickly when needed. You will notice that I used the adjective "fundamental" to describe the needed patent protection. In many cases, you might patent the way you offer a certain value proposition but if a competitor can offer the same benefits in a way that avoids your patent, your protection is illusory. You can read more about that in appendix D.

Promotional Pricing

Promotional pricing is employed to jump start sales of a new product or to boost sales of an existing one. It offers a way of temporarily lowering the selling price without diluting the value message while leaving the door open to a rapid return to the normal price. In this case, you start with and communicate the normal price and then offer an introductory or other temporary price or discount. It's important to clearly publicize the duration of the promotion to encourage customers to act quickly and so they are not surprised when the promotion is over. Remember, the key here is to clearly communicate the message that the product merits a higher price, but that you are simply offering a short-term opportunity to get it for less.

Penetration Pricing

Like promotional pricing in that the price starts low and is then increased, penetration pricing comes at it from a different angle. I think of it uncharitably as "suck you in" pricing. With penetration pricing, the price communicated is a low one. The organization's hope is that the customer will get hooked on their product and will continue to buy it even when the price increases. In some cases, the message will be something like, "Only $49.95 per month for the first 6 months", perhaps hoping you will overlook the second part of the statement. Sometimes, the customer must commit to a long-term contract and be committed to the higher pricing. At other times, the customer must give a credit card number to get a trial offer but, if she fails to cancel in a timely manner, the service is continued at the higher price. While a trial price is nice, I'm not a big fan of the version that requires action on the consumer's part to avoid becoming bound by a contract.

Economy Pricing

As the term implies, economy pricing is the antithesis of promotional pricing. For an organization to succeed using this theory, it must be diligent in minimizing its costs at all levels; production, distribution, overhead, administration and so on. Just as organizations who employ premium pricing must continue to guard their market share through innovation, those employing economy pricing must continue to aggressively control costs on order to counter continual competitive attacks from the low end.

Discriminatory Pricing

While I used the adjective in the heading for this section for consistency, you may be more familiar with the noun; "price discrimination". Here, different prices are charged based, not on the product, but on the customer. The approach requires that different groups of customers have different degrees of sensitivity to price; that is, they follow different demand curves. Capitalizing on such a difference, a company can charge a high price to someone willing to pay it and low price to someone who would not buy at the higher one.

While some firms might offer senior discounts for altruistic reasons, it is also an example of discriminatory pricing. Since seniors often have more modest disposable income, the lower pricing increases revenues to the provider by allowing them to buy a product or service that they would otherwise forego.

We can see price discrimination at work when we consider airline fares. I'm not speaking about "product" differences like business class vs. economy but differences related only to passengers. Since people traveling for business are typically willing to pay more than are families traveling on vacation, airlines can charge different prices by, for example, charging less when the trip includes a weekend stay (something that business people avoid) and more for a direct flight than one with connections (which saves the business person valuable time.)

Discriminatory pricing offers additional benefits as well. Early bird specials in restaurants and low-cost matinee tickets in theaters help to fill seats during slower times, thereby increasing total revenue. By charging less for use during off-peak hours, utilities can shift some capacity from peak hours, thereby reducing their maximum capacity requirements.

While the term "discrimination" causes a negative knee-jerk reaction, it is an effective way of maximizing income while offering products to those who would otherwise do without.

Tier Pricing

Tier pricing is a special case of discriminatory pricing and may be the one of which we are most aware. It is simply the concept that, if you buy more of a product, the unit price is lower; buying a case of beer is more economical than buying it a bottle at a time.

Bundle Pricing

Like tier pricing, which involves quantities of identical products, bundle pricing offers a lower price if certain accessories are purchased with the base product or if several related products are purchased at the same time. In many cases, the bundled products are packaged together and sold as a unit.

Optional Product Pricing

Recently, the airlines have become infamous for this. You get a price for your ticket from A to B but then pay for your luggage, a snack, a window seat and so on.

Captive Product Pricing

Sometimes referred to as "razor blade theory", this strategy involves making more profit on the sale of the required ongoing supplies than on the base product. Earlier, we spoke of Polaroid's incredible 90% gross margin on its proprietary film. As one more example, consider what you pay for a few ounces of ink for use in your printer!

Which Selling Price?

If you are currently working in an organization that sells products or services, you already know (or can easily discover) who it is that buys products directly from you and, therefore, to whom your selling price applies.

When I was teaching, it became obvious that many students had not thought about the difference between what the end user pays and what the producer receives. The term project involved, among other things, identifying an opportunity, doing customer research, developing a concept and rudimentary design, making a rough guess at costs, establishing a selling price and determining their profit. An incredible number of teams set their price based on what the end user would pay and then used that number to calculate their profits. They gave no thought at all to the fact that their fictitious business did not deal directly with the end user. And these were graduate students!

While many commercial businesses sometimes buy directly from producers, consumers rarely do. We buy from a retailer, who often buys from a distributor, who sometimes buys from a master distributor. Since each of the companies in the distribution chain is in business to make a profit, each marks up the price. If, as is often the case, the product physically moves from each of these entities to the next, freight costs are added and they, too, are marked up. In the end, the end user pays a price that may be much, much higher than the one the producer receives. Is that unfair? Of course not; each part of the distribution chain and each freight company incurs its own costs and deserves its own profit. If you are a budding entrepreneur with a hot new idea, make sure you know which "price" represents money you can put in your own pocket!

The number of possible approaches to pricing is staggering and the alternatives confusing. Through it all, keep these points in mind:

- Price must be based on value, not cost. The price target must be established first and the product designed so that its cost will deliver an acceptable profit.

- When evaluating value, consider intangible as well as tangible elements.

- Remember that people associate value with cost; if your cost is too low, it may convey the impression that the value is low as well.

- When in doubt, set the initial price high rather than low; it's hard to raise price but easy to lower it through promotions.

Adoption and Diffusion

We'll address forecasting shortly but, before we do so, let's lay some groundwork...

Once you have an excellent product and a compelling value proposition, people will scurry to buy it, causing sales to instantly skyrocket, right? Not likely! Beyond the obvious elements of value, price, advertising and so forth, several factors affect the rate at which a new product will be adopted and diffused into the marketplace.

Sales of a new product generally grow in a pattern like those shown in Figure 17 below.

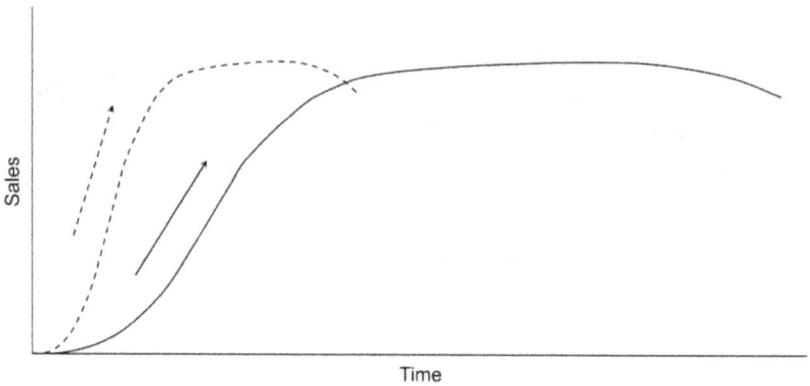

Figure 17 - Sales Adoption Curves

In most cases, sales start out slowly, then begin to increase at an increasing rate. In time, the rate of increase decays, and sales eventually level off as the market matures. Eventually, sales decline and, eventually, stop.

The slope of the curves may vary greatly from one product to another as illustrated by the two curves in the figure. Some products enjoy rapid initial growth as shown by the dotted-line curve in the figure. Depending on many factors, they may also have a short life as illustrated by that same curve. Other products take off frustratingly slowly as shown by the solid-line curve but nevertheless follow the same general pattern at a different rate. If the company had expected rapid growth, it may prematurely conclude that the product is a failure when the issue is simply one of timing. An organization can avoid a lot of frustration by forecasting sales according to the correct adoption curve.

So, what factors affect the shape of the curve and how might we predict what the curve for our new product will look like?

Level of Involvement

The rate at which a product will be adopted is greatly affected by what is involved in reaching the decision to buy. Over which decision will you ponder more deeply and for a longer period, the purchase of a newly introduced candy bar or the purchase of a new car? One explanation for the deliberation needed to make a purchase decision is the level of risk involved. If we make a bad decision on the candy bar, we're out a dollar or so. The consequences of a bad decision on the choice of a car are much greater.

In this example, the risk is primarily financial but other factors can come into play as well. Most of us guard our reputations carefully; a decision that might make me look foolish or cause me to lose the respect of people important to me is one that I would make carefully. In a business context, a decision that that could potentially damage the reputation of my employer would get much closer attention as well.

Five product characteristics influence the adoption rate have been identified[49]. From my perspective, each relate in one way or another to real or perceived risk and willingness to accept it.

Relative Advantage
A product perceived as having a clear advantage over existing solutions will have a faster rate of adoption because it provides a strong incentive to accept a higher level of risk.

Compatibility
A product that will fit well into the prospect's lifestyle or workflow will be adopted more readily than one which will require significant adjustments on the prospect's part. In other words, the more easily a new product can be integrated into a prospect's life, the more readily it will be adopted.

Complexity
We engineers are often proud of whiz-bang products that push the boundaries of technology. A very real problem is that people who are less technically inclined can be easily intimidated by such products and tend to steer clear of them. Understanding and becoming comfortable with a highly complex product entails a lot of effort. Put another way, it requires a high level of involvement.

Divisibility (AKA trialability)
If a product can be tried, risk is tempered significantly. Trial versions, while typically omitting critical capabilities like

printing or saving files, allow us to work with new software until we feel comfortable. When facing a significant purchase decision, this "trialability" can reduce the amount of research needed and significantly speed up the rate of adoption.

Communicability

The more difficult it is to explain a product's relative advantages, to explain how the product is compatible with the prospect's life, or to explain a complex product in terms that are clear to the prospect, the more deeply the prospect will have to become involved before making a purchase decision.

So, using our silly, extreme example of a candy bar and a car, let's compare the thought process involved for a low involvement product with that of a high involvement one.

A candy bar is an incredibly low involvement product. We become aware that a new candy bar is available. We make a quick evaluation based on what we've heard and, if it sounds like something we might like, we buy it. If we were planning to buy a lot of them for presents, that would increase the risk a bit because we don't want to embarrass ourselves, so we might lower the risk by trying one first.

At the opposite extreme, suppose we become aware of a radically new car. We'd build our knowledge through some serious research. Internet, magazines, friends and so on. Based on our new knowledge, we'd do an in-depth evaluation, perhaps creating a spreadsheet outlining the pros and cons. If the evaluation was favorable, we'd do a trial, in this case, take a test drive. In many cases, there might be a fair bit of iteration before enough data was available for a rational decision. FINALLY, if all was favorable, we'd plunk down our money. If the product was a multi-million-dollar IT infrastructure or manufacturing system you can believe the process would be even more rigorous, requiring a very high level of involvement by many people.

Pictorially, the process looks something that shown in Figure 18. Is it any wonder that one takes longer than the other?

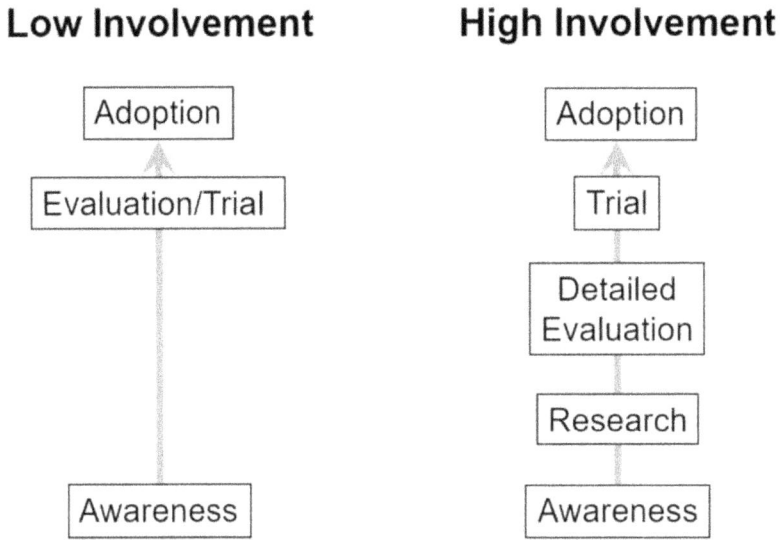

Low Involvement   High Involvement

Figure 18 - High vs. Low Involvement

Figure 18 - High vs. Low Involvement

Buyer Profiles

Not all buyers are created equal and different buyers accept risk at different rates. Some buyers are risk takers; others are most definitely not. You and I both know people who are already waiting for the next generation iPhone and others who are jealously defending their flip-phone. Most of us fall somewhere in the middle.

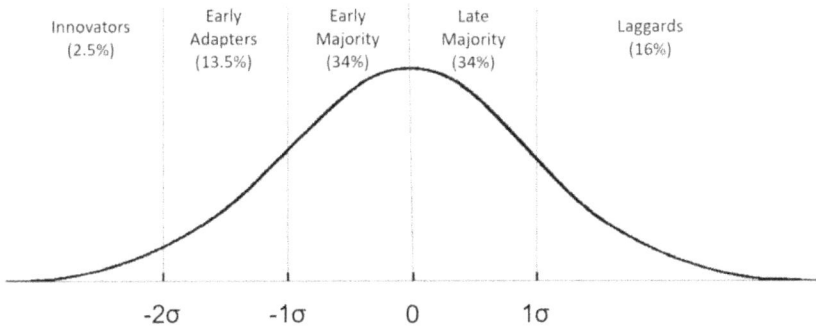

Figure 19 - Adopter Categories

Based upon eight different studies, Everett M. Rogers proposed the Diffusion of Innovation theory, suggesting that the way that people adopt new things is spread on a normal curve[50].

Innovators

At 2.5%, Innovators are a very small part of the population but they are critical to the success of a new product. These folks are self-confident and like to be on the leading edge. When I was a boy, the toy ads on Saturday morning TV often incorporated the words, "Be the first kid on your block with a…" They were targeting the Innovators, the pioneers, those who wanted to be first as opposed to waiting to see what the other kids were playing with.

Innovators are a product developer's friends for they are the folks that pave the road for those who need assurances before venturing forth. They are the ones who fill the toe of the adoption curve shown in Figure 17. While quick to love you, though, Innovators are just as quick to leave you. If your product is one that relies on repeat rather than one-off sales, you must realize that the Innovators will be the first to abandon your product when the next shiny idea comes long. If you want to keep Innovators as customers, you must be the one to offer that new idea.

Early Adapters

While not true pioneers, Early Adapters embrace change and enjoy playing a leadership role. Representing 13.5% of the population, they represent the first mass market for your new product. They are critically important, both because it is they who will sharply increase the slope of the sales curve, and because there are enough of them to begin convincing the next group to follow in their footsteps.

Early Majority (AKA Late Adapters)

The Early Majority is more risk-adverse and therefore somewhat reluctant to change until they determine that it is safe to do so. They want evidence that the new product will fulfill their needs and will seek that evidence through success stories and testimonials. At 34% of the market, they are important, both for their purchasing potential and because it is they who will convince the next group to accept the new product.

Late Majority

Making up another 34% of the market, the Late Majority is important to total sales, but convincing them to buy is not easy. Their risk aversion is such that they need a lot of motivation before trying something new. While they are looking for overwhelming evidence that they are not making a mistake, they can be motivated by competitive or strong peer pressure.

Laggards

The final 16% of the population are the Laggards. They are perfectly happy with the status quo and are loath to upset it. I used to refer to laggards as the "buggy whip crowd", referring to people seeking accessories for their horse-drawn carriage. That can probably be updated to the "flip-phone crowd".

Question: "How many laggards does it take to change a light bulb?" Answer: "None; 'I'd rather stick with the old one!'"

On a very serious note, when the laggards start buying your product, it may well be obsolete, and you should have long since replaced, or at least supplemented, it with something newer.

Applying the Theory

Generally, we think of these adopter categories as applying to individuals. I contend that the concept applies to organizations and sometimes to entire industries; some accept change rapidly while some seem to move at speed of a glacier. Consequently, when a product is first introduced, sales calls should be concentrated on people and organizations that are Innovators. At the other extreme, a sales call on a laggard early in a product's lifecycle is likely to be a waste of time and effort. To the extent possible, the targeting of marketing and sales should evolve as the product matures.

As much as we'd like to see our new product fly off the shelves on the first day, that rarely happens. A deeper understanding of what affects the rate of product adoption will help us to more effectively design our promotional program and forecast sales. With a sales forecast based on these realities, we are better positioned to interpret sales figures to determine whether low initial sales are indicative of a problem or simply something to be expected.

Forecasting

The cynical say, "There are two kinds of forecasts, lucky ones and wrong ones!" While the statement is indeed cynical, it reflects a basic fact; accurate forecasts are hard to achieve.

All forecasting methods rely on various levels of guesswork. We gather a few facts, make a guess at others and put everything into a formula that combines all the errors! If we think there is a lot of precision in the result, we are deceiving ourselves; even the best forecast is flawed to some degree. Remember, though, that while creating a good forecast is hard, running a business without one is much harder. An accurate forecast, or at least one that is as accurate as we can make it, is vital to managing the business.

Depending on the circumstances, there are several potential approaches to forecasting. When more than one approach is applicable, it's advisable to use as many as possible and then to compare results of each method to reach the ultimate result through triangulation.

If your new product will replace an existing one and be sold through the same channels, the task is straightforward. You have but one guess, the percent increase in unit sales. That figure, combined with current sales and the pricing difference should result in a reasonably accurate forecast. Remember, though, to consider your product's value, your promotional plans and the adoption and diffusion factors discussed in the last section.

If you followed the methodology set forth in chapter 6, you identified the addressable market prior to Gate 2 and have updated it continuously as the project progressed. Addressable market, you'll remember, is the sales you'd achieve if you captured 100% of all potential sales of the product. Now, considering such factors as your and your competitors' relative strengths, your product's benefits, your promotional plans and the factors covered in the section on adoption and diffusion, what percent of that addressable market might you expect in each period (month, quarter, year, etc.)? Given enough related history, you may be able to use your market share of similar products as a guide or at least as a reality check.

Another, less obvious, approach is to start with your sales force. Given the history of each salesperson with similar or related products, how many units (or how many dollars) would you suppose each might sell per month? How will those sales progress with time? Combining the results may result in an alternate solution.

Similarly, it may be possible to start with your customers. What might you expect each to buy each month or year? It is likely that you will have to break your customers into categories to refine your guesses. Remember to consider buyer profiles for both salesforce and customers!

If you've been able to employ more than one method, the similarity of results (or lack thereof) will give you a good idea of their accuracy. If they are similar, you'll feel a bit better about them; if they differ significantly, you'll want to evaluate each more closely.

Throughout all of this, be sure your fundamental assumptions are valid. Remember the adage, "Don't forecast the traffic on a proposed new bridge by basing it on the number of people who have been swimming across the river!"

Human nature being what it is, it can be tempting to submit forecasts that are no higher than what is necessary to get project approval. After all, that reduces the likely of being criticized for failing to meet the forecast and increases the likelihood of being praised for exceeding it. Please resist that temptation! The truth is that a low forecast can be at least as detrimental to the organization as a high one! It may cause design engineers to forego superior designs that are only suitable for high production, the manufacturing engineers to refrain from installing equipment suitable for high throughput and low costs, the procurement people from securing the low prices associated with high volume and the product planners from planning adequate quantities to meet demand. Intentionally low-balling a forecast is never acceptable.

Given the importance and inherent inaccuracy of forecasts, I strongly recommend creating and evaluating three forecasts; pessimistic, optimistic and most likely. If all three are as honest as they can be, the company can use them to make intelligent decisions on much more than funding.

If you struggle with forecasting, take heart; you are not alone. In 1943, IBM Chairman Thomas Watson said, " I think there is a world market for maybe five computers." Most of us have more than five computers in our own homes so, hopefully, we can do better than that!

Post-introduction Follow-through

I know it's terribly politically incorrect to say, but I will do so anyway... If you take a girl to a dance, you really should dance with her! The end of a new product development project is not when the product is introduced at a trade show; it's not even when the first product is produced or shipped. Although I told my staff for decades that it comes when customers are happily and consistently sending you money and when you are reaping the profits you'd expected, it's even later than that. In a larger sense, although the development team may be off on other projects, the true end of a development project comes, perhaps years after introduction, when the product is retired from the market. In the meantime, the product and the market for it must be continually monitored and adjustments made to maintain the product's relevance and vitality.

Product Lifecycle Phases: The right actions and expectations at the right time[51]

Without going into the details of how to promote a product, let me touch on how the approach to promotion must change over time in alignment with buyer profiles. Figure 20 illustrates the four major phases in the life of a typical project. You may notice that the sales curve in that figure is the same as the solid-line curve in Figure 17; I've simply added the dividing lines and labels.

Each of the four phases illustrated has distinct characteristics and each roughly corresponds to the profiles of the people who are most likely to buy during that phase.

Referring to the section on buyer profiles, we can expect that the buyers in the introduction phase will be primarily Innovators. Rapid growth will be driven by the early Adapters. The Early and Late Majority will carry us through the mature phase of the product's life and the Laggards will preside over its decline. Just as each group has its own personality, each phase demands its own approach. Let's look at each of the phases.

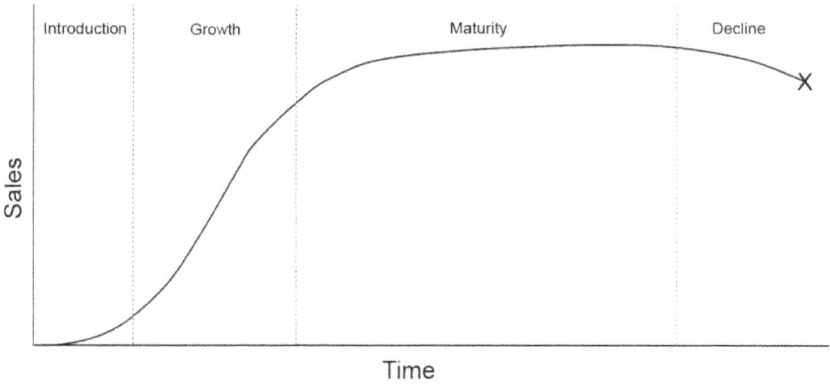

Figure 20 - Product Lifecycle Phases

Introduction

As the primary buyers during the introduction phase are the 2.5% of the population known as Innovators, an approach that addresses the broad market may be largely a waste of resources. Admittedly, if the product is a mass market one, it may be difficult to target the message to Innovators alone but, if it's a high-ticket item that is sold through single-step distribution, it may be reasonable to expect experienced sales professionals to know which of their customers are Innovators and which are Laggards. That being the case, it would be foolish for them to expend energy on trying to secure a sale to a Laggard during this phase and wise to concentrate on the Innovators. Even companies with more complex distribution chains may find it possible to target advertising through media oriented to Innovators. If advertising can be targeted, its cost can be relatively low at this point.

The organizations in your distribution chain and even your own sales people can be categorized by buyer profile as well. I distinctly remember Scott, a territory manager who was my hero because he jumped on every new offering with both feet and almost always out-sold his peers. Of course, being a typical Innovator, as soon as we introduced another new product, his attention shifted to that!

Awareness of a new product during this phase is low both at the customer level and throughout the distribution chain. Our challenge, then, is to begin to build product awareness at all levels through messages that are largely informative.

Sales, of course, will be low during this phase. If the product is truly new, there will be little competition and we may enjoy high prices. On the other hand, we may have applied introductory discounts to promote sales, reducing those profits. In either case, since production volume is still modest, profits may be low or even negative.

During this phase, if corporate expectations have been set without appreciation for these dynamics, a great deal of frustration and even anger may be evident, and there could be calls for drastic, often ill-advised, actions. I strongly urge restraint; ask yourself whether the alleged poor performance is worthy of a course change or is simply a natural phenomenon that should be allowed to run its course.

Growth

During the growth phase, product awareness broadens. Sales increase rapidly as the Early Adapters, both at the end-user level and throughout the distribution chain, begin to accept the product.

The challenge now is to expand distribution and build on the differentiation message. Distribution channels must be carefully managed to assure channel partners' commitment. The onset of competitive reaction makes it prudent to increase advertising, concentrating on persuasive messages.

Profits can be expected to increase as production volume and efficiencies drive down costs. However, it's important to remember that these high profits could be transient. It is therefore important to begin looking at ways to reduce costs in preparation for competitive pressures.

Maturity

Eventually, sales begin to level off as the product matures, competition intensifies and the market becomes saturated. By this time, there will be a high level of product awareness and distribution channels will be well established. However, intense competition may cause prices, and therefore profits, to fall. The challenge during this phase is to maintain customer loyalty and to attract customers from the competition. Therefore, advertising should be heavy and highly competitive.

By the time the product reaches this phase, a well-managed organization will have already put plans in place to enhance or replace the product line, a subject we will address shortly.

Decline

Even Rome eventually fell. A product's lifespan may last months, years, or even decades, but interest will eventually wane and sales will decline, often at a precipitous rate. Prices and profits will fall to the point that the product may no longer be viable. Long before this happens, new products must have been introduced to fill the void left as this one dies.

Death

The treatments I've seen on product lifecycles list only the first four, but just as death is inevitable at the end of our personal lifecycles, so it is with our products. And, as it is true with our pets, it's sometimes wise to euthanize our products. If the product has been highly successful, and especially if that success has been long lived, the decision to terminate it is a difficult one. This is especially true if the product is one on which the success of the business has been built. Nonetheless, keeping a product in the product line after its vitality is gone is harmful to the organization. Products that are past their prime tie up inventory dollars that could be used to support new products. They tie up production resources, lengthening lead times. They even distract the sales force, who should be focusing on products of the future, not clinging to those of the past.

Paradoxically, your new product process must include an "old product process". Just as proper pruning gives vitality to a tree or shrub, a carefully developed and executed product pruning process is vital to your overall product lifecycle management process. It's not nearly as exciting as developing new products, but it's every bit as important.

Project Performance Reviews

In chapter 6, we discussed the need for post-launch audits to be sure that the new product is performing at least as well as expected, not only from a technical standpoint, but from customer satisfaction, sales and profit standpoints as well.

In addition to the more detailed audits outlined in that chapter, ongoing, <u>formal</u> reviews should be held after product release to assure that the organization and its customers are getting what was promised. I recommend they be held monthly or at least quarterly until the product is consistently producing the desired results. How are customers responding? How is the marketplace reacting? How are competitors countering? The reviews must be based, not on opinion or blind trust, but on hard data such as sales and profit figures, QA reports, customer feedback and so forth. In addition to monitoring sales and profit figures, mine the data from salesforce and channel partner reports, customer feedback and support desk calls. Proactively seek customer input. Do not, under any circumstances think that "No news is good news!". Silence may simply mean that your customers have walked away without uttering a word!

Performance reviews are not simply an opportunity to study data and wring hands, they are a time to create and initiate action plans to assure that performance meets or exceeds expectations. Remember, people are much more likely to spread the word about a product or service they dislike than about one they like. If your product disappoints your customers, you can believe that the word will spread quickly. And, trust me, it will spread even more rapidly through the sales force.

To assure action is taken promptly, each review must have active involvement by participants at an organizational level commensurate with the importance of the product to the organization. In many cases, this should mean that top management must participate. As with all important matters, action items must be identified, responsibilities assigned and results tracked.

Cost Reductions

If you've done everything correctly, your new product will deliver the profits that were promised early on. That doesn't mean that you shouldn't try to make those profits higher! It also doesn't mean that the profits will stay as they are once competitors' responses start inducing you to reduce your prices. I'm not going to delve into the mechanics of cost reduction but I do want to make the following points.

It is likely that you can cut costs without reducing the value you offer to your customers. However, be mindful of your value proposition as you seek to reduce costs. There are probably those within the organization who, being focused only on short-term results, are strongly motivated by potential cost savings, even at the risk of a damaged reputation and its long-term effect. In the 1970's, Value Analysis (VA) was all the rage. Back then it was about analyzing a product design to assure that only features that added value were retained, while ways were sought to provide equal value at a lower cost. Unfortunately, by the '80's the term VA had morphed into a euphemism for, "make it cheaper regardless of its effect on value". Have you noticed the diameter of the wire in clothes hangers or the size of English muffins or candy bars? Have you noticed that the package you brought home thinking that it contained a pound of bacon contained only 12 ounces? Those are examples of the redefined VA in action. If your initial customer research has led you to understand that certain benefits were expected, be very careful of stripping them away just to save money. If you mess with the value, you mess with the price/value ratio and that must only be done after careful deliberation.

Nevertheless, it's wise to acknowledge that your initial research may have been flawed; it may be that a feature that you incorporated because you felt it had value is not now valued in the marketplace. Be sure you are right before you act but, if you have strong evidence that you have a feature (read: cost) that does not deliver a corresponding benefit, get rid of it!

Product Line Management

Refer again to Figure 20. Would you be happy to see sales of your new product stagnate and decline as depicted in the figure? Should you calmly accept it? If not, what can you do about it?

While the curve will win in the end, you can delay the inevitable in several ways.

Broadening the Product Line

If you have intelligently managed the scope of the initial project, you have optimized time to market by avoiding the temptation to pack everything possible into the initial offering. You can broaden the product line and increase sales by introducing those products, features or accessories whose development you have delayed. More will be said about this in the next chapter.

Even if you have not already anticipated the need for and identified accessories or follow-on products, they will become obvious if you stay as close to your customers as you were when you did the initial needs research. They, too, will provide sales opportunities.

Product Enhancements

Likewise, if you stay close to the customer, you may find opportunities to enhance the value of the core product by adding benefits without changing the cost/benefit ratio. Be cautious here, however; if such a move would cause you to lose existing customers, it may be better to leave the original offering unchanged and introduce a variant having those added benefits.

Product Variants

As discussed earlier, a product designed for everyone is probably not ideal for anyone. Hopefully, the initial product was well positioned for its target market but, once that product is in place, it's time to target other customers with products better suited to them. Products with fewer benefits at a lower price and others having more benefits at a higher price are strong possibilities.

Introducing products to foreign markets may involve significant hurdles for a company with no such experience but, if your organization is already selling outside the domestic market, creating suitable global variants may be an attractive option. Beware, however, that the task might be much more complex than simply making a metric version or one that works with a different electrical standard.

Addressing a foreign (or any different) market requires the same rigorous research that was applied at the beginning of the initial project. In chapter 5 we stressed the fact that customer needs often vary from one geographical area in ways that are not obvious. If this is true from state to state, it is most certainly true from country to country. Be sure your research is solid before venturing abroad!

Extending the Curve

Figure 21 illustrates an example of how on organization might extend sales growth.

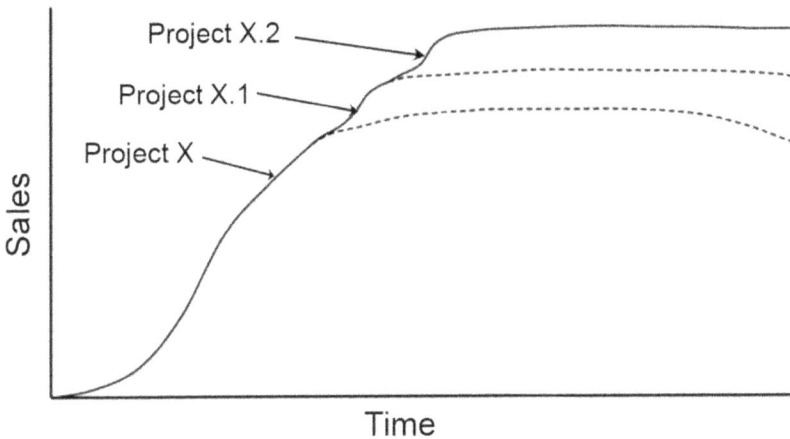

Figure 21 - Product Line Management

In the figure, the initial project, "Project X", follows a typical profile, starting off slowly, gaining momentum and then, if left untouched, would begin to stagnate and eventually die as shown in the lowermost dotted line.

Before that happens, however, a bundle of accessories is introduced as Project X.1, causing the sales curve to continue to increase until its sales, too, begin to decay. Before the decay begins, though, an economy variant, Project X.2, is introduced, offering a lower price but a more limited set of benefits.

Projects X.1 and X.2 in the example were introduced at the points where sales would have leveled off just for clarity of the illustration. They could have been introduced at any point, though it is obviously desirable to do so earlier rather than later. Though only two are illustrated here, such a string of introductions can continue for as long as the product line itself is viable.

The options can be daunting and each possibility may have its own champions, each vying for the organization's limited resources. Therefore, each must be evaluated and managed in a logical way, optimizing the overall result for the organization rather than those of any special interest. The phase-gate process is as applicable here as it was in the initial development project, though simpler versions of the process may be more appropriate. Project portfolio management, as described in the next chapter, will prove useful as well.

Chapter 8 –Project Portfolio Management

When it comes to investing, there is no such thing as a one-size-fits-all portfolio.

– Barry Ritholtz

For any knowledgeable investor, portfolio management is a familiar concept. Based on factors such as age, liquidity needs and risk tolerance, the wise investor, often with professional guidance, develops an investment strategy that divides her wealth over several asset categories. By thus diversifying her portfolio, she maximizes the likelihood of meeting her investment objectives. Thus, a young person, who presumably has time to recover from a downturn in the market, might invest 80 or 90 percent of her assets in stocks while a retiree's investment in stocks might be less than 20 percent.

Following the same logic, an organization is well advised to allocate the resources it applies to new product development in such a way as to manage risk and maximize the likelihood of achieving its strategic objectives.

Perspectives

The wise investor might balance his investment portfolio by industry, for example, as well as by investment instrument such as stocks, bonds, etc. Just as we can manage our investment portfolios from several perspectives, so can we administer our project portfolios. There are many perspectives from which an organization can view its project portfolios, some of which are suggested here.

Newness

As the financial investor balances her portfolio between high-risk, high-return stocks and lower-risk, lower-return bonds, the wise executive team balances their new product investments between quick and easy projects that offer a modest return and a moderate investment risk and projects offering potential breakthrough products with a huge payoff accompanied by significant risk.

The risk associated with a project is closely related to its "newness"; one that is a small departure from what has been done before is relatively safe while one that pushes boundaries may offer a high potential return and a correspondingly high risk of failure.

The newness of a new product can be viewed from two perspectives; newness to the company, and newness to the market. Pictorially, it would look something like this:

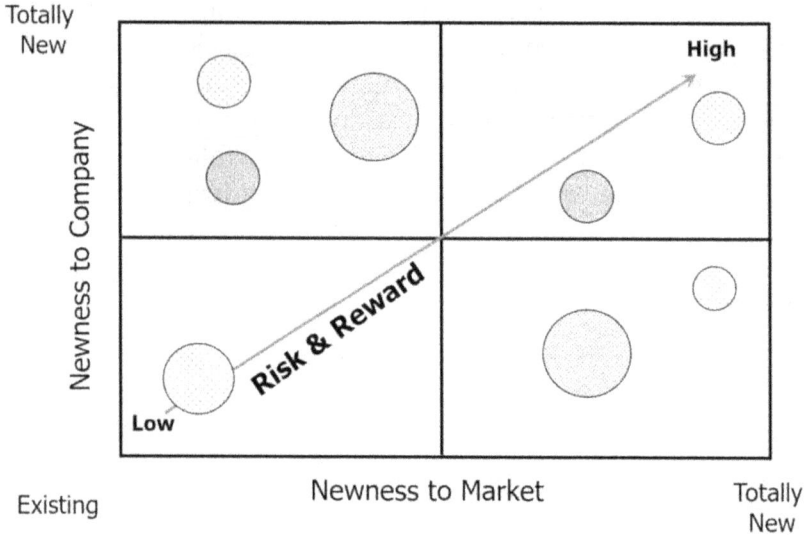

Figure 22 - Product Newness

Of course, the placement of any product on the map is more a matter of art than of science but clearly, those projects closest to the lower left corner may be worthwhile though unexciting while those closest to the top right corner are the risky but potentially rewarding breakthroughs offering huge rewards. Scattered throughout the portfolio are other projects with varying levels of risk and reward.

Though the distinctions are somewhat arbitrary, it is helpful, in the name of simplicity, to divide projects into a few discrete categories. "Product Maintenance" projects, including cost reductions, minor product improvements and so on, would fall in the lower left corner of the chart while potentially breakthrough "New to the World" products would fall at the opposite extreme; the upper right. Elsewhere would be "Product Improvements", "Line Extensions" and "New Product Lines". There is nothing magical about this selection of categories, and yours might be quite different.

The important thing is to select those categories that are meaningful to the way you want to divide your resources.

Once the categories have been selected, decisions must be made as to how the organization's resources should be spread among them. Since the goal here is to link the allocation of resources to organizational strategy, this is not a trivial task. If it is to be a meaningful tool, establishing it will involve considerable strategic thought by the executive staff. The result of the exercise will be a breakdown of targeted spending such as that shown in Figure 23.

Targets:

New to the World	15%
New Product Lines	28%
Line Extensions	25%
Product Improvements	25%
Product Maintenance	7%

100%

Figure 23 - Type Targets

The effort expended in setting targets is totally wasted unless actual spending is continuously compared against the targets and

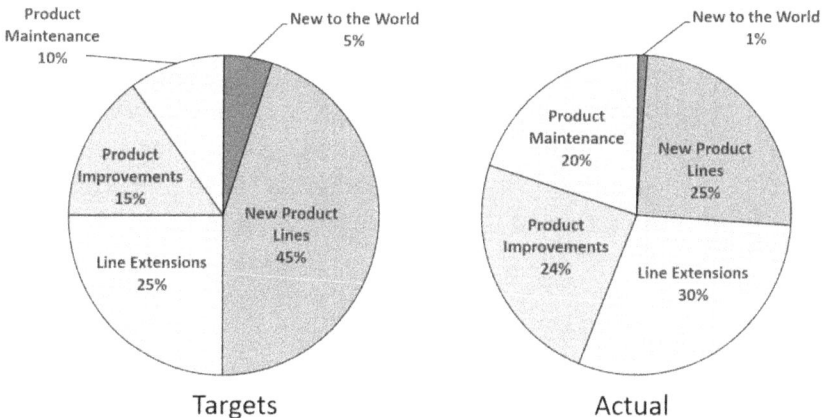

Figure 24 - Actual vs. Target Spending

adjustments made as needed. Figure 24 shows a fictitious comparison between established targets and actual spending during a given period.

In the example, actual spending bears little resemblance to what the organization expects. The charts reveal that resources spent on product maintenance are almost three times what was targeted, perhaps because of severe product problems, but perhaps because of the strong temptation to react to short-term opportunities. Likewise, Product Improvements and Line Extensions have consumed resources that should have been spent on the potentially more lucrative New Product Lines and New to the World products. As is typical in many organizations, New to the World products have been receiving far less attention than was envisaged. The lure of the "quick and easy" often seduces us from work on projects that would have far greater impact. In such cases, decisive corrective action is clearly needed.

Project Significance

Sometimes it's advisable to look more closely at the nature of new product projects. Even within the established categories, projects vary in significance. At one point in my career, it became obvious that we were working on too many minor new product projects and not enough major ones. Our president issued the directive that at least 80% of the time spent on new products; that is, those represented jointly by "New to the World" and "New Product Lines" must be spent on "Major" ones. He and I discussed each project to come to an agreement as to which merited the label, "Major." Then, we maintained pie charts such as those shown in Figure 24 but each of which had only two "slices"; one representing the hours spent on "Major" and the other the time spent on "Other" new product projects. Quarterly review of the chart caused us to focus attention on those projects that were truly impactful and, very shortly thereafter, our project portfolio reflected the president's vision.

Market & Product Line

There are other ways to look at strategic resource splits as well, including by market and by product line. Figure 25 illustrates examples.

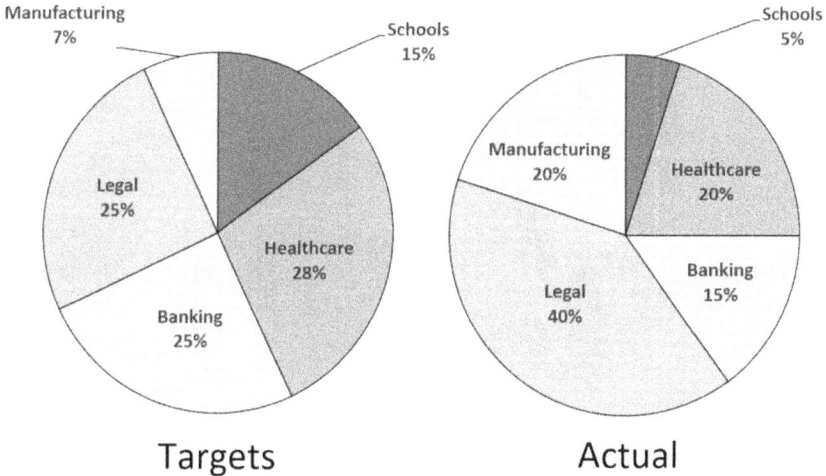

Figure 25 - Other Resource Splits

As was illustrated with respect to newness, monitoring of portfolio performance would require pairs of charts, one for targets and one for actual performance. In each case, any disconnect would result in corrective action.

Launch Timing

When I first considered consulting, a friend counseled me that one of the most difficult things to do was to continue to search for more work while overwhelmed with the work on hand. He stressed, however, that failing to do so would result in hard times once the current contracts were completed. The same thing is true when you're deep into the development of current projects; that's precisely the time when you must get new ones into the pipeline!

If an organization is to maintain a reputation as an innovator, it must introduce a continuous stream of new products. Some may be less significant than others but a flow of frequent "New from..." messages is compelling. The use of a chart such as that shown as

Figure 26 is an effective way of maintaining focus on the flow of product introductions. In the example, column heights represent project 3-year cumulative sales of products introduced in each year as one way of indicating each project's impact. The chart shows clearly

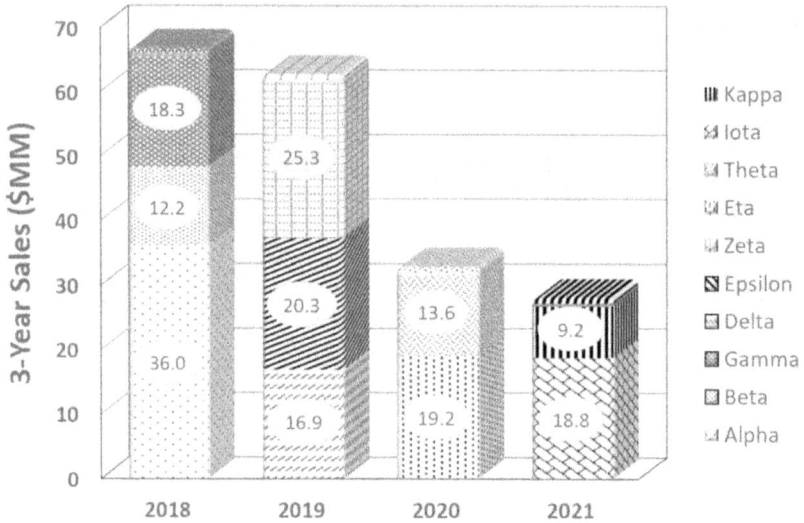

Figure 26 - Launch Timing

that the management team of the organization represented by the example must give immediate attention to the identification of projects to be introduced in the third and fourth years.

Program Impact

More important than maintaining a flow of new products is constantly increasing new product sales. Figure 27 depicts a chart

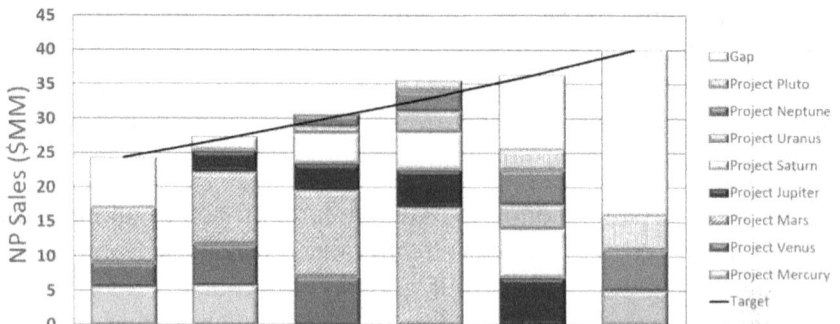

Figure 27 - New Product Projections

showing the predicted composite sales of all new products of a different company by year.

The chart shown is illustrative of a company that counts a product as "new" during the year in which it was introduced and for 3 full years thereafter. Sales in previous years are actual; those in future years are forecasts. At the bottom of the chart we see Project Mercury. Because it was introduced in 2016, only two years' worth of sales appear in the chart. Project Venus was introduced in 2017 so three years' sales appear. Project Mars was or will be introduced in 2018 so sales for all four years appear. Additional products are expected be introduced in 2019 and 2020 and their sales are as shown.

When plotted in light of the company's vitality index expectations (see appendix F), the resulting chart is enlightening. This organization has a vitality index of 25%. That is, it expects that, in any given year, that 25% of its total sales will come from new products. New product sales levels corresponding to that target are indicated by the solid line. The most important elements in the chart are the segments that represent the "Gap"; the shortfall between the identified new product sales for each year and the targets.

As we can clearly see, the year 2018 is not a good year for new products as there is a substantial gap between projected sales of identified new products and the goal based on the vitality index. If all goes according to plan, the years 2019 through 2021 will be good ones, with projections meeting or exceeding targets. After that, however, we see substantial gaps. Given the time horizon, some gap is to be expected in later years, but the chart highlights the strong imperative to quickly identify and initiate projects that will allow the company to reach or exceed expectations for new product sales. In practice, I recommend colored charts with the gap shaded in bright yellow or red to bring attention to impending shortfalls.

Strategic Buckets

Let's reflect again on your financial portfolio. Suppose that, based on a careful analysis of your situation, your financial advisor and you agree that you will invest 10% of your funds in cash, 20% in bonds, 50% in large cap stocks and the remainder in small cap stocks. Just to keep the math simple, let's say you have one million dollars to invest and that you've already invested it according to your strategic plan. That is, you've invested $100K in cash, $200K in bonds and so on. Now your friend, who is a broker, lets you know of a "hot" small cap stock that you "just can't pass up". Based on their performance, you are loath to sell any of your small cap stocks to buy this new one, but you have a $20K CD that has just come due. Do you use that cash to buy the not-to-be-missed stock? Presumably, you allocated 10% to cash so you'd have secure funds for security, a planned purchase or whatever. If you use some of it for the stock purchase, your plan has been thwarted. To be true to your strategy, you'd either sell some of your small cap stocks or pass on the new opportunity.

In this context, NPD guru Bob Cooper uses the term "strategic buckets[52]". Applying that term to our analogy, we'd have a "bucket" labeled "Cash" with $100K in it, another labeled "Bonds" with $200K in it and so forth. The concept dictates that funds can only be used for the investments marked on the buckets.

How does this apply to project portfolio management? We've already said that you can look at portfolios from several perspectives including project categories, markets, product lines and so on. From which perspective should we divide our resources? The answer depends on the realities of the corporation and the mindset of its executives, but the decision need not be exclusive. We could, for example, first divide our resources by project category, setting aside 5% for New to the World Products, 45% for new product lines and so on. Once that is done, we could take the 45% of resources allocated for new product lines and divide that according our strategy for allocation by market.

As an example, imagine that ours is a very large company and that the 45% of total resources that we've allocated to New Product Lines amounts to 12 million dollars. Suppose further that we've determined that 39% of that should be spent on the school market, 31% for healthcare, 18% for legal professionals and the remaining 12% for manufacturing. Our strategic buckets for the split of the 12 million dollars allocated for New Product Lines would be as illustrated in Figure 28.

Schools (39%)		
Allocated Funds ($K):		$ 4,680
Project Name	Cost ($K)	Funds Remaining
Alpha	$ 1,500	$ 3,180
Beta	$ 750	$ 2,430
Gamma	$ 1,000	$ 1,430
Delta	$ 950	$ 480
Epsilon	$ 250	$ (230)

Healthcare (31%)		
Allocated Funds ($K):		$ 3,720
Project Name	Cost ($K)	Funds Remaining
Eta	$ 1,200	$ 2,520
Theta	$ 850	$ 1,670
Iota	$ 1,500	170
Kappa	$ 1,100	$ (930)

Legal (18%)		
Allocated Funds ($K):		$ 2,160
Project Name	Cost ($K)	Funds Remaining
Nu	$ 250	$ 1,910
Xi	$ 500	$ 1,410
Omicron	$ 425	$ 985
Pi	$ 500	$ 485
Rho	$ 300	$ 185

Manufacturing (12%)		
Allocated Funds ($K):		$ 1,440
Project Name	Cost ($K)	Funds Remaining
Tau	$ 750	$ 690
Upsilon	$ 400	$ 290
Phi	$ 200	$ 90
Chi	$ 125	$ (35)
Psi	$ 75	$ (110)

Figure 28 - Strategic Buckets

In the figure, the small tables represent the second-level strategic buckets; one for Schools, one for Healthcare and so on. At the top of each is the allocation percentage but, more importantly the funds allocated for that bucket. So, after the two sorts, $4,680K would go to school projects, $3,720K to Healthcare and so forth.

Within each table has been listed, in order of descending priority, the New Product Line projects that have been identified for that market. In a column to the right of the name of each project is its cost and, to the right of that, a figure that represents the funds remaining after it and any previous projects have been funded.

In the example, five projects have been identified for the school market. After all of them have been funded, there is $230K remaining. On the other hand, of the four projects identified for the healthcare market, funds are available to support only three, there being a $930K shortfall. It would certainly be possible to use part of the excess from the school "bucket" to fund the remaining healthcare market project but, while occasionally taking such action may be tolerable, doing so repeatedly will obviate the strategy and is ill-advised.

As the phase-gate process facilitates the management of individual projects so that they deliver the desired results, portfolio management facilitates the management of the entire project portfolio so that the composite results are aligned with organizational and new product strategies.

Chapter 9 - Managing Risk

The policy of being too cautious is the greatest risk of all.

— Jawaharlal Nehru

There is no question that the development of new products is a risky business, albeit much less risky than <u>failing</u> to do so. It is a leader's responsibility to manage risks in such a way as to optimize the organization's performance. That's easy to say but difficult to do.

Though it should be obvious, let me say this at the outset; thou shalt take no risk without adequate justification! Engineers and designers like to design; the temptation to create something new just because they can do so is a strong one. However, doing so is not always appropriate. Designing a new sub-assembly or component where an existing one will accomplish the same result at the same cost, adds risk as well as time and expense. Unless the new design offers value to the customer, it should be avoided. Likewise, marketers and others are eager to add features just because they can. In chapter 5 we learned that a feature that does not deliver a benefit to the user must be rejected to avoid increasing cost. At least as important is the avoidance of risk. The bottom line is, risk should be assumed only when it delivers value to the customer.

In new product development there are two types of risk; technical risk and market risk. Technical risk is based on the question, "Will it work?" which is more properly phrased, "Will it meet the specification? Market risk, on the other hand, stems from the question, "Will it sell if it does work?" The dividing line is a precise one; the product specification.

The Product Specification

Over the years, I've seen far too many projects get derailed because, from the beginning and far into the project, the specifications were nebulous or missing altogether. Well into the project, someone would say, "Why doesn't it so such and such?" to which the reply would be, "Who said it was <u>supposed</u> to do such and such?" So, the first thing you can do to reduce project risk (and a lot of interpersonal conflict!) is to define the expectations in painstaking detail. How fast should it go? What loads must it bear? What are the maximum and minimum sizes and weight? Through how many cycles must it live? In what environments must it function and for how long? And on and on and on ad nauseum. To reduce workload and promote consistency, a company that produces similar products over time is well advised to create templates with each of the important properties (speed, acceleration, etc.) identified.

Identifying the appropriate parameters and establishing specifications for each is a daunting task and may well spark some heated debates. Once established, however, such a document will serve as a touchstone as the project progresses. Often as a project proceeds, events will call for revisions to the specifications and, if they are made with general agreement and a full understanding of the tradeoffs and consequences, all is well. Changing them without due consideration (or, worse, ignoring them) is irresponsible.

Technical vs. Market Risks

So, back to technical vs. market risks. During project execution, technical risks are more evident; unit cost projections swell, design calculations reveal potential problems, testing reveals failures and so on. Clearly, if the product doesn't work, doesn't do what it's expected to do or can't be produced at an acceptable cost, the project is in trouble. It's natural, then, to analyze and test exhaustively, to make revisions and test some more until everyone is confident that everything will work perfectly under all circumstances. That seems like a good philosophy, right?

Not if taken to extremes. As we analyze, test, revise, modify and repeat, pages fall off the calendar and the launch date is delayed time and again. In the meantime, the world is marching on. Competitors are working on their own projects. The work habits of our customers are evolving, creating changes in their needs. While appropriate time and attention must be spent on managing technical risks, spending an <u>excessive</u> amount of time can increase market- and, therefore, total risk!

To minimize market risk, move quickly. The longer it takes to get your new product to market, the greater the likelihood that the information you gathered so painstakingly will become stale and perhaps totally irrelevant. Resist the temptation to continually "tweak" the product in a futile attempt to make it perfect; you may make it perfectly obsolete before it sees the light of day!

If you've done as expected, you understand your customers' needs and have created a concept to fill them effectively. You'll have also created a set of written specifications to guide the designers and engineers. All that effort will be of little value, though, if the world has changed by the time you introduce the product! Sadly, many companies, having studied the market thoroughly, take their eyes off it once the project is underway.

As the project proceeds, it's essential to stay close to the market; to maintain the same level of vigilance that you did while doing the initial research. Watch for changes in the marketplace, including actions by your competitors. Maintain close communications with your customers and channel partners, continuing the dialog that you initiated at the early stages of the project. Periodically seek feedback from trusted customers and channel partners as the project develops. Early feedback can reduce the likelihood that you will go down a road that is better avoided.

If changes are necessary, make them judiciously; if you react to every new piece of information, the continual course changes will delay the project to the point that it may never succeed.

Scope Management

When it comes to extending time to market (and causing budget overruns), one of the most insidious factors is scope creep. The team starts out in agreement about features and benefits. As the project progresses, two things happen. First, the designers and engineers, being the creative folks that they are, continue to come up with more and more whiz-bang ideas. "Hey, look, I figured out a way to…" or "Wouldn't it be nifty if we could…" In the meantime, the marketers, staying close to the marketplace, are providing their own input as to how the product can be enhanced. As time marches on and these "wonderful" ideas are incorporated, the project becomes an unwieldy monstrosity.

One of biggest regrets in my career was failing to step in to limit the scope of a project that was successful only after it endured excruciating birthing pains that lasted literally for years! The project was a major one, based on a platform that was destined to be both flexible and broad. The problem was that the team kept coming up with more and more inspirations for what it might do. Of course, with each revelation, marketing insisted on having that feature or version upon introduction. The scope of the project continued to grow and grow until it was overwhelming. As always, we were on a strict timetable for introduction, so the only way to do everything was to do it all shoddily. That's exactly what we did and the results were abysmal.

Had we not had all those "Aha" moments, or had we managed project scope effectively, we'd have introduced an excellent product which, though more modest in scope, would have had tremendous market impact. What's more, we'd have done it on time and with a minimum of complications. It is abundantly clear in hindsight that, had we aggressively managed the project's scope by developing a project roadmap as described in chapter 5 <u>and disciplining ourselves to introduce all those great innovations over a reasonable time period</u>, we'd have...

1. ...had a timely introduction of a major, innovative product that addressed significant market needs at an attractive price.
2. ...quickly achieved target sales and positive cash flow.
3. ...avoided some very significant embarrassments in the marketplace.
4. ...over time, introduced an ongoing series of profitable new products and product enhancements that would have maintained excitement over the long run. And...
5. ...avoided many lost customers, untold cost, countless blame-sharing sessions and literally hundreds of sleepless nights!

It's simple math; the larger the scope of the project, the more that can go wrong. Unless there is overwhelming justification to do otherwise, resist the urge to add complexity to the project. Save those new ideas for later development and introduction.

Fast & Dirty Prototyping

I can say it because I am one; engineers love to analyze. We like to work out a design in infinite detail and then to analyze the design to determine whether it will work, often performing complex mathematical calculations. Eventually, we may make a prototype and subject it to physical testing.

While the slow, methodical approach may have its place, all of that designing and calculating takes a lot of time. By the time the design is complete, the organization has made a huge investment in both time and money and the engineers have made an enormous emotional investment. The result is that the inevitable problems are more likely to be addressed with incremental adjustments rather than by scrapping the whole design and starting over.

I prefer a very different methodology, which is best illustrated by example. Among the products our company manufactured were heated cabinets that were used in commercial kitchens to keep food warm. For reasons of both hygiene and customer satisfaction, it's important that the cabinet's interior have the proper, <u>uniform</u> temperature. We typically tested cabinet performance by placing an array of temperature-measuring thermocouples within the cabinet and then recording temperatures over an extended time.

In our traditional cabinets, the "heat module" containing the heating elements, fan and controls was located at the bottom of the cabinet. Among the advantages of that approach was the fact that, since hot air rises, a uniform internal temperature was easier to maintain. There was a call, however, to put the entire heat module near the top of the cabinet to make the controls more readily accessible while keeping all electrical components together for easier service.

The core question was, "What will happen to the heat distribution pattern when the heating system is near the top?" The traditional approach would have been to make a best guess at component layout, perhaps do some calculations, complete a design, build a prototype and test it. That would have taken at least weeks and perhaps months to accomplish. Fortunately, I had an engineer who simply ordered a traditional cabinet from stock, tipped it over, arrayed it with thermocouples and started testing! The investment was the cost of a standard cabinet and few days. Using the knowledge from that tiny investment, we had both the confidence that we'd be successful and a better understanding of how the new unit should be designed. While that example involved a rough prototype of the entire product, the same can be done with components and subassemblies. When you have an idea, especially if you have doubts about whether it will work, don't refine it; throw something together and see what happens!

OK, I freely admit that this approach might be inappropriate for the design of nuclear weapons but, in most cases, it can get you to a successful product launch more quickly and inexpensively and with a lot less frustration.

Evaluating Risk

Failure Modes & Effects Analysis - FMEA

A currently-popular method of evaluating risks is "Failure Modes & Effects Analysis", better known as FMEA. The procedure is quite complex and would require a much more rigorous treatment than is warranted here. In summary, though, it involves the following steps:

1. Define the scope of the study. It might be an entire product or a sub-system. I'll use the word "device" to represent that which is being studied.
2. Understand the function of each part of the device. Ideally, describe each function with two words; an active verb and a noun (e.g. "Illuminate opening" or "Provide heat").
3. Deduce the failure modes. In other words, what can go wrong; in what ways can the device fail?
4. Determine the effects of each failure mode. That is, what can result when something goes wrong?
5. Evaluate and rate the **Severity** of each effect. That is, how bad are the results of the effect? Rating is done on a scale of 1 to 10, with 10 being most severe.
6. Identify the causes of each failure mode.

7. Evaluate & rate **Occurrence** (that is, the possibility of occurrence) of each failure mode. Again, a scale of 1 to 10 is used.

8. Develop a comprehensive list of controls that reveal or make visible each failure effect or mode.

9. Evaluate & rate **Detection** (i.e. the likelihood of detecting the problem) and, again, rate it from 1 to 10.

10. Calculate the Risk Priority Number (RPN) by Multiplying the three ratings (**S**, **O** and **D**). While one might think, as the term implies, that a risk with a high RPN is, by definition, more important than one with a lower one, that is not strictly true. Because the three factors, severity, occurrence and detection, are not of equal importance, the RPN should be taken only as a guide; there is no "magic threshold number" to identify to what degree each risk must be addressed.

11. Take corrective action to reduce the highest priority risks, using the RPN only as a guide. Risks involving safety should be given special attention. Assign responsibility for each of the risks to be addressed to a <u>single person</u>. Others may help but a single person must be accountable.

12. Reevaluate the system after corrective actions have been taken to determine to what degree those actions have been effective. This means reevaluating and scoring the corrected items and taking additional actions as necessary.

FMEA has the distinct advantages of being well defined and well respected. Consequently, it may be especially useful for use on critical systems and especially when safety is involved.

Severity vs. Likelihood of Occurrence

While it may not be as widely used, I prefer a method suggested by Smith and Reinertsen[53]. This method relies on only two variables, severity and likelihood of occurrence. Otherwise, the methodology of identifying risks is similar to that outlined for FMEA.

Likelihood is essentially a probability so, of course, uses a scale of 0 to 100. The scale for severity is undefined by Smith and Reinertsen but I recommend the use of integers from 1 to 10. You can use decimals or a broader scale if you deem it necessary but I feel the granularity is outweighed by the angst that goes with it.

When I first applied this method, I tried to rate severity by assigning cost. My thinking was that if, for example, a risk was the failure of a motor and if replacing the motor would cost $200 and the probability of failure was 1%, the amount of risk was 1% of $200 or $2.00. It seemed logical until it came to assigning a value to an injury or death. I quickly concluded that it was not an attractive option after all!

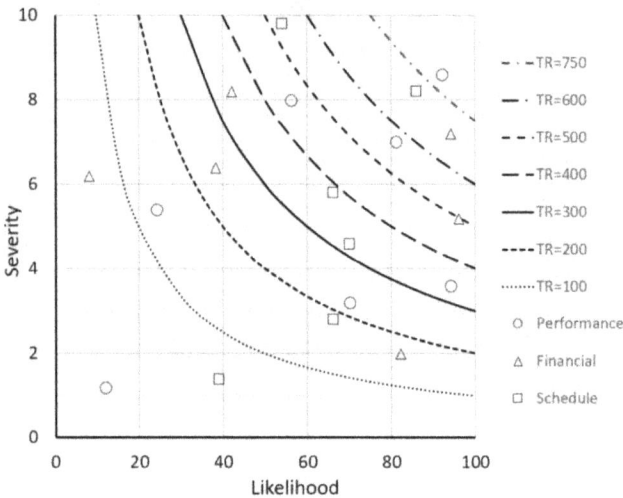

Figure 29 - Project Risk

Beyond its simplicity, what draws me to this method is that I'm a visual person and, having only two variables, this method makes it easy to display results graphically. Figure 29 illustrates such a graphical result. Each of the points plotted on the chart represents one of the identified risks. In the example, risks are identified by type but that is, of course, optional. Each curve represents a constant total risk (TR) where:

$$TR = Severity \times Likelihood$$

In the example, seven such TR curves are shown. Each one was generated, incidentally, by creating a simple table of data pairs, each pair of which has a product equal to the total risk represented by the curve. In other words:

$$\text{Severity} = \text{TR} / \text{Likelihood}$$

If you use this method, I recommend the creation of a template with the chart and TR curves. Once that is done, it's an easy matter to plug in the data.

All points above and to the right of each TR curve have a greater total risk than that represented by the corresponding curve. Just as with FMEA, there is no magic threshold below which we can ignore risk, but those with higher total risk, that is those closest to the upper right corner of the chart, generally deserve more attention. Absent special considerations such as safety concerns, start with all points (i.e. risks) above the curve for the highest risk (in the example TR=750). Next, address the risks above the next-lower TR curve and so on until the major risks have been addressed. That is not imply that only one risk or even one group of risks should be tackled at a time but it does imply a sense of priority.

As with FMEA, responsibility for the mitigation of each of the selected risks must be assigned to a single person. Here again, after corrective actions have been taken, the corrected items must be reevaluated and rescored to determine to what degree those actions have been effective.

A Final Thought

When I was flying, I read a safety article that admonished, "Whenever you say to yourself, "I think we should be able to get around that storm", stay on the ground! Likewise, whenever you think, "This design should work", reflect on the word "should". Unless you are very confident that it will work, you might at least give some thought to "plan B". I frequently used the term "cards up the sleeve" for alternate plans that I could quickly play if the game wasn't going as planned. The more uncertain you are, the more cards you should have up your sleeve. Combining this with what I wrote earlier about fast and dirty prototyping, when you're not sure, do a quick and dirty test. While you're awaiting the results, decide what you'll do if you don't like them.

Risk is inherent to new product development and, to a degree, is inevitable. It's up to us to act responsibly to identify unacceptable risks, eliminate those we can and mitigate the others.

Chapter 10 - Managing the Change

If you don't like change, you're going to like irrelevance even less.

*— General Eric Shinseki,
Chief of Staff. U. S. Army*

It must be considered that there is nothing more difficult to take in hand, more perilous to conduct, or more uncertain in its success, than to take the lead in the introduction of a new order of things...

— Niccolo Machiavelli

What follows is, of course, related to the change embodied in the introduction of a new NPD process and some material is specific to that. In a larger sense, however, much of the material in this chapter applies to or can be adapted to the implementation of any organizational change.

The Challenge

Half of a millennium later, Machiavelli's words still ring true. While we may give lip service to the need for change and even advocate for it when it serves our own interests, when change is trust upon us, our natural reaction is resistance. Machiavelli proposes a root cause of that resistance in the words that followed those quoted at the top of the page…

> *...for the innovator has for enemies all those who profit by the old conditions, and lukewarm defenders in those who may do well under then new. This coolness arises... partly from the incredulity of men, who do not readily believe in new things until they have had a long experience of them.*

Makes sense, doesn't it? Yet, we live in a world of change. From an organizational perspective, acquisitions, mergers and reorganizations are commonplace and each of these activities causes untold anxieties as we anticipate how they will affect us personally. We wonder how difficult it will be to learn the new approach, what problems we will encounter and how successful we will be. Whether we like to admit it or not, those fears engender resistance.

So, we have a challenge; if we are to make any use of the materials covered in this book, we must institute change, even in the face of resistance. If our organization already has an effective, robust NPD process that just needs some fine tuning, the change may be minor and resistance modest. If, however, no formal process exists, the change faced by the organization will be daunting. Some people's roles may change, perhaps dramatically. New methodologies and procedures are inevitable, often requiring the acceptance of new responsibilities and the leaning of new skills.

One of the problems with change in many organizations is that one change follows closely upon the heels of another. They institute program X and, at the first obstacle, abandon it and institute program Y. Before that can get traction, someone has a better idea and program Z is born. As Z begins to take effect, there is a management change and yet a new program is born. In such an environment, time and energy are wasted and people are frustrated. It would be miraculous for any program to be a successful.

Decades ago, I attended a seminar where the presenter spoke of what he termed the "wave theory of change". He suggested that new programs or procedures introduced into an organization are analogous to waves on a beach with the people within the organization like people playing in the surf.

If you watch people in the surf, you will see that some struggle against each wave. They get thrown around, exhaust themselves and occasionally get hurt. Others enthusiastically catch each wave and ride it onto the beach. Eventually, they find the wave dissipated and themselves face down in the sand. The experienced people, however, stand in the surf and, as each wave comes, simply bend their knees and let the wave pass over them. Even the largest waves pass by without noticeable effect, leaving the people unaffected and exactly where they were.

We cannot have that type of change. We need change that is both meaningful and sustainable; change that has been well thought out, that is understood and embraced by the people who will be affected by it and that has the organizational support that is so necessary to see it through.

To minimize pain at all levels of the organization and to maximize the chance of success, I suggest a 6-step approach…

Justifying the Change

Change that is inspired and driven by whim or fad is unlikely to achieve long-term success. A program that has been initiated because the CEO has read a magazine article (or even a book such as this one!) may be worth implementing but, especially if it is significant, the change must be fully vetted before implementation can even be considered. How does it fit the organization's strategic objectives and priorities? What are its probable advantages? What are the potential obstacles? What alternatives are available and how do they stack up in comparison?

Unless a change is a minor one, it's safe to assume that its implementation will require the efforts of many people. The efforts applied will, of necessity, divert resources from other activities including the running of the day to day business. In the case of the implementation of an NPD process, it may mean sacrificing short term results for the, hopefully greater, long-term results. Unless the organization is willing to make that tradeoff, implementation of the program may not be prudent.

If, as Machiavelli contends, change is difficult to institute, we need to be sure that "the juice is worth the squeeze", that the benefits that will accrue from implementing the change will more than offset the pain and suffering that will be endured. Given the potential obstacles, only a well-intentioned change is worthy of further consideration.

Committing to the Change

If, after due consideration, you truly believe that the change contemplated is worthy, you must commit yourself and the organization to the potential struggle inherent in its implementation. You must agree to stay the course, providing the needed support, guidance, encouragement and funding and to steadfastly refuse to turn away unless and until, after due diligence, it becomes obvious that the venture was ill-advised.

To overcome the many potential obstacles, <u>one</u> capable, engaged and empowered person must be made clearly and visibly responsible for seeing it through from beginning to end. Part of the commitment required is the willingness to assign someone with the resources, the skills, the initiative <u>and the authority</u> to get the job done. The entire organization must understand the identity and role of this change agent and that she has the full support of upper management.

If the change is worth making, top management must commit to fully resourcing it and seeing it through!

Rationalizing the Change

According to Machiavelli, one of the reasons that change is difficult to implement is because, in his words, "…the innovator has for enemies all those who profit by the old conditions…"

If we are asked to change the way we do things, our natural reaction is to ask, at least in our minds, "What's wrong with the way I've been doing it; are you implying that I've been doing things wrong.?" No one wants to be told that what he has been doing for years was wrong! What a slap in the face that is! Do you honestly expect support from a person thus offended?

Many years ago, I had the opportunity to work with consultant and change leader Hal McLean[54], who suggests that, in this context, we replace the words "right" and "wrong" with the words "appropriate" and "inappropriate". Regardless of how it appears now, it's probably safe to assume that your current process was considered "appropriate" for your business when it was implemented. Given changes in the environment, changes in your organization or possibly just the fact that you have new knowledge, it may be that the old way is now "inappropriate". So, it's fair to say that we were not wrong, we were just doing things that, while "appropriate" at the time, are no longer so. If we are sincere in our belief and can assure our associates that the proposed change imparts no negative inferences towards them or their work, we have removed a huge obstacle.

Promoting the Change

According to Machiavelli, the other reason that change is difficult to implement is because of "…the incredulity of men, who do not readily believe in new things until they have had a long experience of them."

Especially in today's environment, we just can't wait for that "long experience." It's up to management to educate all those even peripherally associated with the proposed change as to why the organization is instituting it and why the time to do so is now. Specifically, the people who will be affected need to know how the change will benefit the organization and, more importantly, how it will benefit them personally. They need to appreciate that, for each of them, "the juice is, indeed, worth the squeeze." Since their own welfare is largely dependent upon the strength of the organization, in the absence of something stronger, the fact that the organization is more likely to prosper should prove effective if communicated effectively. The earlier and more fully you provide this vital education, the greater your odds of success.

Instigating the Change

If my wife and I were to decide to paint our living room, agree on the color, the cost and by whom it would be done, we would likely to be pleased with the results, even if, after due consideration, we'd agreed that the color should be orange. If, on the other hand, we were to come home one day to find that our misguided if well-intentioned neighbors had surprised us with an orange living room, our response might be less positive than our friends had anticipated!

Beyond merely educating them, the more you involve key people in the design and implementation of the new process, the more likely you will be to gain their support. I have a huge caveat here, though. Please, please, please, resist any temptation to design the new process by committee. I've tried it (I'm ashamed to say more than once), each time with disastrous results. In every case, the result was a bloated process with checks and balances to protect every department's self-interests. Even when the goal of the activity was to streamline the process, the result has been to do just the opposite.

Just as you design a new product by gathering customers' needs and wants and then let the professionals do their job, design the new process by gaining an understanding of the stakeholders needs and wants and then have a very small group design the process. In fact, there is merit to having a single knowledgeable person rough it out and then fine tune it based on input from a few others. And, just as with a new product, you need to seek feedback as you proceed.

Implementing the Change

I can tell you from experience that you can expect a lot of objection to the rigor of a disciplined NPD process. Those who are accustomed to the "just do it, hope it works and fix it if it doesn't" approach will insist that doing the "homework" inherent in a more logical process will require too much effort and will bring every project to a crawl. Consequently, a critical message is that doing things right instead of repeatedly doing them over will significantly reduce the time to success. As we've already discussed, it may be possible to rush a flawed product to market quickly, but a flawed product most certainly cannot be defined as success!

I stress again that the support of the CEO and executive staff is critically important. That support must be evident at program rollout and continuously thereafter. Nothing will do more to undermine the success of the process than to have executives openly disparage it or, equally harmful, fail to show commitment to their own roles in it.

I described education and training in some detail in chapter 6 but let's review a few key points here.

- While the executive staff should have agreed to the development of the process initially, it is essential that the business unit's entire executive staff, including those who have little or no role in new product development, have at least a basic knowledge of the aims, advantages and working principles of the process. A brief session before process implementation will serve to provide this education, address any questions or concerns and secure commitment.

- A general session, addressed to a broad audience encompassing the executive staff, department heads, middle managers and professionals from all departments that will be even peripherally involved in the new NPD process will explain the principles of the process and some of its workings. A major objective is to secure universal support by reducing the anxiety induced by any substantial change.

- A session specifically for those who will function as gatekeepers is aimed at providing the knowledge needed to fulfill that critically important role. The significance of each gate, the nature of gate meetings and the implications of gate decisions are topics of particular importance.

- The scope and diversity of the subjects of interest to those who will be intimately involved in projects will generally require more than one session. A general session will serve to provide more detail on the types of data to be gathered as well as the level of diligence required during each phase. The principles of customer research, the nature and functioning of an NPD team and an understanding of the available tools and templates are also important topics. Because the role of the project manager is unique and critically important, special training is appropriate. Those who will be more intimately involved in customer research need a deeper understanding of its mechanics. Some templates and tools apply to specific functions. For these and other reasons, it may be sensible to arrange break-out sessions for targeted audiences.

As you design the educational program, refer to the appropriate section in chapter 6 for guidance.

Sustaining the Change

In light of our discussion of the "wave theory of change", we must assure that, after all the time and effort we've invested in the new NPD process, it's not discarded or replaced as soon as it encounters a few of the inevitable snags or when someone reads about the newest fad. Beyond the natural resistance to change and the lure of shiny new processes are two forces of which you must be especially wary. One attacks from below and the other from above.

From within the ranks of the people executing the process will come the claim that the "overhead" is slowing them down. In fact, I can clearly remember a time when, working under a particularly inefficient process, it was I who told my boss, "Within the time constraints, I can give you the product or I can give you these damned reports but I can't do both; which do you want?" Don't put your people in that position. If the new process inhibits rather than facilitates progress, such comments and the frustrations that provoke them are inevitable.

As has already been said, if you have developed a robust process, it may not result in getting <u>something</u> to market earlier but it <u>will</u> result in getting the <u>right</u> product to market earlier! And by right, I mean one that you can deliver on time and with a minimum of pain to your production department; a product that delights your customers and delivers the financial results you anticipated. If your new process delivers like that, your task is simply to convince people that it is the best way to operate. If it does not deliver like that, your job is to modify it until it does!

The more insidious attack is generally unintentional and comes from above. Remember, one of the foremost reasons for instituting the process in the first place is to assure that the organization focuses on the right projects, not those that are the apple of the CEO or owner's eye. Decisions as to which projects are initiated and which get continued funding must be based on facts, not emotion. Executives can undermine the process in two ways.

First, they can fail to apply the gate process rigorously. Though the nature of a given project may justify the omission of certain data, unless an exemption is justified and has been given in advance, all required data must be provided. If gates are routinely approved when required data is missing, the project people soon learn that they can get approval without doing their homework. When that happens, the entire process becomes meaningless.

Secondly, executives can denigrate, circumvent or ignore the gate process. If, after due consideration, a gate committee agrees that a project should be approved or killed and a top executive overrides the decision, the entire process is put in jeopardy. I will admit that on very rare occasions a top executive's vision <u>may</u> trump a decision based on analysis but, if such executive actions become anything approaching common, the process loses all value. I wrote earlier of a contentious gate meeting where the project being reviewed was a pet of the company's owner, a very successful entrepreneur. He felt the company should proceed with the project, even in the face of the gate committee's agreement with the team's recommendation to kill the it. In the end, however, he was wise enough to support the process and abide by the group decision. Given that the project in question was the first to be handled through the new NPD process, had he done otherwise, further implementation of the process would have been fruitless.

Process Ownership

The single most important thing you can do to assure the sustainability of any new process is to select and empower a process facilitator or champion; someone to "own" the process as described in chapter 6. This person must be committed to the success of the program and have enough knowledge, influence and authority to both ensure compliance and to identify and facilitate process revisions as they become necessary. Make no mistake, there will be many opportunities to refine the process.

Beware however, of the strong temptation to repeatedly add checks and balances. Whenever an error or omission is made, there will be those who cry, "We need to put something into the process to make sure that it never happens again!" If you repeatedly act on those recommendations, the process will become so bloated it really will slow things down.

Chapter 11 - Parting Words

While countless excellent books have been written on various aspects of new product development, my purpose in writing this one was to amalgamate those diverse topics to form a cohesive picture. In other words, to engender the holistic understanding that is so necessary for everyone engaged in the activity, regardless of function or level of responsibility.

Whether your products are airplanes or snack foods, computer chips or financial services, I hope you have found this book helpful. I hope you will forgive the fact that I've omitted treatment of how products are designed and produced but trust you'll agree that the disparity of industries to which the process is applicable makes it impossible to do otherwise. Other topics have been treated to various degrees. In some cases, I have merely introduced a topic and provided an overview. On other topics, I have gone into much greater depth. In some cases, it was simply because I thought the topic deserved more attention. Sometimes it was because I felt that my own experiences have given me insights that were worth sharing or that led me to beliefs different from those expressed by others.

Though many of us may tend to skip over appendices, I strongly recommend that you resist that urge. The topics addressed there are important to the overall understanding of the NPD process but they simply did not fit well into the flow of the text.

If you are an entrepreneur or executive, I hope you have been inspired to improve the process by which your organization develops new products and have found ways to do so. If you are a marketer, a designer, an engineer or one of the myriad others who are engaged in new product development, I hope that you have gained an understanding of how your role contributes to the overall process and how you can improve your own contribution. If you are a student, I hope I have inspired you to become involved in this very exciting arena.

Now, go make it happen!

Appendix A - Creativity & Innovation

"Experience takes away more than it adds. Young people are nearer to ideas than old people."

— *Plato*

"The problem is never how to get new, innovative thoughts into your mind, but how to get old ones out. Every mind is a building filled with archaic furniture. Clean out a corner of your mind and creativity will instantly fill it."

— *Dee Hock*

Creativity and innovation are essential to the development of new products not only at the beginning but at every step of the process. Opportunities must be identified, designs must be envisioned, problems must be identified and overcome and marketing programs must be conceived. Sometimes, it may be necessary to concoct new production methods, distribution systems and who knows what else. While not everything needs to be new and different, the success of a new product program depends largely on the organization's creative ability and its capability to turn those ideas into reality.

Creativity or Innovation?

Although the two are often confused, the terms are not synonymous. Put simply, creativity is about generating ideas and innovation is about doing something useful with them. Think of the last brainstorming session in which you participated. I'm betting it was a lot of fun and that a staggering list of possibilities was created, many of the possibilities quite creative. I'll also bet that little or nothing came of any of them!

Most of this book deals with innovation; turning ideas into shareholder value, but because innovation cannot even begin without ideas as raw material, let's address the more nebulous issue of creativity.

Creative vs. Logical Thinking

Normally, we think logically; our thoughts flowing naturally from one to the next. It is an effective way to live our day-to-day lives, getting logical results in logical ways. In most cases, it is the most efficient way to think. We wake when the alarm goes off, go through our normal routine of grooming and dressing. We make the coffee following a familiar procedure and take the same route to work day after day. While it may occasionally be worthwhile to explore an alternative route, it would be terribly inefficient to do so each day.

Despite its efficacy in achieving logical results, logical thinking is quite ineffective at getting at the illogical results that we know as "creative" and that are essential to the development of radically new products.

The effectiveness of logical thinking is so great that, the more we do it, the more ingrained it becomes. The ability to think creatively depends on our ability to, at least temporarily, abandon that logical thought process; to set aside what we know, what we think we know and what we assume.

The Dot Problem

It's been around so long that you've probably seen it but, for those who have not and as a refresher for those who have, let me present this little problem:

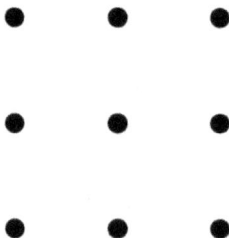

● ● ●

● ● ●

● ● ●

Figure 30 - Dot Problem

Using a pencil, connect the dots presented in Figure 30 with four straight lines without folding the paper or lifting the pencil from it.

If you've struggled with the solution, it's because you, like most people, have restricted your thinking to the imagined limits of the image. If you think "outside the box", however, you'll arrive at the solution.

The Juggle Exercise

Another demonstration of how we unconsciously restrict our thinking is an exercise involving a group of people. I've engaged in it as a participant and used it innumerable times in business settings and in the university classes I've taught. The results have always been the same. While it would obviously be more effective if I could involve my readers personally, I'm hoping a description will serve to make the point.

Needed for the exercise are a stopwatch, three small hacky sacks of different colors (which we'll call "balls" in this explanation) and a flipchart or similar place to display the rules so they are clearly visible throughout the exercise and where you can record results.

Proceed as follows:

- Assuming the participants are seated, ask them all to stand.
- Gently toss a ball to a person who is some distance from you.
- Ask everyone to hold up one hand.
- With their hands in the air, explain the exercise, as follows:
  o Once you say "Go", the person who has the ball is to toss it to another and put his/her hand down.
  o Each person catching the ball is to toss it to a person whose hand is still up and then put his/her own hand down. This continues until all participants have had the ball.
  o Each person must remember from whom they received the ball and to whom they passed it.
  o The last person to catch the ball is to very loudly yell, "Yo."
- When everyone is ready, say, "Go" and surreptitiously use a stopwatch to capture the time between "Go" and "Yo."
- Post the time and ask whether the group thinks they can do it more quickly.

- On the flipchart, below the heading "Rules:", post the rule, "Everyone must touch each ball in the original sequence." <u>Make sure you use the word "touch", not "catch" or "toss"</u>!

- Repeat the exercise. This time there is no need for raised hands since everyone knows from whom they will receive the ball and to whom it goes next. It's likely that the ball will be dropped at least once as people try to do the same things faster. Time the cycle and post the result below the first.

- Repeat the challenge. For this or the next cycle, add a second ball and display the second rule, "The individual balls must be touched in the original sequence (e.g. green ball before red ball.)" Again, use the word "touch".

- Continue with additional demands for faster performance until creative thinking emerges. At some point, you may add the third ball.

You may be shocked to learn that, even with a group of 20 or more people, a total elapsed time of less than 2 seconds can be achieved! You might even reveal that simple fact as a challenge at some point.

This juggle exercise is not only an enjoyable way to get people working together, it's an effective way to drive home the fact that <u>incredible results can be achieved when **imagined** constraints are abandoned</u>.

I admit that the original draft of this book gave solutions to both the juggle exercise and this one. In the wee hours one morning I woke to the realization that, on the off chance that students actually read the text, they would get the solutions without working them out for themselves.

So, if you are an instructor and need a little help yourself, feel free to contact me at book@jhwelschconsulting.com.

Nurturing Creativity

The creative process is delicate and must be managed with great care. For it to have any hope of success, it must exist in a climate that actively encourages it. Unfortunately, it's all too easy to create a hostile environment without even being aware we're doing so.

When someone presents a new and radically different idea, they are putting themselves at risk. In rare cases, that risk may be in the form of an adverse performance review or worse. Far more likely is the risk of criticism or of looking foolish. While a direct attack against an idea can be devastating, an innocent, humorous remark can be equally so. In his book, "Ban the Humorous Bazooka[55], Mark Sebell uses the term humorous bazooka to emphasize the devastating effect that even a witty, though disparaging, comment can have. Before we can even begin to solicit new ideas, let's make sure our culture is such that these embryonic ideas receive the same care that we'd give to any newborn.

To stimulate creativity:

- Provide genuine encouragement. Be especially careful to draw out shy people.

- Avoid the impulse to criticize, even humorously, regardless of how absurd an idea may sound. Remember Albert Einstein's words, "If at first a new idea doesn't seem totally absurd, there's no hope for it." Also worthy of note are entrepreneur and commercial space travel pioneer Richard Branson's words, "If people aren't calling you crazy, you aren't thinking big enough." In fact, it's not a bad idea to post these quotations prominently.

- Work diligently to commercialize the best ideas, not only to reap the obvious benefits, but to demonstrate that creativity is highly valued.

Generating Creative Ideas

Setting the Stage

Imagine if someone asked you, without further guidance, to write a story or draw a picture. Would you immediately start creating or would you be overwhelmed by the unlimited possibilities? The directive, "Come up with some creative ideas for a new product" is equally intimidating. A starry-eyed college student who dreams of inventing a world-changing widget that will make him rich, yet who has no idea what that gizmo might be, is in that uncomfortable position.

Fortunately for those of us working within organizations, our creative efforts are usually more channeled. Our creativity is both stimulated and targeted by our organization's strategy, by competitive moves, by changes in technology and regulations and above all, by the needs of our customers as revealed by our research.

The need for creativity is not limited to the identification of new product opportunities. We must identify product concepts, create detailed product designs, determine and sometimes design production systems and envision marketing programs that will help us realize each new product's potential. In some cases, we might even find creative ways to fund development!

There are many creativity techniques and we will here touch on only a few. Among the many excellent resources of additional methods is the book, "101 Creative Problem Solving Techniques" by James M. Higgins[56].

While brainstorming and other group creativity techniques are useful, individual creativity plays an important role as well. Let's look at both approaches.

Group Creativity

Brainstorming

Brainstorming was developed in the 1930's so it's likely that most people have participated in sessions where the technique was used to generate a list of ideas. As a review, the technique involves presenting a challenge to a group of people and then asking them to call out responses. The challenge can be as broad as, "How can we grow our business?" or as narrow as, "What shall we call this new product?" Key to the success of the exercise are the assertion that no idea is too foolish and the requirement that there be no judgement of ideas as they are presented.

The result is a chaotic affair with people calling out their ideas and someone writing them down on a whiteboard or flip charts where they can stimulate the thoughts of others. By the end of the session, a long list of ideas will have been generated and the organization is faced with the task of separating wheat from chaff.

While brainstorming can be effective, the technique has distinct disadvantages.

- It can be disrupted by strong personalities. Typically, a few gregarious people pour forth a constant stream of responses, intimidating other participants to the extent that potentially excellent thoughts are never aired.
- People tend to fixate on their own ideas. Consequently, many of their subsequent ideas are merely refinements of their own earlier ones.

- There is no way to trace the source of ideas. The idea of tracing the source of ideas may seem trivial or even harmful until it comes time to apply for a patent based upon it. At that point, the "inventors" must be identified. If the seed idea was indeed a key to the invention, the source of that seed will become critically important when a patent is sought.

CRAVE - CReative AVoidancE[©57]

The Creative Avoidance technique was developed by Maurice Zeldman to overcome the limitations inherent in brainstorming. Specifically, it masks strong personalities by giving each person equal attention, prohibits the same person from submitting refined versions of his/her own ideas and tracks the source of each idea submitted. Since a modest amount of stress stimulates creativity, the technique also provides a moderate level of stress by setting time limits and by stimulating a sense of competition both by listing each person's contributions and by arranging seating so that each participant can see each of the others.

A typical room layout is shown in Figure 31. Each participant is seated at a table arranged so that each person can see each of the others as they compile lists of their ideas. Also provided for each person is a pad of writing paper and, in front of the group, a flip chart or other means of listing his/her ideas. A participant's name is listed at the top of each flip chart.

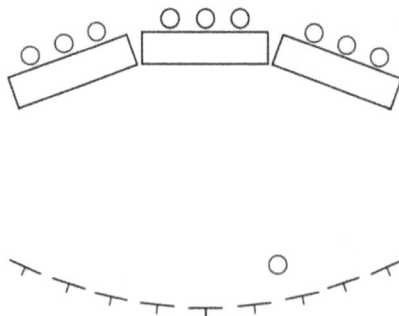

Figure 31 - CRAVE Room Layout

A facilitator explains the rules and presents the challenge that is the purpose of the session. There are three rounds of idea generation.

In **Round One** the participants are given a limited amount of time (generally 3 to 5 minutes) to silently write as many ideas as possible on his/her tablet. When the time has elapsed, writing must stop and they are given 1 to 2 minutes to prioritize their lists.

Next, starting at one end, let's say the left, each person in turn submits one and only idea from his/her list. No one may submit an idea they have not written on their pad during the timed session and there can be no repeats. As each idea is submitted, the facilitator records it on the submitter's flip chart and the other participants cross it off their lists as needed. When the last person has presented an idea, he/she submits a second and "play" continues in the opposite direction (in this case right to left). This pattern continues until all ideas are logged. A participant with no additional written ideas must simply pass. Again, no one may submit an idea they have not recorded during the timed session.

Round Two is similar in all respects to round one except that no participant may submit an idea that builds upon any of his/her own ideas from round one. They can, however, submit totally new ideas or ideas that build upon those formerly submitted by others.

Round Three, the final round, is like the second but there are two possible alternatives. In the first, participants may not build upon their own ideas from rounds one or two. In the second, they are prohibited from building on their own ideas from round two but those from round one are now fair game.

At the end of round three, participants write their names on each of their idea papers. Those papers and the flip chart pages are retained for later identification of the sources of ideas.

My personal experience is that the CRAVE technique is far superior to traditional brainstorming.

Brainwriting[58]

Brainwriting is a technique that encourages people to build upon the ideas of others. Participants sit in a circle and each silently writes ideas on a piece of paper. After a fixed interval, usually of several minutes' duration, papers are passed to the left. Each participant then reads the ideas on the paper received and adds anything inspired by those ideas. At the end of the time interval, the papers are again passed to the left. This continues until ideas have been exhausted or until no more time is available.

If each person adds an identification, such as initials, after each of his or her entries and the papers retained, ideas can be tracked to their source if necessary.

Brainwriting Pool[59]

This technique is similar to brainwriting but it allows participants to continue writing ideas until they have no more. At that point, participants place their papers in a pile in the middle of the table, choose another and build upon the ideas on that paper. The exercise continues for 30 minutes or so.

Individual Creativity

While group creativity sessions are effective, most of us spend more time creating alone than in groups. The Higgins book cited earlier presents techniques to be used by individuals as well as by groups so, rather than presenting yet more techniques here, let me share a few thoughts.

Two-time Nobel prize winner Linus Pauling said, "The best way to have a good idea is to have a lot of ideas." In chapter 5, I introduced my friend and former colleague, Bob Cohn, who I said is the best I know at interviewing customers. Bob also excels at generating ideas. One of his methodologies is to create crude, cartoon-like thumbnails of each idea as it occurs to him. When we worked together, I was amazed to watch him work. As he sketched, he made absolutely no effort to filter the ideas. Obvious ideas were documented right along with the absurd. I asked him once why he took the time to sketch ideas that clearly had no value. He explained that it was his way of cleansing his mind of ideas that were worthless so he'd not continue to dwell on them. Occasionally one of those initial ideas might have inspired something useable, but it was after the cleansing process was complete that Bob got down to creating the best ones. Quickly generating many ideas without judging them is a very effective way of generating truly creative ones.

While a certain level of stress stimulates creativity, too much of it has the opposite effect. Therefore, on the one hand you can't simply sit back until an idea pops into your mind; you must dedicate time for concentrated ideation sessions. On the other hand, there comes a time when the flow of ideas stops. I relate it to occasions when you cannot think of a person's name no matter how hard you try. Just as that name emerges unbidden in the middle of the night, temporarily turning away from the quest for ideas allows the ideas to marinate in the subconscious, only to emerge unbidden later.

Informally collaborating with a friend or colleague can be very effective. I love telling jokes but have trouble remembering them. When someone else tells one, though, I am often reminded of one I'd forgotten. In the same way, when two people share ideas, each is stimulated by the other.

Personal Approaches to Creativity

Let's face it, some of us are more creative than others. Much has been said about the creativity of "right brain" people vs. those who use the left hemisphere. It's temping, then, for us "left brain" folks to sit back and leave the generation of ideas to those "creative types." Each of us, however, can be creative in his or her own way and, even if we are less creative than others, we can strengthen the creativity of the group and, equally important, play a critical role in the innovation to follow.

In his enlightening and entertaining book, "Jump Start Your Brain", author Doug Hall introduces the concept of a "Brain Operating System"[60] (BOS) and presents a simple, self-administered test to determine whether each of us is a Dreamer, a Builder, or a Realist. Hall's research is consistent with my own observations.

Dreamers

Dreamers, Hall says, compose only 15 to 20 percent of the population. These folks, are the ones with their heads in the clouds, the ones who eschew structure to forge their own paths. Those of us who are not as creative can sometimes get frustrated by what appears to be their total disregard for constraints. Once they get fully into the creative process, they don't want to be constrained by minor obstacles like the laws of physics. Gravity? Bah; a paradigm!

While such disregard for realities may be frustrating, it's that very characteristic that let's dreamers consider possibilities that would be immediately disregarded by the rest of us.

It's not all roses for dreamers, though. It is often difficult for them to convince others of the practicality of their ideas. It may take a fair bit of convincing and perhaps some working models to get the more rabid Realists to pay much attention. Being free spirits, Dreamers also tend to flit from one idea to another, loosing focus and sometimes accomplishing little. Though generating a lot of ideas is a powerful methodology, creators need to realize that there comes a time to narrow the focus and begin the innovation process.

While non-dreamers may seem stifling to them, Dreamers must appreciate that it is they who bring with them the knowledge that will make a reality of their ideas. They must learn to work collaboratively with them as described in chapter 4.

Realists

At the other end of the spectrum are the Realists; the folks with their feet nailed firmly to the ground. According to Hall's research, nearly 50% of corporate managers are Realists (big surprise!) and my own logic and totally unscientific observations leads me to believe that most engineers are as well. If my experience as an engineer is typical, I can say that our education is largely about how to analyze things to assure that they don't fail. When presented a product idea of any kind, we immediately think of failure modes. Given that mindset, it's difficult for us to suspend our judgements and to think, not about how or why it will fail, but about how the concept might be tweaked to deliver the desired result despite those pesky laws of physics; in other words, how to innovate.

I know from bitter experience that, as hard as it is to do, realists need to stifle that "It won't work, because..." kneejerk reaction long enough to hear the whole idea, think through the possibilities and then collaborate towards a workable solution.

As we think of Hall's work in light of the innovation imperative, it appears logical to me to see his realists as innovators. As I see it, the key role that the realists play is to turn the creation into an innovation. Creation is a prerequisite for innovation so, by definition, realists are totally dependent upon Dreamers. Realists are often good at making improvements on existing products but their potential is maximized when they align themselves with Dreamers and Builders. And, who knows, in time some of that creative thinking might just wear off!

A last word to Realists... Let your hair down and immerse yourself in the creative process; you might have a lot of fun and find that you're a lot more creative than you thought!

Builders

Builders fall between the two extremes and have the enviable position of seeing both sides of the coin. Because they are not aligned with either but are sympathetic to both, Builders serve as excellent intermediaries, mediating between the opinions of the creators and those of the innovators. To play a meaningful role, Builders must avoid the temptation to sit back and watch the conflict; they must actively facilitate the collaboration that is so essential.

The Effect of Aging

Kids are incredibly creative. Without the knowledge learned later, how could they know that you can't ride a seahorse or that airplanes can't fly to the moon? As we age, we accumulate that troublesome knowledge that "allows us" (or compels us) to quickly filter out creative ideas as being impossible or impractical. So, the more we learn, the less creative we become. That reflects what Plato said well over two millennia ago.

In fact, the research that went into Doug Hall's book revealed that there is evidence that, as we age, we tend to move from Dreamer to Builder to Realist.

Innovation

Given that most of this book is about the innovation process, I'll say just a bit about it at this point.

Innovation has value only when based on excellent ideas. While judgement must be deferred during idea generation, applying intelligent judgement as the innovation process begins is essential. This involves a delicate balance, however. While there may be a lot of chaff to be disposed of, care must be taken lest the wheat be discarded with the chaff. Here, art is more helpful than science and optimism more suitable than pessimism. If an idea is such that it would have great value if it worked, think about how it might be <u>made</u> to work. I'm not talking here about pondering the possibilities for a few hours; the level of effort should be proportional to the value that could be generated if a way were found to turn the idea into reality. Intense collaboration with Dreamers and Builders can often turn an idea that seems insane into a blockbuster new product.

Above all, don't apply quantitative, especially financial, analysis too early in the process. Recognize that, during the embryonic stages, there is simply not enough hard data to make such analysis valid. Many, perhaps most, of the innovative products upon which we rely today would not exist had they been subjected to premature scrutiny.

Appendix B – Project Scoring

What now seems like eons ago, I took an MBA course called "Management Science". I clearly remember my boss scoffing, "What, is management a science now?" To him, management was an art and I readily agree that, to a very large degree, it is; intuition plays a huge part in making good management decisions. Nevertheless, careful analysis of relevant data is critical to making wise ones.

The use of a scoring model can focus discussion and decisions on the relevant facts. There are many variations of scoring models but the one I like best is illustrated by Figure 32.

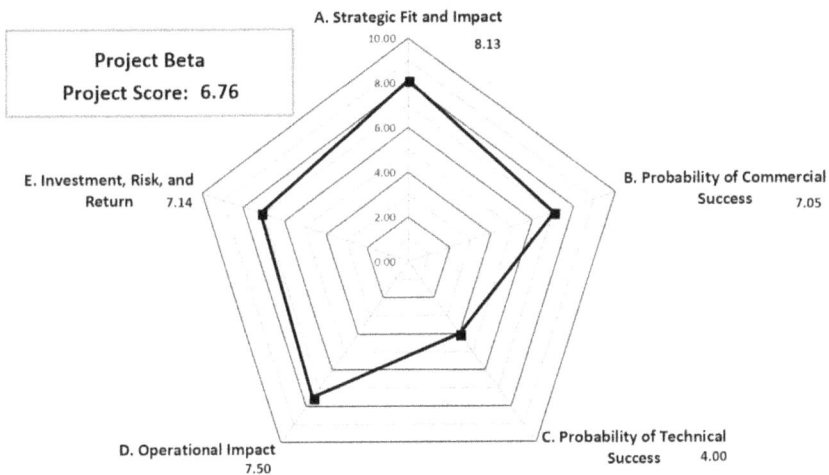

Figure 32 - Project Scoring Model

Before any model can be meaningfully applied, the organization must put a lot of effort into its creation so the resulting scores will accurately reflect how the organization wants to compare projects. In the case of the example used here, a fictitious organization has agreed that five factors are key to determining the project score as shown as the axis labels in the figure. Of course, your organization might decide on more or fewer factors and they may differ from those shown. All things not being equal, the organization must also agree on a weigh for each of the factors so that the project's overall score is the weighted average of those of its individual elements.

The score for each of the factors is determined by considering a number of elements and calculating their weighted average. In this model, each element receives a score between 0 and 10 with 10 being best. Just as the organization has selected and applied weights to each of the factors, it must do the same for the elements. Figure 33 shows one possible way of determining the score for the probability of technical success. This discussion will refer to an Excel workbook that I have used and recommend, but the methodology can, of course, be employed using software of your choice.

C. Probability of Technical Success					Clear
1. Newness of Technology to World					
Required technology is highly developed and well-known.		Technology is available but is relatively new and untested.		Substantial new technology must be developed.	
○	○	◉	○	○	◆
2. Newness of Technology to Business					
We already have competence in all needed technology.		Our people can readily adopt the needed technology.		Technology is totally new to our business.	
○	○	○	◉	○	◆
3. Technical Resource Requirements					
Negligible technical development needed (< 500 hours.)	Technical development will require 500 To 2,999 Hours.	Technical development will require 3,000 To 6,999 Hours.	Technical development will require 7000 To 9,999 Hours.	Technical development will require much effort (>= 10,000 hours.)	
○	○	◉	○	○	◆
4. Technical Resource Availability					
Competent technical resources are readily available.		Technical resources can be diverted and trained to handle this product.		We do not have the technical resources to handle this product.	
○	○	○	◉	○	◆
5. Confidence in Assumptions					
Confidence in these responses is very high.		We have moderate confidence in these responses		These responses are guesses at best.	
○	○	◉	○	○	◆
				Score:	**4.0**

Figure 33 - Element Scoring Sheet

To make it easy for those doing the scoring, 5 radio buttons are used for the rating of each element. Through the spreadsheet's coding, selecting the left-most button applies a score of 10. The next four buttons apply scores of 7.5, 5, 2.5 and 0, respectively. The right-most column is provided simply to clear the selection for later evaluation. Some may ask why there are not more choices for each element. Certainly, that would result in more precision but, given the subjectivity of the exercise, it's unlikely the accuracy would be any better and the larger number of choices is likely to result in more anxiety and debate.

Calibration statements are provided for at least the first, third and fifth columns. While some of the statements are somewhat subjective, others can be quite specific. For example, the calibration statements for element 3 in the example clearly define the range of hours associated with each choice. Such precision can also be applied for addressable market, sales potential, investment, NPV and so on. Valuation for other elements will be more subjective but calibration statements such as those illustrated are nonetheless valuable.

Note that, because a high score is always better, the statements must sometimes be positioned in an order that seems illogical. For instance, the highest sales would appear in the first column while the highest investment would appear in the last. Let me emphasize that, just as with the factors, the selection, calibration and weighting of the elements deserve careful consideration.

The creation of the scoring model is not an exercise for an afternoon; it's something that must be roughed out, studied, debated and refined until all parties agree that it is meaningful. Once it's been put into use, any further revisions will mean that the scores of the projects evaluated before the revision cannot be compared with those evaluated afterwards.

Because of their intimate knowledge of the project, the scoring of each project should be done initially by the project team itself and then presented as a gate meeting deliverable to be reviewed and approved or modified by the gatekeepers. Rather than have every factor and element evaluated by the entire team, it's logical to have each element scored initially by the team member best qualified on the subject. For example, the engineers are probably best suited to score technical success while manufacturing would be best at operations impact. Only after the specialists provide their input would the rest of the team ask questions and make comment, until there is general agreement on the results.

While the gate committee must agree on the validity of the score, any attempt to work through the whole thing at a gate meeting would be futile. The process would take forever and, long before agreement was reached, the executives would flee in frustration and anger. A solution I've found to be effective is this: The team results, including the team's detailed scoring data are provided to each gatekeeper well in advance of the gate meeting. Then, the gate committee members each study it, make notes and come to the gate meeting prepared to question only those things about which they have concern. At the gate meeting, then, there is no need to discuss each element. While it takes some effort to create a spreadsheet workbook that has tables like that shown in Figure 34, the effort pays off by greatly facilitating the discussion.

A. Strategic Fit and Impact   Clear

1. Project Alignment with Company and NPD Strategy					
This project is in perfect alignment with company and NPD strategy. X		There is moderate alignment between this project and company or NPD		There is no alignment between this project and company or NPD strategy.	
○	◉	○	○	○	◉

2. Importance of Project to Company and NPD Strategy					
This project is critically important to company and NPD strategy. X		This project is moderately important to company and NPD strategy.		This project has no impact on company or NPD strategy.	
○	◉	○	○	○	◉

3. Project Impact on Business					
This project is critically important to our business. X		This project will have moderate strategic impact on our business.		This project will have little strategic impact on our business.	
○	◉	○	○	○	◉

4. Platform Potential					
This project results in a platform for many future products		Several additional products can be built from this platform. X		This is a one-off project	
○	○	◉	○	○	◉

			Team's Score:	8.1
			Management's Score:	6.9

Figure 34 - Scoring Review Sheet

In the example, each of the team's scoring choices is shown as an "X" and remains unchanged during the review. The radio buttons for gatekeeper input are initially set to reflect the team's scoring choices. At the gate meeting, a sheet such as shown in the figure is displayed on a screen, gatekeepers are invited to voice their concerns and discussion ensues. When agreement is reached, any changes result in new radio button selections for gatekeepers. Thus, both team and gatekeeper scores are retained. In my experience, use of this method makes the process swift and virtually painless.

Once a project's score is agreed upon, it can be used in two ways; first, to more objectively evaluate a single project and secondly, to compare multiple projects.

In evaluating a single project, avoid the temptation to draw a hard line in the sand with projects with a score lower than X being categorically killed and those above categorically approved. The project score should be considered merely as one piece of data to aid in making a meaningful decision.

The model has another, potentially greater, utility. Look again at Figure 32. Elements A, B, D and E have scores that are quite high. However, element C, Probability of Technical Success, is disturbingly low. The company can accept the project score as calculated and evaluate the project accordingly or it can investigate more deeply. Why is the score low? Without fudging the numbers, can action be taken to change the reality? For example, can an established technology be applied rather than the new one proposed? Such effort can turn an initially mediocre project into a winner.

The model can also be used to compare projects to aid in (but not make!) decisions as to which of the projects competing for funding deserve to receive it. Yes, you can simply make a list of projects, each with its score and expected cost, sort it by descending order of score and draw a line where you run out of money. The approach is clean and neat but depends too much on math and not enough on business acumen. It's much better to evaluate the data more carefully. Creating and referring to a composite radar chart with curves for each of the competing projects greatly facilitates a comparison, not only of the overall scores, but those of the individual elements.

Project scoring must play a key role in evaluation of projects but must not be used as a substitute for judgement. Only by using the score as one of many factors can a gate committee make a valid assessment of projects.

Appendix C – Financial Analysis

Let's be honest, while we may sometimes be driven by altruistic motives, we normally develop new products to make money! Even when profits are not the principal motive, we are expected to be financially responsible. What follows is a brief overview of how an organization can make financial decisions regarding an NPD project.

Because much of it is quite basic, many of you will have a full understanding of the material presented here and will find it of limited interest. Due to the book's broad intended audience (read: addressable market!), however, I'm including this as an appendix to be used as needed. <u>Even experienced business people, however, may find some of what follows enlightening. I've marked the headings of those sections with exclamation points (!).</u>

Terminology and Other Basics

Cost of Sales

If the term has not been explained to you before, you may think that "Cost of Sales" (COS) is what is paid for the salesforce, perhaps with advertising and such thrown in. That is incorrect; Cost of Sales refers to the cost of producing the product or providing the service that is sold. In a manufacturing environment COS normally includes material, labor and factory overhead. A synonymous term is "Cost of Goods Sold" (COGS) and, frankly, that term makes a lot more sense to me, at least when physical products are involved.

Revenue vs. Income

I confess that there was a time when these terms confused me so, to avoid confusion later, let's get it straight. If I sell something, the money I'm paid is income to me, right? Wrong! The money an organization receives from sales is <u>revenue</u>. The money left after subtracting COS from revenue is <u>income</u>.

! Cannibalization and Synergy !

These often-overlooked factors are critically important because net income from a new product development <u>project</u> may be more or less than simply the income from the new <u>product</u> itself.

If the new product will replace or reduce sales of an existing one, we say that the new product is cannibalizing the old. To fully appreciate the value of your <u>project</u>, you must consider the income and revenue you would have enjoyed from the existing product had you not introduced the new one. The lost sales or profits are referred to as "Cannibalized Sales" or "Cannibalized Profits" or simply "Cannibalization".

In some cases, use of a product requires the use of supplies or inspires the sale of accessories or related products. For example, an inkjet printer requires the use of ink cartridges; usually expensive ones. If your new printer requires a <u>new</u> cartridge, then the cartridge is part of the new product offering cartridge, so its sales and profits are attributed to the product. However, if the new printer uses a cartridge that is already part of the product line, we refer to the <u>additional</u> sales or profits of the existing cartridges used by the new printer as "Synergistic Sales" or "Synergistic Profits" or simply "Synergy". Don't forget, however, to account for possible effects of cartridge cannibalization associated with cannibalization of existing printers! Similarly, income from newly introduced accessories would be considered part of the project itself, while any net increase in <u>existing</u> accessories that arises from introduction of the new product would be considered as synergy.

Cash Flow

Cash Flow refers to the flow of money into or out of an organization. On any given day, the organization is probably receiving money from sales and paying out money for material, labor and so on. Money coming in is a good thing so that is referred to positive cash flow. Conversely, money going out is referred to as negative cash flow. The net effect of the flow in and out is called, you guessed it, net cash flow. While the organization may occasionally experience a negative net cash flow, its ability to sustain negative net cash flow is limited by its resources. Just as a prudent homeowner keeps an eye on the checkbook balance, competent business leaders carefully manage their organization's cash flow. As we will see shortly, study of the project's projected cash flow is key to evaluating the value, and even the viability, of a project.

Time Value of Money, Present Value and Net Present Value

If I offer to give you $100, I need not ask whether you want it now or a year from now; I already know your answer. The adage might more accurately be stated as "Pay me now or pay me more later." That's because money has a time value; a dollar promised next year is worth less to us than a dollar right now. How much less is dependent on the interest rate or the expected rate of return. We call today's value of future money its "Present Value" or "PV".

The theory

I think that "magic" has its place as entertainment but not in business. While software like Microsoft Excel can do the math for you, I don't feel it's wise to calculate things without first understanding the underlying principles. Hoping that you share my perspective, please allow me to delve a bit into the theory; it won't take long.

Let's think back to high school and the formula for simple interest. You will remember that, if we invest a principal, ("P") at an annual interest rate of "r", then, ignoring compounding, at the end of one year the cash value of that investment (C) is determined by the formula:

$$C = P(1+r)$$

Realizing that the principal, "P", is the present value, "PV", of the cash that would be there at the end of the year. Substituting PV for P gives us:

$$C = PV(1+r)$$

Solving for PV reveals:

$$PV = C/(1+r)$$

For this to be meaningful, of course, we must consider varying cash flows during many periods (a period being a month, quarter or year as we will discuss shortly) and interest is, indeed, compounded. For compound interest, during any period the above formula becomes:

$$PV_i = C_i/(1+r)^i$$

...where C_i is the net flow during period i and PV_i is its present value.

These formulas apply to each of the periods under consideration, so the net effect of all of them combined, that is the Net Present Value or NPV, is obtained by simply adding them up thus:

$$NPV = \sum_{i=1}^{n} PV_i$$

NPV is an important metric and we will return to it a bit later.

Rate of Return – ROI and IRR

Rate of return is the income you receive from an investment, expressed as a percentage. It is sometimes measured as "Return on Investment"; ("ROI") or "Internal Rate of Return"; ("IRR"). While the former is easier to calculate, the latter is more meaningful and is therefore the one that will be addressed in more detail shortly.

Interest Rate, Discount Rate and Hurdle Rate

All three of these terms are similar in that all relate to how much you pay to borrow money or what you get (or hope to get) if you invest your money. To a degree, the differences are a matter of semantics, but think of interest rate as what the company (or you) would have to pay to borrow money or, from another perspective, what it would earn if it put its money in a "safe" investment such as a certificate of deposit (AKA "CD") .

While there is also a completely different and unrelated definition of "discount rate", in this context it is defined as the organization's cost of capital. The term sounds like it might mean the rate the organization would have to pay to borrow the money needed but that is not so. It refers to the opportunity cost which, in turn, is the return it <u>could have earned</u> from another investment having the same risk. In other words, non-financial considerations aside, it is the minimum rate, that would justify the investment.[61]

Note the qualification "having the same risk" in the definition. When we invest our own money, whether it be in CDs, stocks, bonds, or whatever, we expect to get back more than we put in. How much we get back depends on the risk involved. When playing roulette, there is a reason that a bet put on a single number pays 35 to 1 while a bet on "red" pays only 1 to 1. The reason, of course, is that the risk of the former is much greater than that of the later. Given the inherent risk, it's therefore reasonable for an organization to expect to get a higher return on the money it invests in a new product than it would if the same money was put in a more conservative investment.

While companies commonly use a single rate for their decision making, it is reasonable to consider higher or lower rates based on risk. It is, therefore, understandable if management approves funding of a very low-risk project that promises a return somewhat below what is normally expected, while refusing to fund a high-risk project unless it clears a threshold higher than the norm.

Some organizations use the term "hurdle rate" rather than discount rate. Because it avoids confusion and evokes the image of a horse clearing a hurdle, I prefer to use "hurdle rate" and will do so as we proceed.

! Sunk Costs !

Regardless of your level of expertise and experience, please read this section carefully as I have seen very competent, experienced financial people choke on this concept. If you are one who is already sitting there with arms crossed, please read on with an open mind; I think I can prove my point.

Let me say up front that, when a project has been completed and a postmortem is being conducted, all costs should be considered. Regardless of whether expenditures were wise or not, whether they were approved or not and regardless of when they occurred, all costs go into the calculations to decide, in retrospect, to what degree the project was a financially sound.

Let's say, though, that you are in the middle of a project, perhaps at a gate meeting, and faced with a decision as to whether to continue with a project that is already running well over budget. To complete the project, you need to put in more money such that, at completion, you will still be over budget. And to put more pressure on the decision, let's say that, if you'd known the true total cost in advance, the project would never have been approved. Do you cut your losses or see the project through? I know a lot of folks who would categorically say the former when the right answer is sometimes the latter. OK, I know some of you are ready to write me off, but please humor me by reading on.

Costs already incurred are called "Sunk Costs". They are historical and, while we can wring our hands and even hold people accountable if they've incurred them foolishly, we can't change history; that money is gone forever!

To see how this play out, let's put some bones on the scenario I laid out a moment ago. To make in more interesting, we'll make the stakes substantial. Let's say we've already invested $600 million in a project. The project is still unfinished, and our best estimate is that we'll need to invest yet another $90 million to bring it to completion! To make things even worse; based on a declining market, our best intelligence now is that, if we proceed with the project and introduce the project, income from it will only be $350 million. (Ouch!)

In the real world, the facts before us would have put confidence in our team into very serious question and I've already said repeatedly that, if we don't trust the team, we should not approve funding. To keep the discussion focused on the numbers, though, let's assume, regardless of sins of the past, we've taken whatever corrections necessary so that we now have confidence in the (perhaps new) team and the current figures. For simplicity in this example, we'll also ignore the time value of money and a host of other factors. Now, working with only the three figures I've presented, ($600MM behind us, $90MM yet to spend and, if the project is approved, income of only $350MM) would you approve the project?

If you consider the sunk $600 MM, it's clear that whether you approve continuation of the project or not, you'll have a net loss. The decision on the table is not one between loss and gain but between a large loss and a smaller one.

(Figures are $ Millions)		
	Cut and Run	Stay the Course
Profits from Sales	$0	$350
Initial Investment	-$600	-$600
Additional Investment	$0	-$90
Total project return	-$600	-$340
Cost reduction by ignoring sunk costs:		$260

Figure 35 - Sunk Costs Example

Figure 35 shows quite clearly which decision would have been the correct one when all is said and done. Abandoning the project would have resulted in no income at all, for a net loss of the entire $600 MM already invested. Approval of the $90 MM in additional funding would have been more than offset by $350 MM in profits from the resulting product, reducing the net loss to $340 MM. Thus, the additional $90 MM would reduce losses by $260 MM. So, knowing now that a decision that considering sunk costs would result in a loss of $600 MM and one ignoring them would result in a loss of "only" 340 MM, would you consider sunk costs? Either way, the results are horrifying and I'd not want to be anywhere near the meeting at which the post mortem is conducted. However, ignoring sunk costs leads to a less horrible result.

If we've resolved the issue of confidence in the team and their forecasts to our satisfaction, the numbers speak for themselves. Sunk costs should be ignored.

Analysis of Project Financials

Why

To be financially justifiable, a project to develop a new product must do two things:

1. Provide an acceptable rate of return on the investment needed to commercialize it and...

2. ...generate sales that, on an ongoing basis, will return gross and operating profits that meet or exceed organizational expectations.

In addition, we must have confidence that we can afford to fund the project. We can't determine whether we should proceed with a project unless we understand its costs, its returns and its impact on our cash flow.

When

Financial analysis is necessary...

- ... at gate meetings as part of the data needed for go/no go decisions.
- ...when conditions have changed significantly between gates, calling for a reevaluation of prior approval.
- ...when setting priorities among competing projects.
- ...when making operational decisions within a project such as among alternative product designs or production systems or when deciding, for example. whether it is worth spending more to accelerate development, thereby getting to the market more quickly.

! When *not?* !

Despite what bankers might say, financial analysis is sometimes inappropriate and even harmful. We must discount or even ignore traditional financial analysis...

- ...early in a project's life when not enough is known about either its cost or opportunity.
- ...when evaluating projects outside the norm such as those offering disruptive opportunities.
- ...when strategic implications outweigh financial ones.

How - *Alternative approaches*

Before beginning, let me say that, if you are working in a mature organization, it probably has an established procedure for justification of funding and it is probable that that is the procedure you will follow. Nevertheless, though the finance department may dictate the procedure and even perform the calculations, all team members should have at least a basic working knowledge of the concepts.

Let's explore how we might determine what projects are financially worthy of our organization's attention. There are several approaches in common use, including payback period, internal rate of return and net present value.

Payback Period

Despite some rather glaring deficiencies, many organizations, especially less sophisticated ones, evaluate projects based on their ability to return an investment within a specified "payback period". If a company expects to recoup an investment within 3 years, for example, a project promising a payback of 3 years or less will be funded while one with a 4-year payback will be rejected.

This approach is certainly the simplest both to understand and to calculate. A glaring shortcoming is its focus on short-term results. To understand that, let's look at two hypothetical projects. Each will require and investment of $1,000K. Their return is shown in Figure 36.

	Project Income ($K)			
Year	Project A		Project B	
	Annual	Cummulative	Annual	Cummulative
1	300	300	200	200
2	400	700	300	500
3	350	1050	400	900
4	300	1350	500	1400
5	200	1550	600	2000

Figure 36 - Payback Example

Within the table, there are two columns for each project. For each year, the number in the first column represents the income derived in that year and that in the second column is the cumulative income to date. As you can see, Project A illustrates a short-term project that starts strong but then fades. Project B is a more typical project that starts off weakly and then flourishes.

Remembering the investment of $1,000K, a glance at the cumulative columns for year 3 shows that a company that expects payback within 3 years would accept Project A, which would earn $1,050K by the end of year 3, and reject Project B, which would earn only $900K during the same period. If the company were to close its doors after 3 years, Project A would have been the right choice but most of us expect our organization to continue. In the example, Project B produces more income starting in the 4th year and quickly surpasses the income from Project A, making it the better choice in the long run.

There is a second shortcoming to this approach. The figures in such a table are inaccurate as they ignore the time value of money. In practice, the analysis would initially be done before most of the design work was completed, manufacturing systems were installed and so on. These and other costs would most likely be incurred well before sales are realized, yet the payback approach ignores the important fact that cash later is worth less than cash now.

Internal Rate of Return (IRR)
Unfortunately, IRR is difficult to calculate manually as there is no formula for it; it must be determined iteratively! Prior to the introduction of computers and their ability to quickly do iterative calculations, calculation of IRR was impractical. However, as will be explained shortly, today's software makes it easy to find a project's IRR.

Net Present Value (NPV)
While calculating NPV takes a fair bit of effort, its results are the most useful. Fortunately, the use of spreadsheet software makes things a lot easier and the effort required to gather the data provides a much deeper understanding of a project's financial realities.

Remember, an organization considers a project acceptable if its return is <u>equal to</u> or greater than the organization's hurdle rate. While it may be initially counterintuitive, a project that produces a return equal to the hurdle rate will have an NPV of ZERO! <u>Therefore, a project with an NPV of zero is perfectly acceptable as it delivers the desired return.</u> This shocking revelation will become clear as we look at how the theory applies.

Determining NPV & IRR

Though the process requires estimation of cash flows in each of the periods under consideration, once that is done, electronic spreadsheets make the process of calculating NPV and IRR quite simple.

Before beginning to create the spreadsheet, two things must be determined; the project's duration and the length of the periods into which it is divided. Of course, the project begins when the first dollar is spent but for how long after you begin to realize sales will you consider those sales to be part of the project's justification? Obviously, the more years' sales you consider, the easier it is to justify the investment but, the further in the future you look, the less confident you can be of the sales forecasts. If you are already planning an early replacement product and have set a corresponding end-of-life date for the one now under consideration, that date could mark the end of the duration for this one. Otherwise, the organization must establish a standard so that all (or at least most) projects are justified consistently. If your organization considers a product to be new for three full years after its introduction, that three-year point might be a good time to mark the end of the duration.

Obvious periods to consider are months, quarters and years. Given that you must come up with estimates for spending and income during each period over what may well be several years, a period of a month would mean a <u>lot</u> of guesses. At the other extreme, because a dollar spent in January is far different from one spent in December, a year does not provide enough granularity. Therefore, I recommend the use of quarterly periods and that's what we'll use in the example.

While other software can be used, the explanation here will be based on the use of Microsoft Excel both because of its widespread use and because it's what I use myself.

Developing the spreadsheet

	A	B	C	D	E	F	G	H	I	J	K	L	M
1	Period:	1	2	3	4	5	6	7	8	9	10	11	12
2	Except for unit cost and price,	Year 1				Year 2				Year 3			
3	dollars are in $thousands.	Qtr1	Qtr2	Qtr3	Qtr4	Qtr1	Qtr2	Qtr3	Qtr4	Qtr1	Qtr2	Qtr3	Qtr4
4													
5	Period Cash flows												
6	Development	-1,100	-1,100	-1,100									
7	Prod'n Equip			-1,000	-2,000								
8	Mktg Support				-1,000	-1,000	-500	-300	-300	-300	-300	-300	-300
9	Prod'n Cost (COS)					-1,600	-1,640	-1,680	-1,800	-1,920	-2,000	-2,040	-2,080
10	Sales Revenue					3,200	3,280	3,360	3,600	4,560	4,750	4,845	4,940
11	Synergy Income												
12	Cannibalized Income (-)												
13	Net Cash Flow:	-1,100	-1,100	-2,100	-3,000	600	1,140	1,380	1,500	2,340	2,450	2,505	2,560
14													
15	Prod'n & Sales Vol. (units)					4,000	4,100	4,200	4,500	4,800	5,000	5,100	5,200
16	Unit Cost ($)					-0.40	-0.40	-0.40	-0.40	-0.40	-0.40	0.40	-0.40
17	Sales Price ($)					0.80	0.80	0.80	0.80	0.95	0.95	0.95	0.95
18													
19	Annualized Hurdle Rate:	30%											
20	Periods per year:	4											
21	Period Hurdle Rate:	7.5%											
22													
23	PV:	-1,023	-952	-1,690	-2,246	418	739	832	841	1,221	1,189	1,131	1,075
24	Cumulative PV:	-1,023	-1,975	-3,666	-5,912	-5,494	-4,755	-3,924	-3,082	-1,862	-673	457	1,532
25	NPV by summation:	1,532											
26													
27	NPV by Excel function:	1,532											
28													
29	IRR by Excel function:	46.54%											
30													
31													
32													

Formula callouts:
- `=F15*F16`
- `=F15*F17`
- `=B13/POWER((1+$B$21),B1)`
- `=C13/POWER((1+$B$21),C1)`
- `=B24+C23`
- `=SUM(B23:M23)`
- `=NPV($B$21,B13:M13)`
- `=$B$20*IRR(B13:M13)`

Figure 37 - NPV Spreadsheet

Figure 37 illustrates an example spreadsheet. It is a bit atypical, though, as I've used a short, three-year project duration simply so it would still be readable when printed in this book. The duration used for a typical project will generally be longer so that it covers the development time plus the desired sales duration.

Referring to the figure, you can see that a column has been provided for each of the periods. The first period, marked Qtr1, does not necessarily begin on January 1 of some year; it marks the beginning of the project, a time that serves as the "Present" in "Present Value. I'll sometimes refer to that as "now".

After the column headings, there are several rows for the various cash flows. A row is provided for each of the categories into which we've divided the investment and at least one is for revenue. You can use more, fewer or different categories but remember that the more finely you divide the investment and revenue, the more estimates you will have to make. Since expenditures represent negative cash flows, they must be entered as negative numbers!

Also included is a row for <u>income</u> due to synergy and one for <u>income</u> lost due to cannibalism. Though many projects will not be affected by synergy or cannibalism, I have included them here to show how those factors would be handled but have not populated them in the example. Note that entries in these rows represent <u>income, not revenue</u> so don't use sales figures! <u>Remember also that cannibalism is a bad thing so it must be represented by negative numbers!</u>

At the bottom of the cash flow section is a row (13 in the example) that contains the net cash flow for the period; the algebraic sum of the figures above it.

The section below that is optional and, in some cases, may be more trouble than it's worth. In the example, we've assumed that there is a single project to which we can assign a cost and selling price. That section is used here to calculate Production Costs and Sales Revenues needed in rows 9 and 10, respectively. If your project is more complex, it will be easier to calculate sales and COS elsewhere and enter them directly into the cash flow section.

The third section holds the annual and period hurdle rates. Certainly, we could plug those rates directly into the appropriate formulas but putting them here makes it a simple matter to test the sensitivity of NPV to hurdle rate. Also, I've seen <u>way</u> too many people apply an annual rate even though use of the period rate is essential. In the example, cell B21 contains a formula that simply divides the annual rate by the number of periods in a year; in this case 4. Using $B$21 as the reference in the formulas minimizes the likelihood of using the wrong rate.

Strictly speaking, you can determine NPV and IRR without using what is in rows 23, 24 and 25 of the example. However, rows 23 and 24 provide better insight into how much money will flow out before it starts flowing back in. As we will see shortly, the results in Row 24 are of particular importance. Row 25 is there simply to fulfill my compulsion to explain how all of this works.

Each cell in row 23 contains the present value of the net cash flow for that period. Thus, for example, the present value of the net cash flow in the third quarter of year 1 is a <u>negative</u> $1,690,000 and that for the fourth quarter of year 3 is a positive $1,075,000. The formulas are illustrated in the comment blocks for B23 & C23. <u>Note that the formula uses the period rate (from $B$21), not the annual rate!</u>

Row 24 is used to calculate the cumulative cash flows, thereby showing the level of investment (<u>in present dollars</u>) that has been reached during any period. The formula is the simple one shown in the comment block for cell C24. Thus, for example, by the end of the third quarter of year one, the organization will have invested $3,666,000 in the project. <u>The data in this row is critical in determining whether the organization can fund the project!</u>

The value in cell B25 is the NPV calculated the "hard way" by summing up the individual period PVs, the formula for which is shown in the comment block. It is shown here simply to illustrate that the results are the same as those calculated by the Excel function.

Finally, cells B27 & B29 hold the NPV and IRR, respectively, as calculated using the Excel functions as illustrated in the associated comment blocks.

In setting up the spreadsheet, you'll want to apply the appropriate number formats and, if needed, add a statement somewhere to indicate scaling of dollars. In this example, that statement, "Except for unit cost and price, dollars are in $thousands." appears in the upper left corner. Because cash outflow must be entered as negative numbers, I suggest you apply data validation to those cells to assure that all entries are less than or equal to zero.

Once the spreadsheet is set up as described, I strongly recommend that all cells other than those intended for input be locked and the sheet protected to reduce the likelihood of formulas being inadvertently overwritten. In the example, the only cells not locked are B6:M8, B11:M12, B15:M17 and B19. As an aid to those providing the data, I normally shade input cells as I've done here.

Populating the data

When entering data, it is critical to remember that costs are negative numbers and revenues positive. That's easy to remember when you think of costs bad and revenues as good! Yes, I know I'm beating that to death but I've seen the error made too many times.

Begin by estimating and entering all investments other than the cost of sales. Included in that would be the cost of design, engineering, marketing, tooling, machinery, etc.

Next, estimate and enter the cost of sales and the revenue expected during each period. For some projects, the table such as that shown at A15:M17 and the formulas shown for rows 9 and 10 might be helpful. For more complex projects, it is more practical to simply use total forecast sales and then work backward through gross margin to get cost of sales. In that case, you'd adjust cell locking and shading so data could be entered directly.

If applicable, enter income (profits), not revenue (sales), for synergy and cannibalism in rows 11 and 12. Remember to enter cannibalism as negative numbers.

Assuming "periods per year" (cell B20) has already been entered in the template, the only other data needed is the hurdle rate, which is entered on this sheet into cell B19. If the organization invariably uses the same rate, that cell would be locked and its shading omitted.

Interpreting results

To state the obvious, the two things we set out to determine, NPV and IRR can be found in calls B27 and B29. Let me state again something that is not terribly intuitive; since the hurdle rate is set to deliver the organization's desired return, an NPV of zero is perfectly acceptable! In fact, mathematically, IRR is the rate at which the NPV is zero and, in fact, can only be determined by iterating the rate until NPV becomes zero! A positive NPV is a measure of how much additional money the project returns. Consider it a bonus if you wish.

Two other valuable pieces of information can be found in row 24. The first is a measure of how deep the organization's pockets must be in order to afford the project at all. In present dollars, by the fourth quarter of year one, the organization will have invested $5,912,000. Without the ability to make that investment, the project is not feasible.

Remember, when the project's IRR is exactly equal to the hurdle rate, the cumulative PV in the last quarter will be zero. Looking further to the right we see that, again in present dollars, in the third quarter of year 3 we've reaped the desired return on our investment and begun to earn a bonus. This is consistent with the fact that, in the example, the project's IRR of 46.54% is greater than the hurdle rate of 30%.

It's worth noting that, in some cases, Excel's IRR formula will report the error "#NUM" instead of the expected IRR. Do to the fact that Excel's IRR function works by iteration, this error sometimes occurs if the cashflows follow an abnormal pattern from period to period as, for example, when there is more income than investment in the early periods. The Excel help function offers some suggestions that may help to identify the problem.

Caveats
- Remember, costs are negative, enter them as negative numbers. Cannibalization must be entered as negative numbers as well.
- Effects of synergy and cannibalism are entered as income (profits), not revenue (sales)!
- All cash flows are assumed to be at end of the period in which they are incurred.
- Any cash flow at time zero (i.e. "now") doesn't get put into the formula; it simply gets added <u>algebraically</u> to the NPV.
- If using periods other than 1 year, the hurdle rate and IRR must be adjusted accordingly (e.g. by a factor of 4 for quarterly periods.)
- If you are scaling numbers, be consistent and enter a note to describe it!
- Unless the analysis is for a post-mortem, sunk costs are irrelevant and must be ignored!!
- If a cost would have been incurred even if the project was not undertaken, it is irrelevant to a go/no go decision. Therefore, unrelated costs must also be ignored!

"What-if" scenarios
What would be the effect of spending more on engineering if it would get us to market more quickly? Should we buy a more

expensive machine that would reduce production costs? Should we spend more on advertising if it would boost sales?

The best way to evaluate these and other scenarios is to rename the tab on the sheet you've just created to "Base Case" and then make a copy of the base case sheet for each scenario you want to consider, renaming each appropriately. Then, leaving the base case unchanged for reference, make the changes needed for each scenario and compare each to the base case and/or to each other.

Analysis DURING a project

What if your project is already underway and you want to determine whether to continue? What if you want to compare several ongoing projects to decide which are the most valuable? Remember, sunk costs are irrelevant so, as painful as it may seem, you need to ignore the money you've already invested. Furthermore, the "present" in present value has new meaning; it is now. Therefore, the spreadsheets you prepared at the beginning of each project are no longer valid as they stand. The good news is that it's incredibly easy to modify the sheets to ignore sunk costs and to change the present time.

This is simply another scenario so, again, make a copy of the latest case, rename it and make the following changes to the copy. For this discussion, we'll assume we are now about to enter the 4th quarter of year 1 so all data for the first 3 quarters is irrelevant and the present value must be calculated to the "new now".

Figure 38 is a revised version of the table in Figure 37 that has been modified in accordance with the following recommended procedure. Though in practice, project data may have changed with the passage of time, it has not been changed in the example.

	A	B	C	D	E	F	G	H	I	J	K	L	M
1	Period:	1	2	3	1	2	3	4	5	6	7	8	9
2	Except for unit cost and price,		Year 1				Year 2				Year 3		
3	dollars are in $thousands.	Qtr1	Qtr2	Qtr3	Qtr4	Qtr1	Qtr2	Qtr3	Qtr4	Qtr1	Qtr2	Qtr3	Qtr4
4													
5	Period Cash flows												
6	Development												
7	Prod'n Equip				-2,000								
8	Mktg Support				-1,000	-1,000	-500	-300	-300	-300	-300	-300	-300
9	Prod'n Cost (COS)					-1,600	-1,640	-1,680	-1,800	-1,920	-2,000	-2,040	-2,080
10	Sales Revenue					3,200	3,280	3,360	3,600	4,560	4,750	4,845	4,940
11	Synergy Income												
12	Cannibalized Income (-)												
13	Net Cash Flow:				-3,000	600	1,140	1,380	1,500	2,340	2,450	2,505	2,560
14													
15	Prod'n & Sales Vol. (units)					4,000	4,100	4,200	4,500	4,800	5,000	5,100	5,200
16	Unit Cost ($)					-0.40	-0.40	-0.40	-0.40	-0.40	-0.40	-0.40	-0.40
17	Sales Price ($)					0.80	0.80	0.80	0.80	0.95	0.95	0.95	0.95
18													
19	Annualized Hurdle Rate:	30%											
20	Periods per year:	4											
21	Period Hurdle Rate:	7.5%											
22													
23	PV:	0	0	0	-2,791	519	918	1,033	1,045	1,516	1,477	1,405	1,335
24	Cumulative PV:	0	0	0	-2,791	-2,271	-1,354	-320	724	2,241	3,717	5,122	6,457
25	NPV by summation:	6,457											
26													
27	NPV by Excel function:	6,457											
28													
29	IRR by Excel function:	163.62%											
30													

Figure 38 - Revised NPV Spreadsheet

To modify the worksheet in accordance with this scenario, one would...

- ...reset the period numbers (in row 1 of the example) so that period one marks the first period we are now considering.

- ...delete data (including formulas) pertaining to past periods from the period cost table. In the example, this would be the range B6:D13.

- ...optionally, shade the cells from which you have just deleted data as a reminder that they are no longer under consideration. I recommend you also shade the corresponding cells in row 1, which contains the period numbers.

- ...update remaining data as needed. Remember, I have not modified data in the example.

- ...if you must add periods to reflect an extended duration of the analysis as would happen if the introduction date were delayed, ...

- ...append additional columns to the right of the table as needed, labeling them and formatting the cells appropriately.

- ...extend the period numbering across the new columns.

- ...copy formulas into the new columns. These would include the formulas for net cash flow, PV, Cumulative PV and, if used, COS and Sales Revenue.

- ...modify the formulas for NPV and IRR to include the data in the new columns.

- ...enter new data as needed.

! Limitations of Quantitative Analysis !

- Precision does not imply accuracy. Remember that most, if not all, of the figures upon which the analysis is based are, at best, educated guesses. Take the results of calculations with more than just a grain of salt!

- Quantitative analysis can be misleading and downright counterproductive when evaluating opportunities outside the norm (including disruptive opportunities) and early in the life of any project when not enough is known about either the cost or the opportunity.

- Always consider strategic, risk and other qualitative factors.

- You can't spend percentage! In a different context, I suggested earlier that you ask the question, "Is the juice worth the squeeze? Regardless of the IRR, some projects just don't return enough money to make them worth the organization's time. It's terribly tempting to pursue a series of small projects, each of which has an excellent IRR, while ignoring larger projects that would have a much more significant impact on the bottom line and the future of the organization.

- After all the analysis is done, don't forget to step back and be sure that the project is truly worthy from a non-financial standpoint.

For a more comprehensive treatment of this subject, I strongly recommend chapter 11 of "Product Design and Development" by Ulrich and Eppinger.[62]

Appendix D - Intellectual Property

Innovation without protection is Philanthropy.

— Mark Blaxill, Ralph Eckard

Disclaimer

Having managed the patent program for a company and worked closely with excellent patent attorneys for 35 years, I've learned a lot about the subject but I'm still most definitely neither a lawyer nor an intellectual property (IP) expert. Therefore, nothing here should be taken in any way to be legal advice. To hedge a bit more, even if I was a lawyer, I'd be unlikely to treat this technical, highly complex and rapidly changing subject in any reasonable detail in the few pages to be dedicated here.

What follows is a very high-level treatment of intellectual property, aimed solely introducing the subject, terminology and concepts and at preparing you to ask better questions of an attorney. While editing this chapter, I became aware of just how many times I recommend the seeking of professional advice under various circumstances. Those repeated statements are not there to protect me, I've included them because I truly believe it's important to do so.

Helpful information is also available from the US Patent and Trademark Office website at www.uspto.gov but, before making important decisions on intellectual property, <u>I strongly suggest that you seek legal counsel from professionals. By professionals, I'm referring here not to lawyers in general but to those specializing in intellectual property.</u> If your organization has in-house counsel, they can most likely point you in the right direction.

While I will briefly touch on foreign patents a bit later, the following applies to United States intellectual property laws and procedures.

Definition

Intellectual property (IP) is, essentially, property that is a "product of the mind". In law, it is considered "personal" rather than "real" property (i.e. real estate) and, like other personal property, it can be bought, sold, traded, etc. Sadly, it can also be stolen. Well, since it's perfectly legal to copy a product <u>that has not been legally protected</u>, "stolen" is not the right word but, it sure feels like you've been robbed when a competitor copies a product you've worked so hard to design. That's what brings us to this discussion.

Because they can potentially offer such strong protection for new products, we will concern ourselves primarily with patents while touching briefly on trade secrets and trademarks.

Trade Secrets

Obviously, if you could keep your invention a secret, no one could steal it. That's what the Wright brother tried to do and why they failed to reap appropriate financial rewards from their invention. Secrecy would be a great way of keeping competition away <u>if</u> you could still sell the product. Coca-Cola is the poster child for how well this can work if you can sell your product and not have it "reverse engineered". Unlike patents, there is no time limit on a trade secret unless, of course, someone discovers it. Once the secret is out, your protection is gone. By jealously guarding its secret, The Coca-Cola Company has protected its formula for over 100 years; far longer than would have been the case if it had been patented for reasons we'll see shortly. Since many if not most products are vulnerable to reverse engineering, however, patents are the answer.

Patents

The problem that most of us face is that we are concerned with products that can be reverse engineered. How can you sell a Segway and not have a team of engineers figure out how to copy it? The answer, of course, is that you probably cannot. So, Segway would have had a trade secret until shortly after they shipped unit number one. Given the number of engineers who are smart enough to reverse engineer it, that would have been the end of Segway's dominance. Enter the patent.

The patent office (technically, the United States Patent and Trademark Office or USPTO) issues patents to encourage companies to invent but here is also a more egalitarian reason. Most of us would probably agree that, though our competitors may make our lives difficult, competition is generally good for society. For as long as it remains a secret, a trade secret restricts competition, thus creating a monopoly. Patents address that condition by, in essence, granting the inventor a limited-term monopoly on the "invention", but only in exchange for public access to any "secrets" behind it. Hence, they serve society by not only allowing but enabling competitors to copy the invention after the term of the patent has expired.

We'll get into the details in a bit but, in a nutshell, here's how it works... In the patent application, the inventor must spell out in excruciating detail exactly how the product works and, often, how it is made. The requirement is that there must be enough information in the patent to enable anyone "normally skilled in the art" to reproduce the product after the patent expires. In exchange, the government protects the patent owner's rights to the invention for a limited time.

What rights does a patent grant?

Under US law, a patent grants its owner the right to exclude others from making, using, offering for sale, or selling" the subject invention in the United States and from importing the invention into the United States[63]. Notice that I didn't say the patent grants you the right to make, use, or sell your invention, it only grants you the right to exclude others from doing so! So, you can exclude others from "practicing" the invention but you may not necessarily have the rights to produce it yourself? Though counterintuitive, that's correct.

To use a silly example, let's pretend that no one has yet invented the concept of a chair but you have just done so! I'll get into the idea of the scope of an invention shortly but, for now, let's say that

Figure 39 - Who Can Make a Rocking Chair?

your invention is defined as something that provides for a substantially horizontally surface for supporting a person's posterior (i.e. a seat) , something to keep that surface at a distance from the floor (e.g. legs), a substantially vertical surface for supporting a person's back (i.e. the chair's back) and two devices for supporting the person's arms. (i.e. the chair's arms). Let's assume you get a patent on that invention. Absent someone else's prior patent, you can, indeed, make and sell that chair. That is, of course, something you could have done with or without the patent.

Now, suppose I get the brilliant idea of attaching two curved pieces near the bottom to create something which I will a rocking chair. It's got everything your chair has and adds the "elements" of rockers.

Who, now, can make (or sell or use) a rocking chair or import it into the United States? You can't because I have the right to prevent you from adding rockers. But I can't either, because you have the right to prevent me from making the chair that is mounted upon my rockers! As a practical matter, you and I could enter a cross-licensing agreement enabling both of us to make, sell or use the rocking chair or one of us could buy a license from the other. Absent some legal arrangement, however, neither of us can make, sell or use a rocking chair for as long as both patents are valid.

What types of patents are there?

There are three basic types of US patents, "Utility Patents", "Design Patents" and "Plant Patents". We'll ignore plant patents here.

In laymen's terms, a utility patent relates to how something (including a process) works and a design patent has to do with what it looks like. More specifically, according to the USPTO, utility patents are "…issued for the invention of a new and useful process, machine, manufacture, or composition of matter, or a new and useful improvement thereof…[64]" The noun "manufacture" is a bit unusual but it means, essentially, a "thing". Cars, pens and paper clips are all "manufactures". Weird, I know, but that's how Uncle Sam says things.

On the other hand, the USPTO says that design patents are "...issued for a new, original, and ornamental design embodied in or applied to an article of manufacture...[65]" In other words, it protects how it <u>looks</u>, not how it <u>works</u> or how it is <u>made</u>.

There is also a "Reissue Patent" that is "Issued to correct an error in an already issued utility, design, or plant patent...[66]" Why that is a patent <u>type</u> in and of itself is a bit confusing to me but that's "Uncle Sam speak" again.

What makes an invention patentable?

To be patentable, an invention must be, first, patentable matter as defined for the types listed above. Then, it must be "New", "Novel", "Non-Obvious" and "Useful" and it must not be on an exclusion list. Excluded are such things as "Natural phenomena", "Mathematical algorithms" and "Abstract Ideas". The scope of patentable matter has seen quite a bit of flux in recent years. At one point, business processes were specifically excluded. Then they were off the exclusion list, then further refinements were made to the definitions. The bottom line, again, is that you need to get competent, professional counsel in specific cases.

The words "New", "Novel" and "Non-Obvious" have, of course legal definitions that are quite complex and beyond our scope here. This is simplistic but, just to give you an idea of the high points from a lay perspective, look at it this way... "you can't have a patent if the concept was already known" and "you can't have a patent if it wasn't your own invention." There are other restrictions as well, including one that keeps the courts busy and the lawyers happily employed; section 103. That section says that you can't have a patent, "...if the differences between the claimed invention and the prior art are such that the claimed invention as a whole would have been obvious before the effective filing date of the claimed invention to a person having ordinary skill in the art to which the claimed invention pertains.[67]" You and I may have the same level of intelligence, have gotten the same degree from the same university and have worked side by side all of our lives but what is obvious to you may not be at all so to me. Upon this delightful fact are lawsuits based and lawyers enrichened. However, know this, if your idea seems obvious to you, there is a good chance that it will be obvious to the USPTO and to a court. If in doubt check with an IP attorney.

You also cannot get a patent of the invention was made public more than a year before the patent filing date, even if it was you who made it public. So, you can't see a product on the market and say, "Hey, that's a nifty idea, I think I'll patent it." Nor can you introduce a product, then applying for a patent after waiting a year and a day to see if it's commercially successful.

Who is an inventor?

Before we can identify the inventor(s), we must identify (i.e. define) the invention itself. The invention is clearly defined in a part of the patent called the "claims". The claims are analogous to the property description in a real estate deed in that they define the patent's boundaries. We'll treat this in more detail a bit later.

An inventor is one who has participated in the conception of the invention as defined in the claims. If the person has creatively contributed to any of the features or steps described in any of the claims, he or she is an inventor.

Those who merely defined the problem and those who simply worked to execute the invention conceived by the inventor(s) are not, themselves, inventors. Thus, the executive who says, "Hey, we need to make an affordable solar-powered vehicle" is not an inventor. Unless they provide creative input, the engineer and prototype builder who work night and day to turn the concept into reality are not inventors either unless they had creative input that is reflected in the claims.

When more than one person has provided an inventive contribution, it is critical that every one of those inventors be named in the application for two reasons. First, an inventor not named can later claim rights to the invention, creating no end of problems. Second, such an omission can render a patent invalid.[68]

Who can apply for a patent?

According to the statute, United States patents are issued only to "persons". However, they can be contractually "assigned" to another entity, such as another person (or persons) or organization. In industry, it is common for an employer to require all employees who develop patentable inventions as part of their jobs to file assignment documents concurrently with patent applications. Any resulting patent would then bear the assignee's name along with those of the inventors.

It's worthy of note that you need not be a US citizen or resident to file an application for a US patent; any person, regardless of citizenship, is entitled to apply.

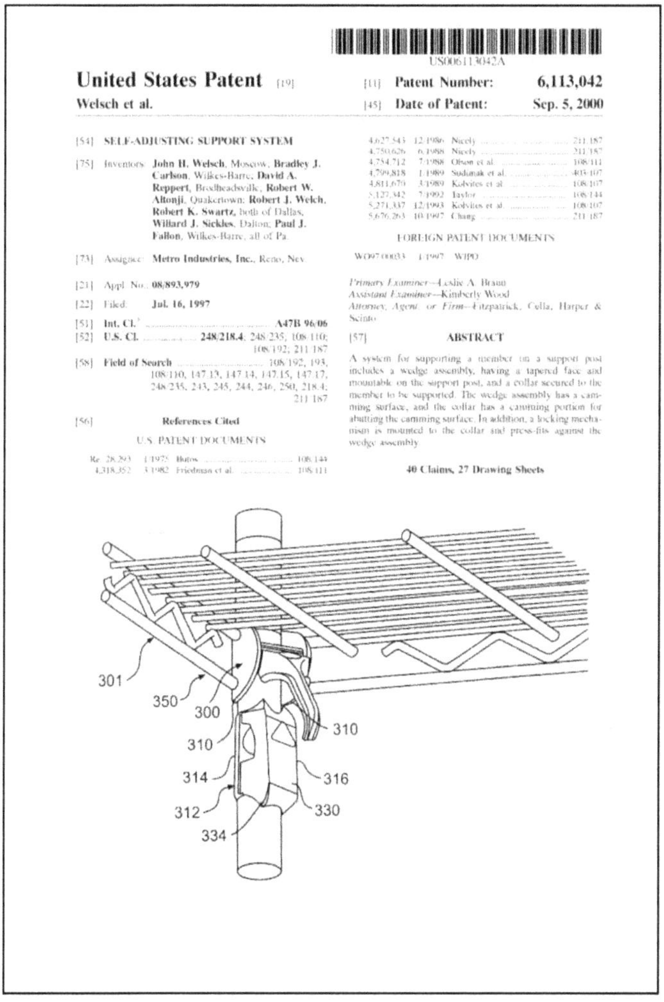

US006113042A

United States Patent [19]
Welsch et al.

[11] **Patent Number:** **6,113,042**
[45] **Date of Patent:** **Sep. 5, 2000**

[54] **SELF-ADJUSTING SUPPORT SYSTEM**

[75] Inventors: **John H. Welsch**, Moscow; **Bradley J. Carlson**, Wilkes-Barre; **David A. Reppert**, Brodheadsville; **Robert W. Altonji**, Quakertown; **Robert J. Welch**, **Robert K. Swartz**, both of Dallas; **Willard J. Sickles**, Dalton; **Paul J. Fallon**, Wilkes-Barre, all of Pa.

[73] Assignee: **Metro Industries, Inc.**, Reno, Nev.

[21] Appl. No.: **08/893,979**

[22] Filed: **Jul. 16, 1997**

[51] **Int. Cl.**[7] **A47B 96/06**
[52] **U.S. Cl.** **248/218.4**; 248/235; 108/110; 108/192; 211/187
[58] **Field of Search** 108/192, 193, 108/110, 147.13, 147.14, 147.15, 147.17, 248/235, 243, 245, 244, 246, 250, 218.4; 211/187

[56] **References Cited**

U.S. PATENT DOCUMENTS

Re. 28,293 1/1975 Butos 108/144
4,318,352 3/1982 Friedman et al. 108/111
4,627,543 12/1986 Nicely 211/187
4,750,626 6/1988 Nicely 211/187
4,754,712 7/1988 Olson et al. 108/111
4,799,818 1/1989 Sudimak et al. 403/107
4,811,670 3/1989 Kolvites et al. 108/107
5,127,342 7/1992 Taylor 108/144
5,271,337 12/1993 Kolvites et al. 108/107
5,676,263 10/1997 Chang 211/187

FOREIGN PATENT DOCUMENTS

WO97/00033 1/1997 WIPO

Primary Examiner—Leslie A. Braun
Assistant Examiner—Kimberly Wood
Attorney, Agent, or Firm—Fitzpatrick, Cella, Harper & Scinto

[57] **ABSTRACT**

A system for supporting a member on a support post includes a wedge assembly, having a tapered face and mountable on the support post, and a collar secured to the member to be supported. The wedge assembly has a camming surface, and the collar has a camming portion for abutting the camming surface. In addition, a locking mechanism is mounted to the collar and press-fits against the wedge assembly.

40 Claims, 27 Drawing Sheets

Figure 40 - The First Page of a Typical Utility Patent

What is included in a patent?

Remember that a utility patent can be issued for "...a new and useful process, machine, manufacture, or composition of matter, or a new and useful improvement thereof...". The explanation that follows here is complex enough already so, strictly for simplicity, I will use the word "product" to encompass all potential invention types.

As explained earlier, an application for a patent must contain enough information for one "...normally skilled in the art..." to reproduce the invention. While design patents are quite simple, the required information for a utility patent can be quite extensive. All utility patents include the following:

Claims

While the claims appear at the end of a patent document, I will explain them first, as an understanding of claims is a prerequisite for an understanding of everything else.

Claims may be compared to a deed for real estate. A deed defines exactly what is owned; it explains in exacting detail the location of the property and its boundaries. A deed contains descriptions like, "Beginning at a point on division line of lands, now or formerly of R. Williams and D. Jones; thence along line of Lot #2 North sixty three (63) degrees West one hundred (100) feet to an iron pin corner; thence along lands now or late of R. Williams North twenty seven (27) degrees East fifty (50) feet to an iron pin corner; thence along the line..." The description continues until the property is completely bounded. Such a description clearly defines what is owned by the deedholder.

Likewise, the claim or claims of a patent, clearly define the scope of the patentholder's rights. For example, the first claim of US patent number 6,113,042[69], the first page of which is shown as Figure 40 reads:

What is claimed is:

1. A system for supporting a member on a support post, comprising:

a wedge assembly having a tapered face and mountable on the support post, with said wedge assembly having a camming surface;

a collar adopted to be secured to the member to be supported, said collar having a first surface for abutting said camming surface and a second surface for press-fitting against said wedge assembly; and

a locking mechanism rotatably mounted to said collar, said locking mechanism including said second surface for press-fitting against said wedge assembly.

Just as a real estate property must lie inside <u>all</u> of the boundaries cited in the deed, another product, in order to infringe upon the patent, must contain <u>each and every</u> element (<u>or its "equivalent"</u>) of <u>at least one</u> of the patent's claims. We'll come back to all of that shortly when we talk of litigation.

Typically, a utility patent has multiple claims and each can be one of two types, independent or dependent. Each independent claim, such as the one above, stands on its own. A dependent claim may depend from an independent claim or from another dependent claim. Each dependent claim is deemed to include all elements of all the claim(s) from which it depends. For instance, the second claim of the example patent is a dependent one that reads...

2. A system according to claim 1, wherein said collar includes a pin for rotatably mounting said locking mechanism.

For me, at least, the easiest way to understand claim 2 in the example is to, mentally if not literally, copy claim 1 in its entirety except for the period (there is only one in any clam) and paste in into claim 2, replacing the words, "A system according to claim 1".

If claim 3 was dependent upon Claim 2, then you'd paste your revised version of claim 2 in place of the words, "A system according to claim 2" and so on.

As you can sense from the example, claim wording is a bit strange to most of us and can sometimes seem downright bizarre. Though it's not terribly important, one piece of trivia that I find a bit strange is the requirement that every claim, no matter how long, must be a single sentence. I've seen claims that filled most of a page and, yet were still a single sentence. I'm not sure my seventh grade English teacher would have been pleased!

OK, back to the beginning of a utility patent document...

At the top are the administrative details; the title, the names of the inventors and so on. Except for those details and the claims, the balance of the patent is called the specification and, taken together, must fully describe the invention as previously discussed. The claims are interpreted in light of the specification.

Abstract

The abstract explains, in very general terms, what the invention entails and what makes it new and unique. The abstract must be concise; preferably 150 words or less.

Drawings

Drawings are required whenever they are necessary for a full understanding of the invention. They must clearly show all features necessary to understand the claims. Generally, multiple views are necessary to illustrate all aspects of the invention. Each of the views must be labeled and the different parts must be indicated by letters or numbers so they can be referenced within the detailed description.

Background of the Invention

A thorough background narrative explains the nature of the invention and puts it into context. Generally, the background of the invention contains two parts, the "Field of the invention" and a "Description of the prior art." The field of the invention explains where the invention would be used and why it is useful. The prior art describes in detail what has been done before anywhere in the world. It's important to reveal everything you know that might result in rejection of your patent.

The description of the prior art explains what has been done before. Great care must be exercised to provide a comprehensive description of the prior art. It is essential that you clearly set forth anything that might be considered relevant and in light of which the examiner might think your invention has been anticipated or is obvious. Such prior art might encompass other products, patents, or publications whether in the US or elsewhere. Whether the prior art is your own or someone else's doesn't matter; your own prior inventions can be just as great an impediment as are those of other inventors.

Do not, under any circumstance, be tempted to withhold information for fear it will jeopardize the issuance of a patent. In the first place, withholding such information is in violation of the statute. In the second, whether you knew of it or not, new information, discovered after the patent is issued, can invalidate all or part of a patent if earlier knowledge would have hampered the issuance of the patent. Spreading everything out before the examiner and arguing why, despite the prior art, you are entitled to a patent is far better than having the patent declared invalid during a lawsuit.

Brief Summary of the Invention
As the name implies, this section presents a high-level explanation of the invention; the object of the invention, what it does and how it does it. Its scope should be limited to the invention as defined in the claims.

A Brief description of the several views of the drawing(s)
The brief description of each view is just that. They can be as simple as "Figure 1 is a perspective view of the system of the present invention." and "Figure 2 is a frontal view of the present invention."

Detailed Description of the Invention
Remember, a patent is granted in exchange for a full disclosure of the invention so that, after its expiration, anyone "...normally skilled in the art" can "practice" (i.e. duplicate) it. Sometimes, perhaps often, there is more than one way to provide a product that provides the benefits of the invention and that would be protected by the same claims. The alternatives are called "embodiments" and each of the several embodiments may be shown in the drawings and explained in the detailed description. For each embodiment presented, enough information must be provided to fulfill the requirement for disclosure. Remember, however, that the requirements for disclosure are only that it must be capable of being understood by one "...normally skilled in the art." It is not necessary to explain anything that would normally be known by someone so skilled. Furthermore, it is sometimes possible to fulfill the requirement of full disclosure, at least in part, by referring to another

patent or readily available publication that adequately provides the required information.

Typically, the detailed description is exhaustive and refers to each of the figures and its parts, explaining exactly what does what and why it does it. If a process is involved, the description may spell out sequences, times, temperatures, pressures and whatever other parameters are needed to make it work.

As in all things, the best way to understand things is to study an example. As all of us are familiar with a computer mouse, I suggest a brief study of the relatively simple US patent number 3,541,541, issued to Douglas C. Engelbart in 1970[70].

Copies are readily available from at least two sources, the USPTO and Google. I find Google more user-friendly. Just go to patents.google.com and enter a patent number. Some browsers don't render the page well, so I suggest you click the link to view or get a copy of the pdf. Incidentally, when you see a patent number on a product you use, you may want to glance at the patent itself. I find it both interesting and enlightening.

How would I obtain a patent?

Inventors may prepare and file their own applications and conduct the subsequent (and sometimes lengthy) patent office proceedings (referred to as "prosecution of the patent") themselves. However, unless the inventor has intimate knowledge of the complex laws as well as the rules and procedures of the patent office, that approach is likely to lead, not only to frustration, but to failure to obtain adequate protection.

Based on its rules and regulations, the patent office recognizes agents and attorneys who it then permits to practice before it. The difference between a patent attorney and a patent agent is simple, yet significant. As the name implies, the former is an attorney at law; the latter is not. While both can prepare and file an application and prosecute it in the patent office, agents are prohibited from doing such things as litigation and the preparation of contracts. Though these folks can be very expensive, I strongly recommend the use of a competent patent attorney or agent.

The patent office also has detailed requirements for the preparation of the drawings. Hence, without a full knowledge of the sometimes-strange requirements, I'd be surprised if an otherwise competent engineer or draftsman could produce something acceptable to the patent office. Your patent attorney or agent will have access to patent draftsmen who will do the job much better than you are likely to do yourself.

Considering the time and effort it would take you to prepare the application and conduct the subsequent prosecution, combined with the very distinct possibility that meaningful protection would be compromised, money spent on competent, professional help is money well spent.

Based on my recommendation and personal experience, then, I'll proceed with this discussion as if you've agreed to use a patent attorney. Chose an attorney who not only has a good professional reputation but who has both education and experience pertinent to the scientific or technical matter related to your invention.

Though new product development often involves the development of processes as well as physical products, we'll also assume for simplicity that our invention here is a product.

The parts of a patent were described earlier. While the attorney is responsible for presenting that information in an application, it is the inventor's responsibility to educate him to an extent that he can do so accurately and effectively. I've found it effective to first have a brief conversation with the attorney to explain the invention at a high level and get his initial opinion as to its patentability. While it's not required by law, the attorney will often suggest a search of the prior art to better analyze the chance of success and to better understand how an application might be written considering that art. Regardless of the outcome, addressing the prior art proactively will often facilitate prosecution. Note especially that knowingly withholding information of prior art is considered fraud on the patent office.

To educate the attorney so he can prepare the application, I suggest providing him with a "disclosure document" that includes, in layman's terms, the background and a detailed description, complete with drawings as necessary. These drawings need not be on the format dictated by the patent office nor does the text need to be in "legalese". They should, however, fully explain the invention. On occasion, I've found it useful to have a face-to-face meeting and, in some cases, to demonstrate a model or prototype. Obviously, the better the attorney understands the invention, the more likely it is that you'll obtain a meaningful patent without incurring disproportionate cost.

Though you may have engaged the services of the world's best patent attorney, resist the urge to restrict your involvement to answering his questions; do not allow him to carry the ball alone once you provide the initial information. Very carefully read the draft application, not only looking for errors but for opportunities to provide clarification My practice has been to highlight and make margin notes on the draft document and then to go through them one by one with the attorney. Discussion of each point will sometimes result in a change to the application and will sometimes help you to understand why the original is more appropriate. Each outcome is worthwhile.

A painstaking review of the claims is of particularly great importance. I strongly recommend you read each claim as if you were a competitor looking for a way to circumvent it. Through conversation with your attorney, explore the feasibility of blocking those potential flanking moves.

As an imperfect example, consider the patent that was most important to the growth of a company for whom I worked for most of my career, US patent 3,424,111[71]. The product was a shelving system and claim 1 began with the words, "Shelving comprising a flat shelf member having corner supports secured thereto at each corner of said shelf member…" and continued to define the unique support system. What if a would-be competitor had developed a shelf with the supports spaced away from the corners? As we'll discover as we discuss infringement in a subsequent section, such a move would most likely have avoided infringement. Our company also sold cantilevered shelving that had supports in only two of each shelf's four corners. Had they wished to, competitors could have freely copied those shelves with impunity since the supports were not at <u>each</u>

of the four corners. In fact, a competitor could probably have avoided infringement if it had moved the supports away from the corners.

Since it was really the support system that was important, it would have been much wiser to change the focus from the shelf to the support and begin claim 1 with words like, "A system for supporting a member on a support post..."? In that case, not only are those "end runs" avoided, the invention's application is potentially broadened. That is exactly the approach we took in later years. In fact, those exact words were used in the patent depicted in Figure 40.

What does it cost to get a patent?

How high is up? The cost of obtaining and maintaining a patent varies greatly. Patent office fees include those for filing, search examination and issue. Additional fees are levied for total claims in excess of 20 or independent claims in excess of 3. Qualifying small entities and non-profit entities enjoy a 50% and micro entities get a 75% discount on most fees. The fees change with time but, at least as of this writing, the USPTO's fee schedule can be found online[72].

These fees are often far overshadowed, however, by attorney's fees and those fees will vary tremendously based, not only the attorney's hourly rate, but on such things as the complexity of the invention and the obstacles to be overcome as the application goes through prosecution. It as an almost foregone conclusion that there will be at least one "office action", where the examiner turns the application back with objections and/or rejections. Your attorney will then reply with a revised application and/or a justification for reconsideration. That "dance" can go on and on, with the cost mounting alarmingly. At some point, the examiner may make the rejection "final" leaving you with the alternatives of walking away or appealing. Need I say that you'd better have a pretty compelling reason for investing in the second option?

So, what will it cost you? Simple answer: I don't know as many variables will affect the cost. I may be mistaken but don't recall getting any utility patent, no matter how simple, for less than 10 or 15 thousand dollars. I recently got input from an attorney saying that one should expect to spend at least $15 to $25K to get a US utility patent. Design patents are less expensive.

The expenses don't stop when the patent is issued, either. Since 1980, all US utility patents are subject to maintenance fees to be paid at 3.5, 7.5 and 11.5 years from the date the patent is granted. Along with attorneys' docketing fees, these can ad another $5K during the 20-year life of the patent. Failure to pay in a timely manner results, after a grace period, in the expiration of the patent. While these fees are not trivial, they pale in comparison with the foreign fees to be discussed later.

For how long is a patent valid?

In years past, a utility patent was valid for 17 years from the date of <u>issue</u>. Currently, utility patents are valid for 20 years from the date of <u>filing</u>, as long as the periodic maintenance fees are paid.

Design patents issued before May 13, 2015 have a term of 14 years; those issued after that date enjoy a term of 15 years. No maintenance fees are required for design patents.

When the most important patent in my employer's portfolio expired, many people said, "Man, I can't believe you were too stupid to renew your patent!" I'm not really <u>that</u> stupid; US patents simply cannot be renewed. Remember the tradeoff between a trade secret and a limited-term monopoly we discussed earlier? That tradeoff wouldn't make sense if you could extend the monopoly, would it?

Design Patents

The preceding text refers primarily to utility patents. As stated earlier, design patents refer to how something <u>looks</u> rather than how it <u>works</u>. Consequently, the application is much simplified, as is the patent document itself. Gone are the abstract, the background, the summary and the detailed description. Remaining are the drawings (without reference characters), a brief description of the views and a single claim. The claim is in a set format that simply claims the "ornamental design" as shown in the drawing(s). Obviously, design patents are easier and less expensive to get than utility patents. However, unless it's really the ornamental design your customers are paying for, they are also much easier to circumvent; change the "look"; avoid the patent.

Patent Litigation

Infringement

Basically, infringement involves the unauthorized making, using, selling, or offering for sale a patented invention in the United States or importing it into the United States within the term of the patent. In addition, inducing someone to infringe or contributing to infringement by selling or offering to sell something suitable only for use in or with a patented invention are also considered forms of infringement. To define it more precisely, I quote from the statute (35 U.S. Code § 271):

> *(a) Except as otherwise provided in this title, whoever without authority makes, uses, offers to sell, or sells any patented invention, within the United States or imports into the United States any patented invention during the term of the patent therefor, infringes the patent.*

> *(b) Whoever actively induces infringement of a patent shall be liable as an infringer.*

> *(c) Whoever offers to sell or sells within the United States or imports into the United States a component of a patented machine, manufacture, combination or composition, or a material or apparatus for use in practicing a patented process, constituting a material part of the invention, knowing the same to be especially made or especially adapted for use in an infringement of such patent, and not a staple article or commodity of commerce suitable for substantial noninfringing use, shall be liable as a contributory infringer.[73]*

There is more to the statute than that quoted but I leave it to you to access the referenced source if you are interested.

How do we know whether someone who makes something very similar to a patented product is infringing the patent? As we said earlier, the rights protected are defined in the claims. Just as someone can be accused of trespassing if she is within the boundaries of a property as defined in a deed, she can be accused of infringement if her product falls within the boundaries of the patent <u>as defined in the claims</u>.

While a patent may have many claims, infringement occurs when any <u>one</u> is violated. Think of it this way, firing many bullets may improve the chances of killing a deer but it only takes a single one to do the job!

Let's look a little closer at what I said earlier, that, to infringe a patent, a competitive product would have to contain each and every element (or its "equivalent") of at least one of the patent's claims. Looking patent number 6,113,042's claim 1 as quoted earlier, an infringing product would have to, first, be "A system for supporting a member on a support post", then it would have to have a wedge assembly that was mountable on a support post and which has a tapered face and a camming surface. It would have to also have a collar and a locking mechanism, each with all the characteristics listed. Ignoring for a moment an important exception to this interpretation, if <u>any one</u> of those elements were to be missing, the claim would not be literally infringed. So, if a competitor found a way to leave out, for example, the tapered wedge or the camming surface, he would not infringe that claim.

And now for the exception… He would not be a <u>literal</u> infringer but he, nonetheless, might be guilty of infringement under the "doctrine of equivalents". This doctrine prevents an infringer from getting around the claims of a patent by making a trivial and inconsequential change or substitution. The U.S. Supreme Court, in Graver Tank & Mfg. Co. v. Linde Air Prods., Inc., held that and element is equivalent, "if it performs substantially the same function in substantially the same way to obtain the same result."[74] Thus, in most cases, a rivet might be considered the equivalent to a bolt. In that case, if a claim read "bolt" and the competitor's product used a rivet instead, he'd still be guilty of infringement.

Remember that earlier we said that a dependent claim includes all the elements in the claim(s) from which it depends. Therefore, to infringe a <u>dependent</u> claim, a competitive product must incorporate each of the elements of every claim in its chain of dependency.

There are several reasons why most patents have multiple claims. The first is that, unlike a piece of real property, the invention may be defined from several perspectives. Other reasons have to do with litigation.

In chess there is more than one way to get out of "check". Likewise, there is more than one way to prevail against a charge of infringement. One is to prove that the patent itself is invalid or unenforceable. There are several reasons that might be the case but we'll leave further explanation to the lawyers. Another way, obviously, is to argue that invention alleged to infringe lacks at least one of the elements (and any equivalents) in each and every claim. The more elements (i.e. restrictions) there are in a claim, the more likely it is that someone can avoid infringement by avoiding at least one. That argues for shorter claims. Unfortunately from the patentee's perspective, another way to prevail against a charge of infringement of a claim is to argue that the claim should never have been allowed by the patent office in the first place. The broader the claim (i.e. the fewer the restrictions), the easier it is to argue that the claim was anticipated by or obvious in light of the prior art, and is therefore invalid.

So, if your claim has too few elements, it may be disregarded because it is invalid. If it has many elements, however, it's more likely that a competitor can produce a reasonable product by omitting one, thus avoiding infringement. If, however, you can get a fairly broad claim allowed by the patent office and then have a chain of increasingly restrictive claims depending from it, you stand a better chance that the court will find at least one that is both valid and infringed. That's the one bullet that is all that is necessary for the kill.

Patent suits are expensive.

Decades ago, my patent attorney said I should budget a million dollars for a patent suit that goes all the way to trial! Later experience has taught me that patent suits are no longer so "cheap." If you're the guy who owns the patent, you can decide whether the battle is worth the cost. If you infringe someone else's patent, however, you may be in a battle whether you like it or not. Let's look at it from both perspectives...

The defendant's perspective

My best advice is, "Don't infringe someone else's patent!" As we all know, ignorance is no excuse. Therefore, while you can't possibly know about every patent out there, you owe it to yourself to learn as much as you reasonably can and to act responsibly on that knowledge. Before you introduce a product (and perhaps before you even begin to develop it), consider your competitors' products and any other products that are similar to what you are planning to introduce. Look for patent numbers on literature and products. Get copies of all identified patents and, unless you are absolutely certain that there is no possibility of an accusation of infringement of any kind, even considering the doctrine of equivalents, get professional counsel.

Except when advised it's safe to do so by competent counsel, never knowingly infringe a valid patent! Beyond the ethical issue is the fact that a judge can hold an infringer responsible for treble damages plus the plaintiff's legal fees for "willful infringement" if he infringes a patent of which he was aware unless he can convince the court that he had a well-founded belief that he had a right to proceed. That is a very high hurdle, so advice of a competent IP attorney is critically important. In some cases, the attorney may recommend a more detailed study and the preparation of a legal document that documents your responsibility. While it may be expensive, seeking counsel may be the best money you've ever spent.

Also, don't fall into the trap of thinking, "That guy doesn't have the money to sue me; let's just forget about him." In today's world of mergers and acquisitions, the patent may find its way into the portfolio of a big company with plenty of money and motivation to come after you.

The plaintiff's perspective

While neither side of any battle is fun, it's always a lot better to be on the offensive. Many times, just having a patent is enough to keep competitors at bay. Of course, that only works if your competitors are aware of the patent. Be sure to list applicable patent numbers on advertising literature and, if possible, on the product itself. Doing so is expected and will not only act as a deterrent, it will position you for an argument that an infringer is guilty of willful infringement and open the way to increased compensation. Note, however, that claiming that a product is patented when it is not is against the law.

While we're on the subject, a notice such as "patent pending" or "patent applied for" may also deter competition. However, the fact that you have a patent pending does not, in and of itself, provide any legal protection and a competitor is free to copy the product until your patent is published or issues (see "Publication" below). However, he may be unwilling to begin marketing a product in the knowledge that he may suddenly be forced to stop sales and even destroy inventory if and when your patent is issued. In fact, you are in one sense doing your competitors a service by pointing out that possibility. Be aware also that such a notice is allowable only during the pendency of the application.[75]

Other Issues

As you may expect, there are myriad other issues; much more than can possibly be addressed here. I will, however, touch on a few of them.

Outside Ideas

As has been explained, it is critical that each inventor be identified on every patent application. Failing to do so may make it impossible to prevail in a suit against an infringer. Furthermore, any inventor who has not assigned all rights to the invention may have legal rights to it. To prevent that, each employee whose job involves idea generation should, as a condition of employment, agree in writing to assign all patent rights to the organization. Ideas coming from other sources pose a serious threat of legal action if the submitter later claims rights to the idea. While ideas from customers or others may be enticing, I strongly suggest that you consult with a competent attorney who specialized in intellectual property law before you even listen to them. Though our ethics were such that we'd never have knowingly stolen an idea, my office strictly followed a procedure written by our attorneys and designed to minimize the probability that we'd be sued by someone who <u>felt</u> that we had done so.

Provisional Patent Applications

The date of filing is important in establishing priority. Since 1995, it has been possible to establish a "filing date" by filing a "provisional" patent application. The provisional application is much simpler than a normal one and can therefore be filed more quickly and less expensively. While it will not, in itself, lead to the issuance of a patent, it is a way of "putting a stake in the ground" when you are not yet sure whether a normal application is justified. The 12-month pendency of the provisional application gives you time to do further product and market testing as well as to prepare a traditional application. If you do not file a regular application during the 12-month period, however, the provisional application becomes abandoned. Since the term of any resultant patent will run from the filing date of the normal application, filing the provisional will also have the effect of adding up to 12 months to the eventual expiration date.[76]

I leave it to you to explore this avenue with your attorney but I have used it from the time I first learned of the opportunity.

Publication

Prior to November 29, 2000, a patent application was maintained as confidential until issue of the patent. That meant that you might hope to resort back to trade secret protection if you failed to obtain a patent. In my own experience, a more significant advantage of the confidentiality was that competitors were reluctant to introduce a product similar to one marked "patent pending" for fear of later infringing a patent, the scope of which they were ignorant. It was rather like, "You'd better not be on my land when my deed is filed but I won't tell you where its boundaries are so you'd be wise to stay well clear." At the same time, however, other countries published their applications so, if you filed for a patent outside the US, confidentiality was lost anyway.

Subsequent to the change mandated by the American Inventors Protection Act of 1999 (AIPA), a patent will be published by the USPTO "...promptly after the expiration of a period of 18 months from the earliest filing date for which a benefit is sought under this title.[77]" The words, "earliest filing date for which a benefit is sought" make for some pretty convoluted logic in order to determine when publication will occur so, again, you'll want to check with your attorney if it's important to you.

As the title of the act suggests, publication carries with it a distinct benefit to the inventor, however. Prior to the change, an inventor could not seek damages for infringement occurring before issuance of the patent. Under the provisions of the AIPA, however, it is possible for an inventor to collect reasonable royalties during that period. In fact, it is possible to request early publication in order to get earlier protection.[78]

Foreign Patents

Remember, a US patent will allow you to prevent someone from making, selling or using your invention, but only in the Unites States. If a competitor does all three elsewhere and does not import it into the US, there is nothing you can do about it absent a patent in the country where the offence occurred. Therefore, if your business is a global one, foreign patents may be worthwhile.

In most cases, a US inventor will file first in the United States. In fact, to do otherwise requires a Foreign Filing License without which you cannot file earlier than 6 months after your US filing date. On the other hand, you must file within 12 months of the US filing date or forever loose the opportunity to do so. If your invention is considered by the US government as something that should be kept secret (e.g. something relating to defense), you will be precluded from filing a foreign application. Your patent attorney can help you with these details and should have a network of foreign associates who will be able to handle the details.

Through the Patent Cooperation Treaty (PCT), it is possible for a resident of one of the treaty's "Contracting States" (including the United States) to file a single application that will serve as an application to any or all of those states. Note that it is the application that is common, not the patent. I've heard people claim, "I have the world patent rights to that invention." That's hogwash; while there are some organizations, such as the European Patent Organization (EPO) that will issue a regional patent., there is no such thing as an international or "world" patent.

Early in my career I attended a patent seminar where a speaker questioned whether foreign patents were based on sound business decisions or were simply, as he put it, "ego trips." If the latter, they are exceedingly expensive ones. Even when you can file a common application, such things as translations, examination fees, office actions and issue fees mount up quickly. In addition, many countries assess "annuities" to be paid annually and, in some cases, those annuities increase each year on the theory that the patent's value to its owner increases over time. Before you start down the foreign patent road, get a realistic estimate of the total costs over the life of the patent.

US Trademarks and Service Marks

You will note the "US" in this section's title. It is there, not only to distinguish this discussion from foreign registrations but to distinguish it from state common law, which may also provide protection within individual states. What follows is an exceedingly brief treatment of federal protection under the Lanham Act[79].

While the term "trademark" is familiar to most of us, there are several other types of marks that are similar in concept. In all cases, the "mark" is a word, phrase, design or some combination that serves to distinguish goods or services coming from one source from those coming from another. Trademarks apply to goods, while service marks refer to services. Since the scope of this book encompasses the development of services as well as physical goods, both apply here. For simplicity, I'll ignore the distinction, using "mark" to apply to both trademarks and service marks. Just to complete the topic, it must be said that there are also "certification marks" and "collective marks", neither of which are particularly relevant here.

Just as a patent benefits both its owner, who is granted the right to prevent others from making, using or selling the subject invention, and the public, who gains access to the invention after the patent elapses, a mark has two distinct beneficiaries. One is, of course, the mark's owner, who can block a competitor from using the same mark on similar goods or services. Again, the other beneficiary is the consumer, who can acquire the goods or services with the expectation that it comes from a particular source and, therefore, is of a certain quality. The mark does not necessarily imply good quality, merely an expected quality. Therefore, you can enter a restaurant under the golden arches, not expecting a five-star experience but, rather, the one you've come to expect from McDonald's®.

I hinted earlier that a given mark applies to a distinct group of goods or services. In many cases, therefore, a given mark may be used by different companies if their goods and services are sufficiently different to prevent the likelihood of confusion.

As noted, the mark can be simply a word, a collection of characters or a phrase, such as "Exxon®", "IBM®" or even "Just do it®". It can be a logo or other graphic such as McDonald's arches or Target®'s "target" symbol.

In rare cases, it can be a unique sound, a unique color, a unique package design, or even a unique identifying feature of the product. The key here, however, is that the feature cannot have any function other than identification[80].

An interesting case was one between Levi Strauss & co. and Blue Bell, Inc., the manufacturer of Wrangler jeans. In 1936, Levi Strauss began to sew a folded ribbon into the seam of a rear patch pocket and acquired a trademark for the feature. I'll spare you the details but when, in 1969, Wrangler introduced jeans with a similar, but not identical label, Strauss sued. Because, during the intervening years, buyers had come to associate Levi's ribbon as an indication of origin, the trial court found that the pocket tab had acquired "secondary meaning" in identifying Levi Strauss and its goods. The court enjoined Wrangler from further use of the tab and an appeals court affirmed the trial court's decision of infringement[81].

It's worth noting that marks come from common law and, as such, they need not be registered. If a product or service is used in interstate commerce, however, federal registration is advantageous. You have undoubtedly noticed the indication "TM" as well as ®. TM can be used on any mark to which you wish to lay claim. Use of the ®, however, is restricted to marks registered with the USPTO.

Even after establishing a mark, there are requirements that must be met in order to maintain your rights to it. As with patents, the only safe course is to seek competent, specialized legal counsel early in the development process and to follow their advice closely. If you merely want to increase your knowledge from an academic perspective, I would refer you to the USPTO's "Basic Facts about Trademarks[82]."

Appendix E – Product Safety & Products Liability

The safety of the people shall be the highest law.

— *Marcus Tullius Cicero*

Disclaimer

I repeat; I am most certainly not a lawyer and nothing here should be taken in any way to be legal advice. In fact, because I am not a lawyer and since the law is changing every day, some of what is written is likely to be erroneous or obsolete. My reason for including this appendix is solely to create a sensitivity, perhaps even a passion, for product safety. Legal counsel should be sought from professionals, preferably those specializing in products liability. If your organization has in-house counsel, they can most likely guide you in the right direction. Your company's insurance company may also be a source for such counsel.

Our Moral Obligation

Our obligations here are several. In my mind, at least, our primary obligation is a moral one; in other words, "First, do no harm."[83] While no product is totally without the potential to do harm, especially if used improperly, we have a moral obligation to create products which are not "unreasonably dangerous.[84]" Is a kitchen knife dangerous? Of course, it is. Is in unreasonably so? I would argue that it is not and it, since we can't imagine life without knives, society apparently agrees.

Above legal and financial considerations, my touchstone when judging whether we'd commercialize a product was always to think of how I'd feel about my wife or kids using it. If I'd not feel that my wife or child would be safe using the product, how could I morally expose someone else to the same danger? As we'll see in a moment, this alone will not keep us safe from litigation but let's not go to bed thinking that our work has exposed someone to unreasonable risk!

Safety by Design

Safe product design is a subject better left to entire books, not a small section in this one. However, simply to provide a little background, I'll touch on a few things with the admonition that you do a lot more studying on the subject.

Safety is not optional! If you are involved in the development of new products, you are morally and legally responsible to assure that they are safe. If you are an executive or someone else in authority, you have a responsibility to instill a culture that puts product safety first. Before profits? Absolutely; if the product you are working on cannot be designed to be safe as well as profitable, turn your attention to a different product!

If you are not inspired by moral issues, consider the 1970's case of the exploding Ford Pinto. In addition to the direct and indirect costs of the lawsuits, publicity was devastating and the image still lingers. Popular Mechanics magazine provides a good example. Their summary was, "Company builds car, car has terrible problem, company ignores it, people die."[85]

If you are old enough, you probably remember at least the bare facts of the case. Ford was rushing a new economy model, the Pinto, to market to counter foreign competition. Late in the design cycle, they discovered that the fuel tank's positioning caused it to burst into flame when the car was struck from behind. They even identified some inexpensive design changes that would have addressed the problem. Unfortunately for Ford and especially for the people who suffered the consequences, Ford did a cost/benefit analysis and decided that it would be less expensive to pay damages to victims than to fix the problem! The design changes went unimplemented[86]. Good math; lousy decision. The lesson here is that, if you identify a safety issue, <u>fix it</u>!

The best thing for us, of course, is to avoid finding ourselves with such a safety problem far into the design cycle. That simply cannot be trusted to luck. Questions, like "How will people use and misuse the product?", "What could go wrong?" and "How can I be sure it doesn't?" must be prominent throughout the cycle. Calculations must include the application of appropriate safety factors and, where possible, testing must be done to assess product performance even when it is misused.

While the best way to assure that products are safe is to design them to be intrinsically so, that is not always possible. When a hazard cannot be sufficiently mitigated through the basic design, the second line of defense is appropriate guarding. Where even that will not sufficiently mitigate risk, safety warnings may be necessary.

Safety Labels and Warnings

Labels and warnings are the subject of much debate and consternation. Some guidance is provided by the ANSI Z535 series and there are many other standards that apply to specific product categories. However, ANSIZ535 and other consensus standards serve as a floor, not a ceiling. Standards can vary from country to country and state to state. Laws certainly do so.

In many cases, unfortunately, there are no clear answers. Consider, for example, the number of warnings needed for a given product. Do we have enough warnings and labels? Do we have too many? Personally, when I get six pages of warnings in the manual for a camera, I don't read <u>any</u> of them. Therefore, <u>my personal belief</u> is that too many can be as harmful as too few, but courts may not agree. As in all things related to products liability law, seek professional counsel.

While warnings may have their place as a last resort, don't for a heartbeat consider them as a viable alternative to safe design. Consider the case of Uniroyal Goodrich Tire Co. v. Martinez[87]. Mr. Martinez, a mechanic, was injured while mounting a tire in a manner that was explicitly warned against on a conspicuous label <u>that he acknowledged he'd seen</u>. Nonetheless, a Texas jury awarded him $17 million in damages when he argued that Uniroyal could have utilized an alternative design which would have reduced, but not eliminated, the risk of explosion![88]

Safety Review

Beyond simply applying good engineering practices throughout the design process, make it an inviolate policy to do thorough safety reviews, not only at the end of the process when time and other resources have been committed to a faulty design, but periodically throughout it. These safety reviews should be conducted by a cross-functional team, including many people NOT on the project team. If possible, include one or more product safety experts. Notice that I said "cross-functional team"; non-technical people can often provide better insight into possible misuse than can engineers. You want to have people who do not have any stake in the process other than making wise safety decisions. Safety is a subject important enough to justify a dedicated event; do not simply incorporate it as a topic of your periodic design reviews.

A good place to start each safety review is by assuring you've complied with all regulations and voluntary compliance standards that relate to safety. Remember, though, compliance alone is not sufficient; it should be considered as a starting point, a bare minimum.

Having passed that hurdle, use the same sort of creative thinking that went into creating the design to identify how people might get injured (or worse) or how property might get damaged. Think carefully, not only about the intended uses for your product, but about the reasonably foreseeable misuses. If your product is a chair, isn't it reasonable to assume someone will stand on it to change a lightbulb? If it's small, might it find itself into the mouth of a small child?

I've found it useful to create a checklist template that has been customized to the types of products the organization offers. The list would remind you to consider, for example, structural strength, sharp edges, pinch points, electrical shock hazards, toxicity, choking hazards and so on. Such a basic checklist should them be supplemented with concerns specific to the product under consideration. Guided but not constrained by the list, proactively search for trouble spots and then address each aggressively.

When warnings are called for, consider them with the same diligence that was applied to the analysis of the product itself. Do they meet or exceed standards? Are they appropriate and clear to the intended and other likely users of the product? Are they placed where they are most effective?

A safety review goes beyond the product and warnings. It must encompass advertising, catalogs, user guides, web pages, trade show displays and so on. Make sure you are not claiming or implying that your product can safely do something that it cannot. Watch especially for application photos that show your product being used in ways that could cause harm.

Finally, make sure salespeople and all other customer-facing personnel understand the critical importance of not saying or doing anything that might encourage or induce unsafe application or use of the product.

Products Liability - The Legal Theories

All of that having been said, we must recognize the legal realities. For better or worse, we live in a litigious society and, sadly, we may be sued and found liable even when we've been diligent. To better understand the legal minefield let's look at the theories under which we might be found liable in the United States. You can fall victim to any or all.

Negligence

Suits for negligence are based on "Conduct which involves an unreasonable risk of causing damage" or "...which falls below the standard established by law for the protection of others against unreasonably great risk or harm.[89]" That "or" is worth noting. Just because your product meets or exceeds the standards doesn't get you off the hook if a reasonable person would have done something different. While meeting or exceeding standards will not get you off the hook, you'd better believe you'll be on the hook if you fail to at least met them. To prevail against charges for negligence, you must also be able to convince the court that your actions were those of a "reasonable person". Of course, it will be up to the court, and often a jury, to define exactly what that fictitious person would have done.

Express Warrantees and Misrepresentation

Again, this is a non-professional's interpretation. If you say or imply that your product will do something safely, it darned well better do it safely! The key here is to watch the hyperbole in what the sales folks say as well as what is published in marking statements. If a salesman says, "Sure, you can hang our heavy safe on that drywall partition", you are in for a rough ride when it comes crashing down. Carefully consider the claims made in your marketing materials and educate your sales staff about the need for discretion. Given that it's common for plaintiff's attorneys to cast their net over a wide array of defendants, those prone to hyperbole should be warned that they could find themselves sitting in the courtroom as a co-defendant.

Strict Liability

This last category is the one that has kept me awake many nights. Because this is very much in a state of flux, I'll issue an even stronger argument for legal counsel but let me just touch on the issue to show you how critical it is.

In the late 1950's, William Greenman was seriously injured by a piece of wood thrown from his Shopsmith combination power tool, manufactured by Yuba Power Products, Inc. It was not until months later that Mr. Greenman provided the retailer and manufacturer with written notice of claimed breaches of warrantees and filed suit, alleging the breaches as well as negligence. As sometimes happens, the trial court's decision was appealed to the California Supreme court. In his decision, Justice Traynor wrote, "A manufacturer is strictly liable in tort when an article he places on the market, knowing that it is to be used without inspection for defects, proves to have a defect that causes injury to a human being.[90]" Thus was born the concept of "Strict Liability" as applied to product safety.

Shortly after the court's decision, the American Law Institute (ALI) issued the Restatement (Second) of Torts § 402A (1965) and, in 1997, it completed the Restatement (Third) of Torts: Products Liability. Together, these documents guide judges as they decide cases involving products liability. In layman's terms, the key take-aways are that, if you produce or sell a product that causes harm, you could be held liable if the product contains a "defect" that was the proximate cause of the harm. Here, the word "defect" has a meaning broader than you might assume. The third restatement explains:

- *A product "contains a manufacturing defect when the product departs from its intended design even though all possible care was exercised in the preparation and marketing of the product."*

- *A product "contains a design defect when the foreseeable risks of harm posed by the product could have been reduced or avoided by the adoption of a reasonable alternative design by the seller or other distributor, or a predecessor in the commercial chain of distribution, and the omission of the reasonable alternative design renders the product not reasonably safe."*

- *A product "is defective because of inadequate instructions or warnings when the foreseeable risks of harm posed by the product could have been reduced or avoided by the provision of reasonable instructions or warnings by the seller or other distributor, or a predecessor in the commercial chain of distribution and the omission of the instructions or warnings renders the product not reasonably safe."*

Consequently, you need not have been negligent, you need not have made any warrantees, you need not even have known there was a better way to design or make the product. If bad things happen and a jury decides that the product <u>could have been</u> designed or made better, <u>even in hindsight</u>, or that the warnings were inadequate, you will be held liable.

Have I provided all of this just to scare you? Well, maybe just a little, but only to focus your attention on the fact that all of this must be taken very seriously.

Proactive Defense

Unfortunately, we live in a terribly litigious society. People's natural greed has been fed by a barrage of ads saying, "If you've been hurt, call me." So, even if your product is perfect in every way, you may still find yourself in a legal battle. Even when the injured party is clearly at fault, a person's desire to blame someone else could mean you'll be involved in litigation. You may say, "Sure, but we'll win in court," and you <u>may</u> even be right. But, unless you've been through it before, you have no idea how expensive and time consuming that lawsuit will be <u>even if you win</u>. In other words, if you win, you still lose!

Let me give you an example. Our company was the developer of the wire shelving with the serpentine front edge that you see on virtually every TV show involving a restaurant kitchen or hospital. Some of it is used in the walk-in coolers and freezers of restaurant kitchens. Some years ago, a person decided to climb up on the shelving. That's not a brilliant thing to do under any circumstances but, in this case, the shelving didn't tip over or fail in any way; it just sat there as it was intended to do. However, the guy's foot slipped, and he fell, hurting himself. The suit was, essentially, that our shelving, <u>in the freezer</u>, was coated with ice and, as it turns out, our shelving is slippery when coated with ice! Eventually, the case was dismissed but not before we spent a <u>ton</u> of money on legal fees and one of my very best engineers was burdened with the case for months!

So, other than to vent my spleen and warn of yet more of life's injustices, why am I telling you this? Because, while you and I might conclude that our product is totally safe, a suit may still be brought, and a jury might even decide to play "Robin Hood". In such cases, you'd better make sure not only that you've done all you can to provide a safe product but that you have not given anyone the tools to argue otherwise.

In the context of our responsibility to offer only intrinsically safe products, I said earlier that safety is not optional. Those words apply here in a different context. Here is a cardinal rule: **Never, ever** offer a safety feature as an option! Beyond your obligation to assure safety in the first place, making a safety feature optional will come back to haunt you during litigation. I explained earlier that one definition of "defect" outlined in the third restatement of torts involves the availability of a reasonable alternative design. By offering a safety feature as an option, you not only offer the plaintiff's attorney that alternative design, you provide her with a powerful story. Imagine the effect on a jury when she explains that you <u>knew</u> of the risk and of a way of avoiding her client's injury but left it up to her client to evaluate a risk which he was not capable fully comprehending! Ouch!!

It's important that you know that, if you find yourself on the wrong end of a products liability action, your words and actions will be subjected to scrutiny more intense than you can imagine. You will be required to respond to countless "interrogatories" (formal, written questions) about the design process, the people involved and countless other subjects. In addition, company and even personal records are all subject to a process called "discovery". It's important to note here that records <u>cannot be altered or destroyed once litigation begins</u>.

In the aforementioned Ford Pinto case, the folks at Ford apparently compounded their error in judgement by having written documentation of the math and the resulting decision. The moment a lawsuit was filed, those documents became gold in the hands of the plaintiffs' attorneys. Be very careful about everything you put in writing and take steps to assure that everyone else in the process follows that advice as well.

I'm most emphatically not suggesting that you make irresponsible decisions and then simply refrain from documenting them. However, at one time or other, most of us have been guilty of hyperbole or of saying in anger or frustration something we didn't mean. Who hasn't said something like, "I'd could kill that guy!" though we'd never dream of doing so? You can be assured that, if it serves his purposes, a plaintiff's attorney will seize any hyperbolic, inappropriate and even inaccurate comment in a memo, report, or email and present it to a jury in a way that puts you in the worst possible light. Again, I am <u>not</u> suggesting that you cover up flaws, only that you do not memorialize unnecessarily inflammatory statements.

The Ultimate Goal

In the end, remember this. Your goal is not to win a lawsuit; it is to assure that a suit is impossible because no one has been hurt and no damage has been done!

Appendix F - Metrics & Consequences

What's measured improves."

— *Peter F. Drucker*

Not everything that counts can be counted and not everything that can be counted counts.

— *Albert Einstein*

In my experience, both quotes that begin this chapter are true and considering them together would seem to explain why some of the metrics we use create results that can be not only useless, but harmful to the organization.

Regardless of which metrics are used, no single one will be adequate to properly evaluate your NPD program. On the other hand, using multiple metrics indiscriminately may tend to send the organization in conflicting directions. The best approach is the development of a balanced scorecard that will help you to look at selected metrics, including those from other initiatives, holistically. For the metrics to be meaningful, each must be reviewed by executive management no less often than quarterly, and corrective action must be taken promptly.

Newness Revisited

We can't really talk about new product metrics until we establish the definition of "new product". Is any new SKU we add to the catalog new? Is it new if it differs only in size or color or, at the other extreme, must it be disruptive? I think we'd agree that the definition of a new product lies between these extremes.

Referring to Figure 22, we saw that products can differ widely in their newness to the organization and newness to the world. If our tool company decides to start selling hammers that are just like others on the market, it may be a big deal to us but it may mean little to the marketplace. The first solar-powered nail gun in the world, however, might be something else again!

Sadly, even though the definition of "new product" is critically important in defining metrics, it often comes down to a matter of opinion. Those who want to publish metrics that demonstrate to the world what great innovators they are will want to use a relatively low threshold, while those who want to use the metric internally to encourage true innovation will set the bar somewhat higher. Some organizations use two metrics; one for publication and one for use internally.

Newness also has a time component. Should we consider a product new for only a year or two or can we stretch its "newness" to 5 years or more? While the threshold is being driven downward by the acceleration of innovation, the fact is that there is no one correct answer. I know nothing about the hand-held screwdriver industry but I'll bet it evolves a lot more slowly than does the mobile phone industry. Therefore, the former may consider a product new for three to five years while the latter limits its definition to one or two.

Typical (and not so Typical) Metrics

If you study the metrics used by various organizations, you will discover that there are many from which to choose. If you try to use too many, not only will you bury yourself with data gathering and analysis, unless you use a properly designed balanced scorecard, you'll find yourself pushed in conflicting directions. The list here is most definitely not all-inclusive and, as you'll see, some are not even among those I'd recommend; I present them solely to provide a feel for the options.

Commitment Metrics

Some call these input metrics but I prefer my term because they reflect the organization's commitment to NPD.

R&D Spending as a % of Sales
This very popular metric reflects the degree to which the organization backs its rhetoric with resources. Its definition sounds straightforward until you consider what is meant by the "D" in "R&D". Does that include design? Engineering? Modeling? Testing? Obviously, the more you include, the prouder you'll be of the commitment you're making but that pride may not be justified. If you use this metric, be careful about how you view its results, as requirements differ largely from one industry or technology to

another. While it may be possible to stay up with or surpass your competitors with a 3% investment in some industries, in others you may have to spend 15% or more just to avoid falling behind.

Because many organizations sacrifice R&D efforts as soon as business softens, thereby compromising their future, I feel this is an especially important metric. A farsighted organization will assure that this metric does not fall and, if they are truly committed to new products, they will consider increasing it over time. However, if you use it to compare your own organization to others, make sure the comparison is a fair one.

R&D Headcount
Like the previous one, this metric is only relevant relative to your own industry and the size of your organization. However, as with the previous metric, if the R& D headcount is going down, the organization is clearly not committed to innovation.

A year after I graduated from university, the economy took a downturn and engineers were laid off in droves. While I kept my job, I was transferred to a location that did not interest me in the least. As I searched for a new job, I found a most enlightened employer who had decided that the abundance of unemployed engineers made it an excellent time to expand his R&D department. Shortsighted executives find it all too easy to chop R&D, saving money in the short run and doing serious damage to their future. This metric is exceptionally easy to monitor, and it will help you to keep the organization's future in mind as you make staffing decisions.

Average Development Cost and/or Capital Investment per Project
If your business is such that your product offering is homogeneous, these moderately popular metrics may have some value to you. In my personal experience, the complexity of products and the scope of the projects varied so widely that averages would have been meaningless. Think of it; put one hand on a stove and the other in liquid nitrogen and, on average, you'll feel comfortable!

Process Metrics

It is not only our products that we seek to improve continually but the process as well. Process metrics will help manage progress in that regard.

Project Kill Rates

We've discussed the many reasons that a project should be killed and the fact that a kill delayed until late in the process not only wastes time and money, it also has a huge opportunity cost. Kill statistics are useful in two ways. They indicate both whether projects are being killed rather than rubber stamped at every gate (in which case, why use the process at all?) and whether they are being killed in a timely manner.

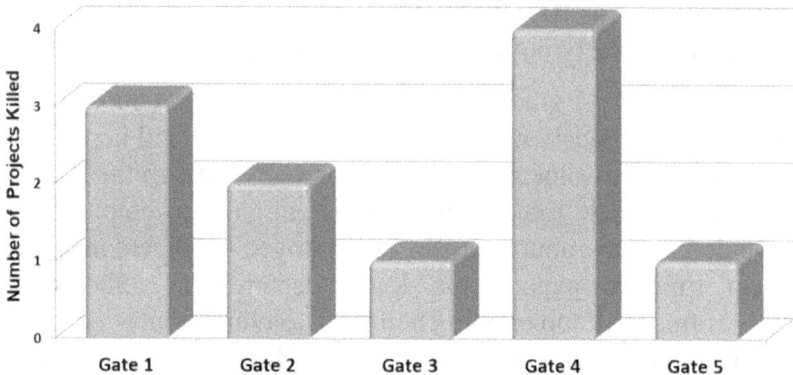

Figure 41 - Project Kill Statistics

Figure 41 shows that, though the example organization is killing some projects, many survive until late in the process. In that case, a root cause investigation is warranted. An investigation might reveal, for example, that executives get cold feet when it comes to spending capital on production equipment, even though they'd approved the capital budget much earlier. Such a finding would indicate that capital expenditures must be more carefully considered earlier in the project. This is, of course, only one of the possibilities but it highlights the need to monitor the statistic, investigate root causes and take corrective action when needed.

Average Schedule Slippage

Throughout this book, we have stressed that getting products to market quickly is highly important. Doing so accelerates positive cash flow, helps the organization to stay ahead of competition and allows it to move on to the development of yet more products. Sadly, a myriad of issues tend to stifle the smooth flow of a project, resulting in schedule slippage. I freely admit that I don't recall a project of significant scope that didn't run into one or more snags that held it up at least a bit, but serious or endemic schedule slippage is a serious problem that is all too often explained away and forgotten. If you routinely track and report on it, though, you are more likely to take it more seriously.

Others may see it differently, but I feel the stopwatch for this purpose starts when someone presents an idea for the first time and stops when the product is in full scale production, customers are happily buying it and it is returning the expected profits. Slippage can be calculated by simply dividing days lost by the number of days forecast and expressing the result as a percentage.

If slippage is a recurring problem in your organization, you might also start tracking slippage for each phase to help you to pinpoint recurring themes. If your organization is typical, you may see serious slippage in the early phases where the perceived urgency is less.

Average Budget Slippage

Since the logic and math here are similar to that for schedule slippage, little need to be said except that it is sometimes prudent, after deliberation, to spend <u>in excess of</u> budget in order to accelerate the schedule. The mathematics of a tradeoff can be evaluated using the methodology presented in appendix C, but strategic issues must also be considered. Nonetheless, tracking budget slippage will help you to detect endemic problems.

Portfolio Metrics

In chapter 8 we stressed the importance of setting goals for how projects are resourced according to project types or in other ways. Setting targets serves no purpose unless performance against those targets is monitored and corrections made as needed. Figures 24 and 25, presented in chapter 8, are examples of charts comparing actual vs. target spending. Portfolio metrics should be reviewed no less often than quarterly.

Results Metrics

<u>Current Year % of Sales Due to Products Introduced in the Past N Years (AKA Vitality Index or VI)</u>
The Vitality Index is calculated simply as:

New Product Sales / Total Sales

While this ubiquitous metric has some value, it has two minor and one very serious shortcoming. The first minor issue is ambiguity of the definition of newness as was discussed a bit earlier. If you define "new" to deliver a high VI for public consumption, it will lull you into a state of complacency. Therefore, I strongly recommend that you also use a more conservative definition to drive you to meaningful innovation.

The second is, as with the % R&D metric, the difficulty in comparing across industries. I was once bragging to a banker about our high vitality ratio and he said, "That's not necessarily a good thing." When I asked for an explanation, he said, "Depending on your industry, you may have to resource that just to stay even with competition!"

The serious issue is insidious and, in my opinion, makes this metric the poster child for unintended consequences. <u>By maximizing VI, you may be sub-optimizing sales or profits!</u> The VI that results from the development of products that simply replace existing ones will almost always be higher than the VI that results from the development of breakthrough products that produce incremental sales. This may seem counterintuitive until you look at the math with a focus on the denominator.

Again, we'll illustrate this by studying an example that, while a bit simplistic, should make my point. Let's assume the company's total sales are $100,000K dollars including the sales of project A, sales of which are 5,000K. Two projects have been proposed, each with forecast sales of $5,500K. Proposed project B would completely replace Product A, while sales from Project C would be incremental. Therefore, Project B will generate only $500 in incremental sales (for total sales of $100,500), while project C will generate $5,500 in incremental sales (for total sales of $105,500).

Assuming project costs and so on were the same, the data presented so far would lead any rational person to select Project C. However, consideration of vitality index alone would lead to the opposite conclusion.

Project B results in a vitality index of:

$$5,500/100,500 = 5.47\%$$

However, because the additional sales that make it preferable increase the denominator, Project C's vitality index is only:

$$5,500/105,500 = 5.21\%$$

So, if it were your company, would you opt for the higher vitality index or the additional sales? Admittedly, the example is simplistic but incremental sales will always increase the denominator, always reducing VI. Use whatever reasonable numbers you like; you'll come to the same conclusion.

Despite its shortcomings, monitoring VI can be valuable if used intelligently. Setting a VI goal based on industry data and then creating a plan to achieve that goal will help you to focus on improving your level of innovation. The example curve shown in Figure 42, shows the historic and planned VI of an organization whose VI has been languishing but who has set aggressive VI goals and is working towards achieving them. Remember, though, that an excellent VI is not a substitute for incremental sales.

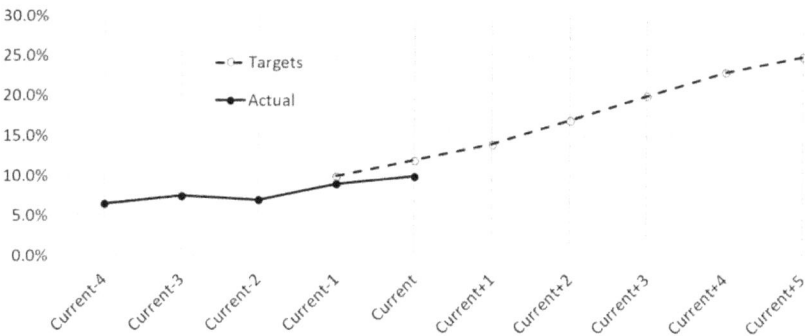

Figure 42 - Vitality Index

A chart like the one illustrated in chapter 8's Figure 27 would be an excellent way of examining performance against VI goals. While the VI curve in Figure 27 was based on a constant VI for simplicity, a little extra effort would result in a curve based on an increasing VI.

Current Year Incremental Sales Dollars (or, better, profit dollars) due to products introduced in the past N years

These are metrics that measure something that really counts! In many industries you must keep developing new products just to stay even with competition but, to have a positive impact on shareholder value, you must generate incremental sales. Remember, though, that incremental sales are not quite so exiting if they are not profitable. While both metrics have value, I like the second a bit better. A chart or charts like that shown for in Figure 42 for VI would be valuable for highlighting performance against these metrics as well.

Actual Sales and Profits Performance vs. Forecast

When each project is approved, sales and profit forecasts are presented and accepted by the gatekeepers. Gate approval for each project is based, at least in part, upon those forecasts. In essence, a contract is made between the team and management; "You approve and fund the project and we'll deliver these sales and profits." If they approve and fund the project, management deserves proof of delivery and corrective action if results do not meet expectations. Figure 43 illustrates a chart that can be used for sales or profits.

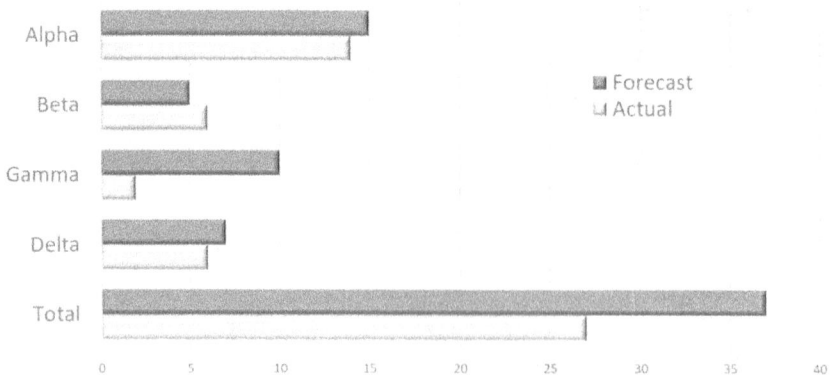

Figure 43 – Sales or Profit Performance by Project

The example shows that, while project Beta is performing ahead of forecast, overall results are far below expectations and corrective action is clearly needed. Though some attention is needed to projects Alpha and Delta, Gamma is where strong intervention is essential. The use of such a chart on a frequent basis enables the organization to identify and address shortcoming early in order to get struggling projects back on track, delivering on the promises made.

Annual Number of Products Introduced

From what I've read, this is a very popular metric, but I think it is a poor one. Is the number of products important or is it the value of those products that matter? Years ago, I had a peer, another VP, who opined that my department (and, by extension, I) should be measured by the number of products we added to the product line. I said, "OK, so if we could design one product to do several jobs very well, you'd be happy if I managed my own income by burdening the company with the development, production and inventory of several products to accomplish the same thing?" He decided to drop the issue. Let me say it again; though popular, I think the use of this popular metric is ill advised.

Annual Patents Filed or Issued

This could have at least some value if it's used to track your own activities over time but, given the differences between industries as well as the sizes of organizations and their views on the value of patent protection, it offers little value in comparing one organization's performance to that of others. Furthermore, given that some patents have tremendous value while others are worth little more than the paper they are printed on, is a raw number of any use?

Personal Objectives & Rewards

In chapter 4, I stressed the importance of including performance on NPD projects as a personal objective for, not just the marketers, designers and engineers, but for every person engaged in the NPD process. Once these objectives are established and communicated, they must be used as an element for periodic performance reviews and become a factor in the determination of raises and bonuses. To be meaningful, however, functional managers must seek and take into consideration feedback from those leading the projects with which the employees were involved. Absent incorporation of this feedback, functional managers can put their provincial interests above those of the organization as a whole. Only when the organization demonstrates the importance of NPD by tying it to the reward system will it enjoy optimal employee performance.

Having said that, you will recall that, in chapter 4, I stressed the importance of risk taking and advised that people not be punished for doing so. Unless it becomes habitual, no person should be punished for taking calculated risks that result in failure. On the other hand, it's sometimes appropriate to "motivate" those who routinely refuse to take risks through performance evaluations.

While performance (or lack thereof) on NPD projects should be reflected in bonuses and salary increases, much has been said about separate rewards to those who are responsible for bringing new products to fruition.

Because their identification is somewhat objective, I have always made it a practice to recognize inventors named on patents with a plaque. However, I must confess that, although I have tried for decades to discover a way to implement rewards beyond that, I have been unable to do so. There are two reasons for this; the element of time and the definition of who is and who is not "directly involved". To give or withhold rewards based on early product performance is meaningless; project success cannot be accurately determined until sales and profits can be compared to forecasts over a reasonable period. This may take many months, and to delay rewards until long-time performance is verified is to render those rewards of little value.

The second issue is that of who should and who should not get a reward even if a way was found to award one. It's clear that the project manager, the lead marketer, the lead designer and so on, would participate. But, where to draw the line? On any project in a reasonably sized organization, there will be many people who dedicate countless hours and perhaps Herculean effort, yet would not be counted as "key contributors" since their roles are supporting ones. As with a family wedding, the larger the circle of "invited guests", the larger the number of disgruntled people who are just outside the circle. Neglecting to include such people when rewards are given is a surefire way of dispiriting them.

Beyond the patent plaques, I feel it's best to, in a group setting, identify the key players, acknowledge the "...many others who worked long and hard..." and ask all those who participated to stand and be recognized.

Putting Metrics to Use

It should be clear by now that, given the variability of how metrics are determined, it's often impractical to compare your organization's "scores" with those you read or hear about. Nevertheless, tracking your own metrics over time and against your own targets is indispensable. Some metrics can and should be tracked monthly while others can be reviewed quarterly. Simply tracking them and making pretty charts to be put in a file, however, is useless. They must be reviewed by executive management and concrete action taken.

About the Author

A graduate of Lehigh University, Jack Welsch (legally "John" and not to be confused with former GE president, Jack Welch) has had over 4 decades of experience in engineering and new product development at all levels and has been awarded 38 U.S. and many foreign patents. He has been directly involved with the phased and gated process for new product development since 1979 and has spent much of his time and energy in the implementation and refinement of the process.

While most of his career has been spent in management and executive positions in manufacturing companies, he has taught the business aspects of product development as an adjunct instructor at both Lehigh and Wilkes Universities.

He has been a speaker on the subject at conferences at Cornell, Lehigh and Wilkes Universities and was honored to be a featured speaker at the prestigious Stage-Gate® Innovation Summit hosted by noted Stage-Gate® guru, Dr. Robert Cooper.

He is currently Principal of J. H. Welsch Consulting, L.L.C., which is dedicated to helping organizations to improve their new product development process.

Index

Table of Figures

Annotated Bibliography

Burchill, Gary and Christina Hepner Brodie. *Voices into Choices*. Madison, WI: Joiner Associates, Inc., 1997. *(A particularly good treatment of "Voice of the Customer")*

Christensen, Clayton M., *The Innovator's Dilemma*. New York: Harper Business Essentials, 1997.

Christiansen, Clayton M. and Michael E. Raynor, *The Innovator's Solution; Creating and Sustaining Successful Growth*. Boston, MA: Harvard Business School Press, 2003.

Cooper, Alan, *The Inmates are Running the Asylum: Why High-Tech Products Drive us Crazy and How to Restore the Sanity*. Toronto: Sams Publishing, 2004. *(Directed primarily towards software but principles apply to physical products as well.)*

Cooper, Robert G. and Scott J. Edgett, *Generating Breakthrough New Product Ideas*. Hamilton, ONT, Canada, Product Development Institute, Inc., 2007.

Cooper, Robert G. and Scott J. Edgett, *Lean, Rapid and Profitable New Product Development*. Hamilton, ONT, Product Development Institute, Inc., 2005.

Cooper, Robert G., Product Leadership, *Pathways to Profitable Innovation*. New York: Basic Books, 2005 *(Still an excellent treatment of the subject.)*

Cooper, Robert G., Scott J. Edgett and Elko J. Kleinschmidt, *Portfolio Management for New Products*. Cambridge, MA: Perseus Books, 1998.

Cooper, Robert G. and Scott J. Edgett, *Product Innovation and Technology Strategy*. Hamilton, ONT: Product Development Institute, 2009.

Cooper, Robert G., *Winning at New Products*. Cambridge, MA: Perseus Books, Third Edition, 2001.

Goldratt, Eliyahu M., *Critical Chain*. Great Barrington, MA: The North River Press, 1997. *(If you liked "The Goal", read this book about New Product Development. It's written as a novel so it's easy to read but the message is compelling.)*

Goldratt, Eliyahu M., *The Goal*. Great Barrington, MA: The North River Press, 1984. *(The classic introduction to Goldratt's "Theory of constraints")*

Hall, Doug, *Jump Start Your Brain*. New York, NY: Time Warner Books, 1995.

Higgins, James M., *101 Creative problem Solving Techniques: The Handbook of new ideas for business*. Winter Park, FL: The New Management Publishing Company, 1994 *(Some interesting techniques for ideation.)*

Hisrich, Robert D. and Michael P. Peters, *Marketing Decisions for New and Mature Products, Second Edition*. New York: MacMillan Publishing Company, 1991

Hooks, Ivy F. and Kristen A. Farry, *Customer-Centered Products*. New York, NY: AMACOM, 2002

Kubler-Ross, Elisabeth, MD, *On Death and Dying: What the dying have to teach doctors, nurses, clergy and their own families*. New York: MacMillan Publishing Co., Inc., 1969.

Mattimore, Barry W., *99% Inspiration*. New York: AMACOM, 1994.

Mello, Sheila, *Customer-Centric Product Definition*. New York: AMACOM, 2003. *(This is a particularly good book.)*

Peters, Thomas J. and Robert H. Waterman, Jr., *In Search of Excellence; Lessons from America's Best-Run Companies*. New York, NY: Harper & Row. 1982 *(Old and obsolete in many ways but chapter 6, "Close to the Customer", is worth reading.)*

Ries, Al and Jack Trout, *Marketing Warfare*. New York: McGraw-Hill, 1985 *(Like "Positioning..." an old but fascinating and easy-to-read book.)*

Ries, Al and Jack Trout, *Positioning, The Battle for your Mind*. New York: McGraw-Hill, 1981 *(This is very old but covers well an ESSENTIAL concept. A fascinating subject and an easy-to-read book)*

Ries, Al and Laura Ries, *The Origin of Brands*. New York: Harper Business, 2004.

Robert, Michel, *The Power of Strategic Thinking*. New York: McGraw-Hill, 2000.

Robert, Michel, *Strategy, Pure & Simple II: How Winning Companies Dominate Their Competitors*. New York: McGraw-Hill, 1998.

Schley, Bill and Carl Nichols, Jr., *Why Johnny Can't Brand*. New York: Penguin Group (USA), Inc., 2005.

Sebell, Mark Henry, *Ban the Humorous Bazooka: [and Avoid the Roadblocks and Speed Bumps along the Innovation Highway]*. Chicago: Dearborn Financial Publishing, Inc., 2001.

Smith, Preston G. and Donald G. Reinertsen, *Developing Products in Half the Time: New Rules, New Tools, Second Edition*. New York: John Wiley & Sons, 1998,

Ulrich, Karl T. and Steven D. Eppinger, *Product Design and Development*. New York: McGraw-Hill, 1995.

Ulwick, Anthony W., What Customers Want; Using Outcome-Driven Innovation to Create Breakthrough Products and Services. New York: McGraw Hill, 2005.

Weinstein, Alvin S. et al, *Products Liability and the Reasonably Safe Product : A Guide for Management, Design, and Marketing*, New York, NY: John Wiley and Sons, 1978. *(Obviously a very old book and now out of print; it's still an excellent one on the subject. It must be supplemented with something more current because of the changing legal climate!)*

Endnotes

[1] Maslow, Louis 1933, *Egg Beater*, US Patent 1,910,302.

[2] Maslow, Louis 1940, *Whip*, US Patent 2,208,337.

[3] This is so ubiquitous that few challenge its authenticity. Though the words themselves were probably not Darwin's, the quote is probably a fair interpretation of his thoughts and is certainly a valid parallel to what I'm proposing here.

[4] Christensen, Clayton M., *The Innovator's Dilemma* (New York: HarperBusiness Essentials, 1997).

[5] The Washington Post, "Why we should believe the dreamers — and not the experts", https://www.washingtonpost.com/news/innovations/wp/2014/07/31/why-we-should-believe-the-dreamers-and-not-the-experts, accessed July 21, 2018.

[6] BrainyQuote, "Ferdinand Foch Quotes", https://www.brainyquote.com/quotes/ferdinand_foch_164802, accessed July 21, 2018.

[7] Denver Post, "Kodak's chief outlines photo giant's challenges," Nov. 9, 1997.

[8] Tim Mojonnier, " Lessons Learned from Kodak's Fall", businesstheory.com, http://businesstheory.com/lessons-learned-from-kodaks-fall/, Accessed Jan. 7, 2015.

[9] Satell, Greg, "A Look Back At Why Blockbuster Really Failed And Why It Didn't Have To", Forbes, Sept. 5, 2014, http://www.forbes.com/sites/gregsatell/2014/09/05/a-look-back-at-why-blockbuster-really-failed-and-why-it-didnt-have-to/, accessed Jan. 7, 2015.

[10] It's worthy of note that RedBox has also carved out a niche for those who are unwilling to pay a subscription fee or don't want to wait for a film to be available on Netflix. In the absence of Netflix, it's worth considering that, with their 35,000+ kiosks they would also have done serious damage to Blockbuster.

[11] Clayton M. Christensen, *The Innovator's Solution; Creating and Sustaining Successful Growth.* (Boston: Harvard Business School Press, 2003) pp. 46-47.

[12] Elisabeth Kubler-Ross, MD, *On Death and Dying: What the dying have to teach doctors, nurses, clergy and their own families* (New York: MacMillan Publishing Co., Inc., 1969), pp. 38, 50, 82, 85, and 112.

[13] Forbes, The World's Most Innovative Companies, https://www.forbes.com/innovative-companies/list/#tab:rank_header:innovationPremium, accessed Aug. 6, 2018.

[14] Stage-Gate is a registered trademark of Stage-Gate, Inc.

[15] Robert G. Cooper, *Product Leadership; Pathways to Profitable Innovation, Second Edition* (New York: Basic Books, 2005.)

[16] Niccolò Machiavelli, "The Prince", 1515.

[17] Robert G. Cooper, "Uncovering Your Innovative Potential; Top 10 Actions to Drive Better Innovation Results", Feb. 26, 2008, Stage-Gate Summit® '08, Clearwater, FL.

[18] NASA, "NASA - Excerpt from the 'Special Message to the Congress on Urgent National Needs'", NASA.gov, April 4, 2004, http://www.nasa.gov/vision/space/features/jfk_speech_text.html#.VMPh1P7F9IE, accessed January 24, 2015.

[19] Those who dispute the value of the space program do not appreciate the extent to which the very fabric of our daily lives is based on technologies that are a result of that initiative.

[20] At the risk of creating confusion, it can be said that the true vision involved dominance over the Soviet Union in the court of world opinion and that Kennedy's moon challenge was, in fact, a strategy aimed at accomplishing that. Nevertheless, his words are excellent examples of what a vision is about.

[21] Michel Robert, *Strategy Pure and Simple II: How Winning Companies Dominate Their Competitors* (New York: McGraw-Hill, 1989), p. 87.

[22] For more on the "Balanced scorecard" refer to Balanced Scorecard Institute, "Balanced Scorecard Basics", http://www.balancedscorecard.org/BSC-Basics/About-the-Balanced-Scorecard, accessed July 14, 2018.

[23] Stew Leonard's Farm Fresh Foods, "Company Story," http:// http://www.stewleonards.com/about-us/company-story, accessed Feb. 15, 2015.

[24] Thomas J. Peters and Robert H. Waterman, Jr *In Search of Excellence; Lessons from America's Best-Run Companies* (New York: Harper & Row, Publishers, 1982), p 196.

[25] Shiela Mello, *Customer-Centric Product Definition* (New York: AMACOM), p. 68.

[26] Alan Cooper, *The Inmates are Running the Asylum* (Sams Publishing, 2004), p. 23.

[27] IDSA, "What is Industrial Design?", http://www.idsa.org/education/what-is-industrial-design, accessed April 30, 2015.

[28] Interaction Design Foundation, " Interaction Design Foundation, A Global Community of the World's Best Designers", https://www.interaction-design.org, accessed April 30, 2015.

[29] Slideshare, "22 Quotes On Management By Peter F. Drucker", http://www.slideshare.net/bright9977/22-quotes-on-management-by-peter-f-drucker, accessed May 1, 2015.

[30] Toolshero, "Kano Model", http://www.toolshero.com/kano-model/, accessed April 30, 2015.

[31] Alan Cooper, pp. 132-147. (While Cooper uses the term "persona", I prefer the term "Avatar".)

[32] Anthony W. Ulwick, *What Customers Want; Using Outcome-Driven Innovation to Create Breakthrough Products and Services* (New York: McGraw Hill, 2007), p. 23.

[33] Ulwick, *What Customers Want*, pp. 39-57.

[34] Autotrader, "Chrysler's K-Car: The First Modular Platform?", https://www.autotrader.com/car-news/chryslers-k-car-the-first-modular-platform-261267, accessed Dec. 23, 2017.

[35] Robert G. Cooper, *Generating Break New Product Ideas; Feeding the Innovation Funnel* (Hamilton, ONT, Canada Product Development Institute, 2007.)

[36] Jacque R. Edwards, an aeronautical Engineering graduate of Penn State University was Vice President of Product Development, my boss and my predecessor for almost 10 years. It was Jacque who lured me into the world of Product Development and taught me much of what I know about the subject.

[37] "Stage-Gate is a registered trademark of Product Development Institute, Inc., 1425 Osprey Drive Suite 201 Ancaster, Ontario, Canada L9G4V5. (Registration #2,712,980, May 6, 2003).

[38] The Gold Scales, "Albert Einstein Anecdotes", http://oaks.nvg.org/einstein-anecdotes.html, accessed July 8, 2016

[39] Robert G. Cooper & Scott J. Edgett, *Lean, Rapid and profitable New Product Development* (New York: Basic Books, 2005), pp. 147-150.

[40] Peters and Waterman, *In Search of Excellence*, p. 318.

[41] Cooper, *Product Leadership Second Edition*, p. 191.

[42] Cooper, *Product Leadership, Second Edition*, p. 262

[43] Eliyahu M. Goldratt, *Critical Chain: A Business Novel* (Great Barrington, MA: The North River Press, 1997)

[44] Preston G. Smith and Donald G. Reinertsen, *Developing Products in Half the Time: New Rules, New Tools, Second Edition* (New York: John Wiley & Sons, Inc., 1998), pp. 55-56.

[45] Bill Schley & Carl Nichols, Jr., Why Johnny Can't Brand: Discovering the Lost Art of the Big Idea (New York, Penguin Group, 2005), p xvi.

[46] Al Ries, Al and Jack Trout, *Positioning: The Battle for Your Mind* (New York: Warner Books, 1981), p. 2.

[47] Reis & Trout, *Positioning*, p. 11.

[48] AdAge, "AFTER 50 YEARS, AVIS DROPS ICONIC 'WE TRY HARDER' TAGLINE", http://adage.com/article/news/50-years-avis-drops-iconic-harder-tagline/236887/, accessed July 29, 2018.

[49] Robert D. Hisrich & Michael P. Peters, *Marketing Decisions for New and Mature Products, Second Edition* (New York: Macmillan Publishing Company, 1991), *Marketing Decisions*, pp. 288-291.

[50] Hisrich & Peters, p. 284.

51 Much of my understanding of lifecycles and the promotional activities during each come from discussions with John Nackley, President of InterMetro Industries, Wilkes-Barre, PA.

52 Cooper, *Product Leadership*, pp. 116-121.

53 Smith & Reinertsen, *Developing Products in Half the Time*, pp 128-132.

54 The Mclean group, "Meet Hal McLean", http://www.the-mclean-group.com/hal-mclean, accessed June 25, 2018.

55 Mark Henry Sebell with Jeanne Yocum, *Ban the Humorous Bazooka: [and Avoid the Roadblocks and Speed Bumps along the Innovation Highway]* (Chicago: Dearborn Trade, 2001), p. 26.

56 James M. Higgins, *101 Creative Problem Solving Techniques: The Handbook of new ideas for business* (New York: New Management Publishing Company, Inc.)

57 Creative Avoidance is a registered copyright of EMZEE Associates, Inc., owned by Maurice Zeldman.

58 Higgins, *101 Creative Problem Solving Techniques,* p. 125.

59 Higgins, p. 126.

60 Doug Hall, *Jump Start Your Brain* (New York: Warner Books, 1995), pp. 145-153.

61 InvestingAnswers, "Cost of Capital", http://www.investinganswers.com/financial-dictionary/stock-valuation/cost-capital-112, accessed July 11, 2018.

62 Karl T. Ulrich and Steven D Eppinger, *Product Design and Development* (New York: McGraw-Hill, Inc., 1995) pp. 234-357

63 "Infringement of patents", 35 CFR §171.

64 US Patent and Trademark Office, "Types of Patents", https://www.uspto.gov/web/offices/ac/ido/oeip/taf/patdesc.htm, accessed Dec. 6, 2016.

65 (US Patent and Trademark Office; same as above)

66 (US Patent and Trademark Office; same as above)

67 Uspto.gov, "Appendix L - Patent Laws", https://www.uspto.gov/web/offices/pac/mpep/mpep-9015-appx-l.html#d0e302376, accessed Dec. 6, 2016

68 IP Spotlight, "Who should be listed as inventors in a patent application?", https://ipspotlight.com/2016/12/15/who-should-be-listed-as-inventors-in-a-patent-application/, accessed Aug. 30, 2018.

69 Welsch, John H. et al 2000, *Self-Adjusting Support System, US patent* 6,611,046.

70 Google Patents, "X-y position indicator for a display system", https://patentimages.storage.googleapis.com/pdfs/460cb2437784ae911 203/US3541541.pdf, accessed Feb. 18, 2017.

71 Maslow, L 1969, *Readily assemblable and adjustable shelving*, US Patent 3424111.

72 United States Patent and Trademark Office, "USPTO Fee Schedule", https://www.uspto.gov/learning-and-resources/fees-and-payment/uspto-fee-schedule, accessed August 13, 2018.

[73] Cornell University Law School Legal Information Institute, "35 U.S. Code § 271 - Infringement of patent" https://www.law.cornell.edu/uscode/text/35/271, accessed Jan. 10, 2017.

[74] Graver Tank & Mfg. Co. v. Linde Air Products Co. 339 U.S. 605 (1950)

[75] US Patent and Trademark Office, "General information concerning patents - Patent Marking and Patent Pending", https://www.uspto.gov/patents-getting-started/general-information-concerning-patents#heading-29, accessed Feb. 19, 2017.

[76] US Patent and Trademark Office, "Provisional Application for Patent", https://www.uspto.gov/patents-getting-started/patent-basics/types-patent-applications/provisional-application-patent, accessed Feb. 19, 2017.

[77] US Patent and Trademark Office, "Eighteen-Month Publication of Patent Applications [R-07.2015]", https://www.uspto.gov/web/offices/pac/mpep/s1120.html, accessed Feb. 27, 2017.

[78] US Patent and Trademark Office, "USPTO Will Begin Publishing Patent Applications", https://www.uspto.gov/about-us/news-updates/uspto-will-begin-publishing-patent-applications, accessed Feb. 28, 2017.

[79] "Trademark Act of 1946, as Amended", Title 15 U.S.C., https://www.uspto.gov/sites/default/files/trademarks/law/Trademark_Statutes.pdf, accessed Feb. 27, 2017.

[80] Legal Information Institute, "Functionality Doctrine (Trademark)", https://www.law.cornell.edu/wex/functionality_doctrine_trademark, accessed Feb. 28, 2017.

[81] *Levi Strauss & Co., Plaintiff/appellee, v. Blue Bell, Inc., Defendant/appellant,* 632 F.2d 817 (9th Cir. 1980.)

[82] US Patent and Trademark Office, "Basic Facts about Trademarks", file:///C:/Users/jack/Documents/J.%20H.%20Welsch%20Consulting,%20LLC/Book/TM%20Basic%20Facts.pdf, accessed Feb. 27, 2017.

[83] This term is often falsely attributed to the Hippocratic oath. It's source is unimportant; the sentiment is.

[84] I really like that term, which I first heard at a presentation by author Alvin S. Weinstein decades ago.

[85] Popular Mechanics, "The Top Automotive Engineering Failures: The Ford Pinto Fuel Tanks", http://www.popularmechanics.com/cars/a6700/top-automotive-engineering-failures-ford-pinto-fuel-tanks/, accessed Dec. 2, 2016.

[86] Justia US Law, "Grimshaw v. Ford Motor Co. (1981)", https://law.justia.com/cases/california/court-of-appeal/3d/119/757.html, accessed Aug. 31, 2018.

[87] Uniroyal Goodrich Tire Co. v. Martinez, 977 S.W. 2d 328 (Tex. 1998), cert. denied, 526 U.S. 1040 (1999)

[88] The Law.Agency, "The Restatement (Third) of Torts Products Liability: The Tension Between Product Design and Product Warning", http://www.thelaw.agency/products-liability/, accessed Nov. 30, 2018.

[89] Alvin S. Weinstein et al, *Products Liability and the Reasonably Safe Product: A Guide for management, Design, and Marketing* (New York: John Wiley & Sons, 1978), p. 6.

[90] Greenman v. Yuba Power Products, Inc. , 59 Cal.2d 57 [L. A. No. 26976. In Bank. Jan. 24, 1963.]

www.ingramcontent.com/pod-product-compliance
Lightning Source LLC
Chambersburg PA
CBHW061138220326

41599CB00025B/4278